THE QUEST FOR THE NAZI PERSONALITY
*A Psychological Investigation
of Nazi War Criminals*

The LEA Series in
Personality and Clinical Psychology

Irving B. Weiner, Editor

Gacono & Meloy • The Rorschach Assessment of Aggressive
and Psychopathic Personalities

Zillmer, Harrower, Ritzler, & Archer • The Quest for the Nazi
Personality: A Psychological Investigation of Nazi War Criminals

THE QUEST FOR THE NAZI PERSONALITY
A Psychological Investigation
of Nazi War Criminals

Eric A. Zillmer
Drexel University
Molly Harrower
University of Florida
Barry A. Ritzler
Long Island University
Robert P. Archer
Eastern Virginia Medical School

LAWRENCE ERLBAUM ASSOCIATES, PUBLISHERS
1995 Hillsdale, New Jersey   Hove, UK

Lawrence Erlbaum Associates, Inc., Publishers
365 Broadway
Hillsdale, New Jersey 07642

Cover design by Kate Dusza

Library of Congress Cataloging-in-Publication Data

The quest for the Nazi personality : a psychological investigation of
Nazi war criminals / Eric A. Zillmer ... [et al.].
        p.   cm.
    Includes bibliographical references (p.) and index.
    ISBN 0-8058-1898-7.
    1. World War, 1939–1945--Atrocities--Psychological aspects.
2. World War, 1939–1945--Germany--Psychological aspects. 3.
War criminals--Psychological aspects. 4. National socialists--
Psychological aspects. I. Zillmer, Eric.
    D804.G4Q47   1995
    940.54′ 05--dc20   94-48889
                                                        CIP

Books published by Lawrence Erlbaum Associates are printed on
acid-free paper, and their bindings are chosen for strength and dura-
bility.

Printed in the United States of America
10 9 8 7 6 5 4 3 2 1

940.5405
Q

Contents

The authors (from left) are Barry A. Ritzler, Molly Harrower, Robert P. Archer, and Eric A. Zillmer.

About the Authors

Eric A. Zillmer, PsyD, is associate professor of psychology and director of the doctoral graduate program in clinical psychology at Drexel University. He is a fellow of the Society of Personality Assessment, the National Academy of Neuropsychology, and the American Psychological Association. Dr. Zillmer has written extensively in the area of psychological assessment and neuropsychology, having published more than 50 journal articles and book chapters, including the recently co-authored text, *Neuropsychological Assessment and Intervention.*

Molly Harrower, PhD, DHL, is professor emeritus at the University of Florida. As a Rorschach pioneer and leading international clinical psychologist, she has published more than 17 books and more than 100 articles, ranging from poetry to psychological theory and test construction, in scientific journals. Dr. Harrower's past interest and research on the psychological functioning of the Nazis extends back to World War II and the war crimes themselves.

Barry A. Ritzler, PhD, is professor of psychology at Long Island University and is the president of the Society of Personality Assessment. He is also associate editor of the *Journal of Personality Assessment* and a member of the faculty of Rorschach Workshops, Inc. Dr. Ritzler has published more than 75 journal articles and book chapters on topics related to schizophrenia, personality assessment, and ego psychology.

Robert P. Archer, PhD, is professor and interim chair of psychiatry and behavioral sciences at Eastern Virginia Medical School and founding editor of *Assessment.* He is a fellow of the Society of Personality Assessment and the American Psychological Association. A recognized expert in personality assessment, Dr. Archer's most recent books include the *MMPI-A: Assessing Adolescent Psychopathology* and *A MMPI Casebook.*

Foreword

Irving B. Weiner
University of South Florida

Fifty years after the death of Adolf Hitler in a Berlin bunker, the specter of the Nazism he created still haunts the memories of those who experienced it and the dreams of those who fear its reemergence. The political, historical, economic, and sociological origins of Hitler's rise to power and the power of his persuasion have been plumbed in a vast array of books and essays, many of which raise more questions than they answer. Perhaps least well understood is the individual psychology of those who led the Nazi movement and beckoned to its call. The present volume is an impressive contribution to furthering our knowledge of the Nazi psychology.

As the subtitle of this book indicates, its pages report a psychological investigation of Nazi war criminals. The investigative method chosen by the authors is the Rorschach inkblot technique, and more than 200 Rorschach protocols produced by Nazi war criminals are their primary data. Some detailed case studies and an appendix containing numerous verbatim protocol records, many of them never before published, will be of considerable interest to Rorschach clinicians and researchers.

However, the presentation by Zillmer, Harrower, Ritzler, and Archer is primarily concerned not with the Rorschach method but with the personality characteristics of these war criminals. No prior familiarity with the Rorschach is assumed by the text, and a brief chapter devoted to essential elements of Rorschach administration and interpretation suffices to make the rest of the volume fully accessible to general readers in psychology. Beyond what the authors conclude about the personality characteristics of notorious individuals, they offer historical and political insights into how data are collected and disseminated. Psychologically oriented readers interested in history and politics as well will find some fascinating accounts of controversy and inconsistency in how these Nazi war criminals were treated, how they were examined, and how the results of their examinations were managed.

Throughout their presentation, the authors exercise sound scholarship and eschew the unfounded speculation that has too often characterized analyses of Nazi psychology. Their observations have been carefully researched and their conclusions are conservatively drawn. These qualities will make their book a valuable source of information and an important addition to the literature.

Preface

Half a century after the collapse of the Nazi regime and the Third Reich, scholars from a range of fields continue to examine the causes of Nazi Germany. With the opening of the National Holocaust Memorial Museum in Washington, DC, and the release of Steven Spielberg's movie *Schindler's List*, an increasing number of young Americans are attempting to understand the circumstances that led to the rise of the Nazi party and the subsequent Holocaust, as well as the implication such events may have for today as the world faces a resurgence of neo-Nazism, ethnic warfare, and genocide. Were the Nazis monsters, or were they ordinary human beings? The debate regarding the behavior of Nazi Germany is still very much alive today. It is an important question because by studying the past we may be better able to understand the present, and most importantly, prepare for the future.

In the months following World War II, extensive psychiatric and psychological testing was performed on more than 200 Nazis in an effort to understand the key personalities of the Third Reich and of those individuals who "just followed orders." In addressing these issues, *The Quest for the Nazi Personality* examines the strange history of more than 200 Rorschach inkblot protocols that were administered to Nazi war criminals and answers such questions as: Why the long delay in publishing the protocols? What caused such jealousies among the principals? How should the protocols be interpreted?

Specifically, the goals of the current text can be summarized as follows: (a) to uncover important historical and political insights into the administration and dissemination of the psychological tests given to the defendants at the Nuremberg International Military Tribunal, (b) to trace the feud between the Nuremberg prison's psychiatrist and psychologist, (c) to report on the bizarre events that unfolded during the Nuremberg trials and in the postwar years that are just now being reported on, based on previously unavailable personal letters between the key figures. The volume will also provide a professionally responsible and schol-

arly interpretation of the psychological test data of the more than 200 Nazis, the
majority of which have been previously unavailable and unpublished.

This text is intended as the definitive and comprehensive study of the psychological functioning of Nazi war criminals, both the elite and the rank-and-file.
These analyses lead to a discussion within the context of previous work done in
social and clinical psychology, including the authoritarian personality, altruism,
obedience to authority, diffusion of responsibility, and moral indifference, in order
to apply a fresh perspective to understanding the causes that created such antisocial
behavior. The implications for current political events are also examined as
neo-Nazism, anti-Semitism, and ethnic hate are once again on the rise. Although
the text does contain some technical material relating to the psychological interpretations, it is intended to be a scholarly presentation written in a narrative style.
No prior knowledge of psychological testing is necessary, but it should be of great
benefit for those interested in the Rorschach inkblot technique, with a special
interest in psychological testing, personality assessment, and the history of psychology. It is also intended for readers with a broad interest in Nazi Germany.

The text includes nine chapters and an appendix. The introductory chapter
reviews the search for the controversial "Nazi Personality." Chapter 2 examines
the political events that led up to the Nuremberg trials and the psychological climate
in the postwar years. Chapter 3 examines the context in which the psychological
evaluations of the prisoners at Nuremberg were carried out, the defendants' reaction
to the testing, and some preliminary findings. Chapter 4 focuses on the feud
between the psychiatrist and psychologist that developed over the psychological
test data. Chapter 5 is a brief introduction to the administration and interpretation
of the Rorschach inkblot technique. Rorschachers may skip this chapter, although
the discussion of the irregularities of the Nazi Rorschach administrations may be
of interest. Chapters 6, 7, and 8 present an interpretation of the psychological
records of the Nazi war criminals, including members of the elite, the rank-and-file,
as well as case studies of Karl Dönitz and Julius Streicher. Much of the information
presented here is based on psychological records that were previously unavailable.
The final chapter presents a general discussion on whether such war crimes can
recur based on the evidence put forth in this text, a discussion of the current
resurgence of neo-Nazism, the degree of psychopathology the Nazis manifested,
and the failure to detect a specific "Nazi Personality." The appendix summarizes,
for the first time, complete verbatim records of all major Nazi Rorschach protocols
available, including seven previously unpublished records.

ACKNOWLEDGMENTS

This book could not have been written without the cooperation, help, and support
of numerous people. Many friends and scholars assisted us with the research and
listened patiently, offered suggestions, and provided encouragement along the way.
Bonnie Bailis, Richard Binder, Padraic Burns, Douglas Chute, Bill Culbertson,
George Kren, Robert Lifton, Irving Gottesman, Thomas Hewett, Frederick Kasten,

Bill Mandel, Burton Porter, Arthur Shostak, Charles Spielberger, Doreen Steg, and Burton Weiss deserve special mention.

A few scholars have gone beyond the call of duty to facilitate the publication of this book. I thank first Reneau Kennedy, Research Fellow at Harvard Medical School and Massachusetts General Hospital, who provided special support to this project. Her motivation to uncover details about many of the Nazis described in the text is unsurpassed. Without her support, humor, and friendship many aspects of the book could not have been completed.

Douglas Porpora, associate professor of sociology at Drexel University, has been a faithful friend, advisor, and critic since the inception of the project; when encountering troubled waters he helped me keep the project afloat.

Another individual who has given valuable assistance is John Exner, Jr., executive director, Rorschach Workshops. He performed many of the statistical analyses used in the final Rorschach interpretations reported here. John also provided important verification of the information pertaining to Gustave Gilbert's and Douglas Kelley's role in the Nuremberg Rorschach drama. Finally, John is to be thanked for developing the Rorschach Comprehensive System, which made the actuarial analysis of the Nazi protocols possible in the first place. His scientific approach to the Rorschach serves as the catalyst for this book.

Still another group of people deserves very special mention. John Dolibois' assistance in providing many details of the Nuremberg jail and the psychological examination of the defendants at Nuremberg is greatly appreciated. His willingness to respond to numerous questions deserves particular mention.

Special thanks goes to my friend Reinald "Cookie" Baumhauer of Munich, Germany, for his hospitality during my trips to Germany and his input to our conversations on the topics in this book, which was stimulating and insightful. He helped me to think more clearly about the issues involved.

To Elizabeth Wolf, professor emeritus at Florida Tech, I owe a special debt. She introduced me to the Rorschach technique and quite serendipitously to the fact that Nazi Rorschach records existed.

Appreciation also goes to my department head Anthony Glascock and Dean Thomas Canavan, both of Drexel University, who provided teaching relief and financial support for research trips.

The two individuals most instrumental in obtaining the Danish Nazi Rorschachs were Nancy Bratt-Oestergaard from Copenhagen, Denmark, and Michael Selzer from New York City. Nancy was one of the psychologists who administered the tests to the Danish subjects. She graciously helped negotiate with the Danish government for permission to let Barry study the test materials. Michael, who supervised the translation of the protocols into English with the help of a Ford Foundation grant, generously furnished Barry with verbatim copies of the entire collection of protocols. Appreciation also is due to Jerry Borofsky of Harvard for informing Barry of the existence of the Danish protocols as well as for his support in the early days of the project.

Many psychology graduate students served on this project and our research could never have been accomplished without their diligent efforts. The students did much of the scoring and nearly all of the computer work involved in the project. Those involved include Barbara Holda, Bill Gardner, Stephanie Wingate, Linda Meisenhelder, Jacqueline Belevich, and Christel Uhl, all of Drexel University. Graduate students serving under Barry's supervision were Stefan Massong and Diane O'Rourke from the University of Southern Mississippi, Lisa Saraydarian and Darlene Nalesnick from Fairleigh Dickinson University, and Judy O'Leary and Alex Hipona from Long Island University. Special thanks also go to Kate McReynolds from City College of New York for her assistance in scoring the Streicher and Dönitz protocols and for her moral support when the going got tough.

The clerical assistance and motivational encouragement of the secretaries in the psychology department at Fairleigh Dickinson University and the psychiatry department at Eastern Virginia Medical School need also to be acknowledged. Thanks to Gloria Gruber, Ellie Messersmith, Leni Kecher, and Denise Holloway.

Several distinguished experts in the field of Nazi studies have made valuable suggestions regarding the historiographical dimension of the text. Ronald Smelser, professor of history at the University of Utah, assisted with the background of Nazi Germany and details on Robert Ley. Eric Bose, professor of history, Drexel University, provided insight into the early history of Nazi Germany and was overall very supportive of the entire effort. Keith Bird, professor, New Hampshire Technical Colleges/Institute, gave excellent feedback on Karl Dönitz and the German navy. Finn Hornum, chair of sociology, social work, and criminal justice at La Salle University, provided valuable background on the Nazi occupation of Denmark.

Genya Markon, director of photo archives, U.S. Holocaust Memorial Museum, and Robert Brown, Still Picture Branch, National Archives, assisted with the search for pictures.

My parents played a special role in this project. My Austrian mother, Madeleine, lived through the Nazi occupation in Vienna, and my father David, a retired U.S. Army officer, fought in World War II with the 42nd Rainbow Division. The accounts of their experiences stimulated and deepened my interest for this project. As a result of my parents' international marriage and my father's military career, I spent 16 years in West Germany. All of my formative education was in German schools. This experience provided me with a unique perspective of German history.

Any scholar with a family knows what it means to write a book and try to maintain a normal family life at the same time. I am forever grateful to the patience and understanding displayed by my daughter Kanya and my wife Rochelle.

Finally, I am most appreciative of the expert contributions of my three distinguished co-authors. They are mentors in the literal sense, wise and trusted teachers who have been a source of support and encouragement throughout.

The assistance of many individuals has enabled me and my colleagues to publish this book. We are grateful to all of them. Although I have benefited from their understanding, criticism, and advice, they cannot be held responsible for any mistakes the book may still contain. That responsibility is mine alone.

Eric A. Zillmer

Chronology of Historical Events Related to the Psychological Studies on Nazi War Criminals

1923 November, "Beer Hall" Putsch in Munich. Attempted Nazi coup.

1933 January 30, President Paul von Hindenburg appoints Adolf Hitler as Reich Chancellor.

1933 April 26, formation of Gestapo (secret police).

1934 August 2, death of Hindenburg. Hitler becomes the head of the state and commander-in-chief of the armed forces.

1935 Declaration of the "Nuremberg laws" against German Jews.

1938 November 9, *Kristallnacht,* "Night of Broken Glass." State-organized program against Jews.

1939 September 1, German invasion of Poland: World War II begins.

1943 April 19 to May 16, uprising and destruction of the Warsaw Ghetto.

1945 January 26, Auschwitz liberated by Soviet troops.

1945 April 30, suicide of Hitler.

1945 May 1, Admiral Dönitz takes over as head of German government.

1945 May 7, unconditional surrender of all German forces signed at Reims by General Alfred Jodl and May 8 at Berlin by Field Marshal Wilhelm Keitel.

1945 May 23, naval admiral and Hitler's actual successor Karl Dönitz and members of his government are arrested.

1945 June 5, Supreme Allied Command in Germany declares that it will assume all government powers.

1945 August 15, Japan formally announces surrender.

1945 September, Kelley arrives at the Nuremberg jail appointed as chief of psychiatry for the European Theater of Operations. While at Nuremberg he administers the Rorschach inkblot test to Hess, Göring, Frank, Rosenberg, Dönitz, Ley, and Streicher.

1945 October 20, Gilbert arrives at the Nuremberg jail in the capacity of prison psychologist, interpreter, and Counterintelligence Corps officer. During his assignment at Nuremberg, Gilbert administers the Rorschach test to 16 of the defendants as well as the Thematic Apperception Test and IQ tests to other Nazi defendants.

1945 October 20, 24 leading Nazis were indicted for crimes against humanity and aggressive warfare by the International Military Tribunal in Nuremberg.

1945 October 25, Ley commits suicide.

1945 November 20, the International Military Tribunal begins at the Palace of Justice in Nuremberg.

1946 February 7, Kelley leaves Nuremberg jail for the United States, 2 months after the trial had started and 10 months prior to the conclusion of the International Tribunal, to begin work on his book entitled *Twenty-Two Cells in Nuremberg*.

1946 Bratt-Oestergaard administers the Rorschach inkblot test to approximately 207 Danish Nazi Collaborators and German Occupational Personnel during the Copenhagen war crimes trials.

1946 April, Kelley presents a preliminary report of Rorschach studies of Nazi war criminals in Nuremberg at the 17th annual meeting of the Eastern Psychological Association, held at Fordham University, New York City.

1946 Kelley publishes preliminary studies of the Rorschach records of the Nazi war criminals in the *Rorschach Research Exchange*.

1946 September 30, Nuremberg verdicts announced—11 to be executed, 3 acquitted, 7 imprisoned.

1946 October 1, International Military Tribunal ends.

1946 October 15, Göring commits suicide.

1946 October 16, execution by hanging 10 of the Nazi war criminals.

1946 October, Gilbert leaves Nuremberg for the United States to work on publishing the *Nuremberg Diary*.

1947 Kelley publishes *Twenty-Two Cells in Nuremberg*.

1947 Gilbert publishes *Nuremberg Diary*.

1958 New Year's Eve, Kelley commits suicide.

1963 Arendt publishes *Eichman in Jerusalem: A Report on the Banality of Evil*.

1963 Milgram performs his experiments on the obedience to authority.

1977 Gilbert dies of natural causes.

1987 August 17, Hess commits suicide in captivity at Spandau prison in Berlin.

1992 Resurgence of neo-Nazism in Germany.

1993 Reports of "ethnic cleansing" and concentration camps in the former nation of Yugoslavia.

Chapter 1

The Quest for the Nazi Personality

I insist ... that we are capable of learning from carefully examining past evil.
—Robert J. Lifton (1986)

THE LAST NAZI?

A hush falls over the crowd as the 79-year-old Josef Schwammberger teeters into a courtroom located in Stuttgart, Germany. Spectators stretch for a glimpse of the former Nazi commander whose war crimes trial may well be Germany's last courtroom confrontation with its past. Twice a week, for 4 hours a day, Schwammberger is brought from his prison cell into Room 1 at the Stuttgart State Court where he retreats silently to his solitary place at a long table at the side of the room. He stares vacantly while survivors of the Polish town of Przemsyl recount their memories of the commandant of Ghetto A, a human corral in a town that housed 28,000 Jews before Schwammberger arrived in 1943, and no more than 100 when he left.

Schwammberger, an Austrian with Argentine citizenship, is accused of murdering at least 43 people and being an accessory to the murder of thousands of predominantly Jewish victims in wartime Poland. In 1945, French soldiers arrested Schwammberger after they found him carrying eight sacks stuffed with diamonds and gold tooth-fillings. He confessed to killing 27 Jews and was charged with war crimes, but 3 years later he escaped to Argentina where he lived under his own name, protected by Argentine authorities. Since 1973 the West German government has sought extradition of Schwammberger from Argentina for the atrocities he committed as a Nazi SS captain in charge of two Jewish ghettos and a work camp in occupied Poland (Freiwald & Mendelsohn, 1994).

The witnesses come from Canada, Australia, Israel, and the United States. One after another they report having seen Schwammberger shoot innocent men, women, and children, or of hearing him order thousands to their deaths, simply because they were Jews.

On Wednesday, January 29, 1992, it was Samuel Nussbaum's turn to tell what he knows about Schwammberger. Nussbaum, a retired plumber who just arrived in Stuttgart, now lives in Kansas City. Forty-nine years after Nussbaum and Schwammberger last met, they are separated by only several feet as accuser and accused in the courtroom. Two men stiffened by age, each with a horseshoe of white hair. Each returning to Germany after four decades of absence. Nussbaum steps up to an easel and points to a precise location on a map. He takes a deep breath and summons all the detail his mind can muster about the man he knew from February to November of 1943. In a clear, strong voice, the 72-year-old plumber recalls the last time he had been so close to the commandant (Freiwald & Mendelsohn, 1994):

> He [Schwammberger] called for me one time to walk with him. Him, his wife and his dog, Prince. Nobody walked with us. There was an injured Jew lying on the street, shot in the lower part of the body. We stopped, me, him, his wife and [the] dog. That person in the street could say only "Wasser, Wasser, Wasser [water]." Schwammberger took his right foot and flipped him over on his stomach. He took out his pistol, and I was looking at Mrs. Schwammberger to see how she looked. She turned back. She did not look. And then he shot him. Right in the head.
>
> "Dead?" asked Judge Herbert Luippold.
>
> "Dead," Nussbaum answered.

Nussbaum then went on to recall other horrors of the past—stories that had gone untold for decades. Once he explained, Schwammberger ordered him to lock the car doors on a train carrying Jews to the Auschwitz extermination camp. Only later did Nussbaum learn that his entire family was inside one of those cars. He also tells of an incident where Schwammberger shot 25 Jews one after another, because they had been hiding during a roundup.

"I expected a beast," Nussbaum said after his testimony. But what he saw was a slight man wearing a crisp new cream-colored golf jacket, a fellow who joked with his guards, but who never showed the slightest sign of emotions during the trial. Later Nussbaum added, "he [Schwammberger] looks old … like a human being."

Schwammberger, who was listed on the top of the "10 Most Wanted" list by the Wiesenthal Center, admits he was a labor camp commander but denies killing anyone. When confronted with witness after witness he calmly says that he does not recognize any of them and that they are simply lying. At one point during the trial, the judge, obviously exasperated by Schwammberger's blanket rejection of testimony from one witness after another, said: "But here is yet another witness who says, Mr. Schwammberger, I knew you well." Schwammberger replied, "there were 10,000 or 15,000 of them. The 15,000 can know one, but that does not mean the one knew 15,000." At this point his attorney cut him off, declaring that he was too exhausted to continue.

Now at the age of 79 Schwammberger is facing a sentence of life in prison. The trial is the first major Nazi war crime proceeding since German unification in October 1990. It well could be the last. Only one major Nazi fugitive, Alois Brunner (chief deputy to Adolf Eichman), is thought to be alive. Brunner, described by Eichman during his trial as "my most consistently effective aide," is believed to be living in Damascus, Syria;[1] he is said to have been responsible for the murder of more than 100,000 Jews and 60,000 others.

The scale of involvement by members of Hitler's regime, including the leadership corps of the Nazi party, the *Gestapo*,[2] the *SS*, the *SD*, the *SA*,[3] and of certain others is astounding. Conservative estimates indicate that between 150,000 and 200,000 Germans were actively responsible for committing war crimes before and during the war years. It is estimated that more than 35,000 (20% of those believed responsible for major war crimes) have been captured, brought to trial, and convicted. The most publicized of these trials was the one held in 1945–1946 at the Palace of Justice at Nuremberg, where 24 high-ranking Nazi leaders were charged with war crimes before an International Military Tribunal.

Since the 1960s, there have been additional highly publicized trials such as those of Adolf Eichmann in Israel and Klaus Barbie in France. There has also been intense media interest surrounding former Nazis who escaped (e.g., the death of Josef Mengele), those who just fell through the cracks (e.g., Kurt Waldheim's questionable involvement in the Third Reich; Herzstein, 1988), alleged Nazis (i.e., the 71-year-old John Demjanjuk, a retired Cleveland autoworker, believed by Israeli authorities to be the dreaded "Ivan the Terrible"), as well as the deaths of some very well-known Nazis who served long prison sentences at Spandau prison in Berlin (e.g., Albert Speer and Rudolf Hess).

Although Schwammberger, "The Mass Murderer of Poland," was well known for the atrocities he committed as a Nazi SS captain in Poland, the significance of his trial may very well be the realization that, 47 years after the collapse of the Nazi regime, one of the last of Hitler's henchmen is being brought to justice. Thousands of Nazi criminals may still be alive but the Nazis who had responsibilities during the war were already in their 40s at the time, which means they are about 90 years old today. We are now entering a new era in which the last Nazi war criminals are

---

[1]The government in Damascus has refused to extradite Brunner.

[2]*Gestapo* is an acronym for *Geheime Staatspolizei* (State Secret Police). It was created in the spring of 1933 under the direction of Göring. The Gestapo membership grew to more than 30,000.

[3] *SS* = Schutzstaffeln started as a very small group entrusted with the personal safety of Hitler. Under Himmler direction it expanded into a very large (e.g., 100,000 in 1940) police, intelligence, national security empire within the larger Nazi regime. It was also a self-styled racial elite; *SD* = *Sicherheitsdienst* or security service created in 1931 to identify political enemies and dissenters using more than 6,000 agents; *SA* = *Sturmabteilung* or storm trooper detachment of the Nazi party, the striking arm of the Nazi party in the years before Hitler's accession to power.

either dead or are too old to be tried (in fact, Schwammberger may avoid prison on grounds of illness[4]). Furthermore, many of the victims who were eyewitnesses to World War II atrocities have passed away or, as occurred during Schwammberger's trial, are now tending to give contradictory or confusing accounts of what happened.[5] Even Nazi hunters themselves admit that both suspects and witnesses are becoming too feeble to undergo the strenuous rigors of a war crimes court trial.

The balding and frail-looking Schwammberger is a reminder that as Nazi war criminals and their victims succumb to old age, an era of German history is ending. From now on, only history will judge the Nazis.

RANK-AND-FILE NAZIS

In discussing Third Reich war crimes, and specifically the probability of recurrence of similar crimes, there are at least two important questions that stand out and that deserve further scholarly examination. One is that of understanding the involvement of numerous rank-and-file personnel in crimes against humanity. The second is related to the analysis of Nazi leadership in World War II atrocities.

The first issue focuses on the involvement of the man in the street,[6] the member of Hitler's National Socialist party or NSDAP.[7] How could so many seemingly average and otherwise unremarkable citizens have been motivated to participate in cruel, inhumane, and antisocial actions? What could have inspired so many people, many of whom were decent and quite ordinary citizens themselves, to carry out orders that resulted in the deaths of millions of similarly decent and ordinary people?

Clearly, many who participated in the Nazi regime were not necessarily involved in war crimes directly, and some even lost their lives resisting the government, but those responsible for many of the atrocities of the Third Reich do represent quite a large number of Nazi officials, guards, military personnel, bureaucrats, and others that claim to have "just followed orders." Did they all exhibit a common personality style in which the essential feature was a pervasive pattern of dependent and submissive behavior? Did they all tend to subordinate themselves to others because they were unable to make any decisions for themselves? Or did they perhaps volunteer to engage in inhumane actions in a bizarre attempt at receiving recognition from their superiors? These questions, of course, cover familiar ground and

---

[4]Schwammberger has a heart condition and was briefly hospitalized in 1987 in Argentina when he admitted his identity.

[5]This also occurred in the controversial John Demjanjuk trial, where Israel's Supreme Court cleared Demjanjuk of being the Nazi guard "Ivan the Terrible," even though there was evidence connecting him to war crimes.

[6]The perpetrators of war crimes were almost exclusively male.

[7]NSDAP is an acronym for Hitler's *Nationalsozialistische Deutsche Arbeiterpartei* (National Socialist German Workers' Party).

have been asked before. For example, the psychological functioning of rank-and-file Nazis has been investigated in a number of comparative experimental psychological studies, most notably in Asch's (1952) experiments on social conformity, Milgram's (1963, 1974) studies of obedience to authority, and Zimbardo's (1972) investigation of prison life.

Briefly, Asch, a social psychologist, showed how powerful the tendency to conform to others can be, even in regard to simple perceptual judgments. Faced with a simple, unambiguous task (i.e., matching the length of a line with one of three unequal lines), a large majority of the subjects ignored their own senses and agreed with the obviously incorrect choice made by a group of strangers (actually confederates of the experimenter). The subjects reported later that they had started doubting their own eyesight or had thought they had misunderstood the instructions. Interestingly, the subjects who did not conform reported feeling uncomfortable about disagreeing with the other members of the group. The "Asch effect" shows how readily most people will go along with a decision that their own judgment tells them is wrong, even when no coercion or force is used.

Guessing the length of a line is, of course, not comparable to participating in war crimes. However, Milgram (1963, 1974), a Yale psychologist, showed that obedience to authority relieves many people of moral responsibility, thus making them more likely to behave with considerable cruelty. Milgram had originally designed his experiment in response to the Adolf Eichmann trial, in part to understand why "ordinary people" in Germany (like Eichmann) had participated in murdering millions of innocent victims during World War II. Milgram had initially planned to bring to perfection his experiment in the United States and then travel to Germany to continue his studies, assuming that Germans may be more prone to obedience than Americans. The results he obtained in the United States, however, made it clear that he did not have to leave home. Milgram recruited subjects through advertisements in a local newspaper for a study in memory. The subjects were then asked to participate in a teaching exercise. The volunteers operated a "learning apparatus" that supposedly delivered "shocks that can be extremely painful" to a learner in an adjacent room (in reality an ally of the experimenter). With considerable verbal coercion by the experimenter, the majority of the subjects gave the "learner" what they believed to be a 450-volt shock labeled "Danger: Severe Shock," despite the "learner" having pounded on the wall twice and then having stopped responding altogether. In later experiments, almost one third was willing to hold the "learner's" hand against a metal plate to force him to receive the shock. Milgram's study clearly demonstrated that, under certain circumstances, the tendency to obey an authority figure can be very strong.[8]

In yet a different experiment, psychologist Zimbardo (1972) asked a group of ordinary college students to spend time in a simulated prison. Some were randomly assigned as guards, given uniforms, billy clubs, and whistles and were instructed

---

[8]One criticism surrounding Milgram's study centers around the issue that the subject's volunteer status may have been associated with greater susceptibility to authority. Most of the war criminals, however, were also "volunteers" for the Nazi movement.

to enforce certain rules. The remainder became prisoners, were asked to wear humiliating outfits, and were locked in barren cells. After a short time the simulation became very real as the guards devised cruel and degrading routines. The prisoners, one by one, either broke down, rebelled, or became passively resigned. After only 6 days Zimbardo had to call the study off demonstrating that for many of us, what we do is what we gradually become.

The rank-and-file Nazis performed a very special role in the evolution of the Third Reich, because it was more likely that they, compared with upper echelon participants, were the direct perpetrators of many of the atrocities. This volume examines a relatively large group of nearly 200 psychological protocols of rank-and-file Nazis, many of which have been previously unavailable. The issue of whether rank-and-file Nazis present a heterogeneous or homogeneous personality pattern can only be addressed within the context of a relatively large sample, because it allows for the separation of specific subgroups (e.g., those who participated in episodes of brutality and murder compared to those who did not; see chap. 7).

THE NAZI ELITE

A second related question, but one deserving equal attention, is that of whether Hitler's "henchmen" were mad or insane. Can one equate evil behavior with psychiatric abnormality? These questions are related to the personalities and motivations of those high-ranking persons who were considered to have been members of the "Nazi elite."[9] The men closest to Hitler constituted a group of perhaps 100 individuals. For the most part, these individuals were responsible for not merely following orders, but also for issuing them. These Nazis were charged with such conspiracies as the "final solution," the creation of concentration camps, the initiation of aggressive warfare, and slave labor. In short, they created an environment in which the atrocities of the Third Reich were allowed to occur, and they and many of their subordinates had the managerial freedom to make it happen. Many of these Nazis could be classified as administrative facilitators who seldom, if ever, committed acts of violence themselves and were, as a group, rather far removed from the incidents of death and torture perpetrated by their rank-and-file subordinates.

A psychological study of Nazi leadership is undertaken by examining the Rorschach data of high ranking members of the Third Reich who stood trial during the International Military Tribunal in Nuremberg. Twenty-four of them were brought to trial for their involvement in the Third Reich and of these, the majority were administered psychological tests, several of which have remained unpublished; these are reviewed in subsequent chapters.

---

[9]For biographical studies of the Nazi elite see Smelser and Zitelmann (1993).

THE SEARCH FOR A GERMAN NATIONAL CHARACTER

How could Nazism become the ruling passion of the German people? Why are the Germans so unreasonably aggressive? What accounts for their brutal treatment of non-Germans? Such questions are typically asked by individuals who blame a Nazi personality, a German enigma, or a National Character for the shameful occurrences under the Third Reich (e.g., Brickner, 1943). They argue that Nazism is merely an expression of a German culture that has existed for more than 100 years. They take comfort in describing a Nazi personality as aggressive, militaristic, disciplined, undemocratic, and anti-Semitic in nature.

Particularly during the war and postwar years, there was much activity in the search for a Nazi personality or that of a German national character. For example, British psychiatrist Dicks, who in 1941 was appointed to take over the psychiatric care of Rudolf Hess after his flight to England, evaluated more 1,000 German prisoners of war. Dicks (1950, 1972) defined national character as the broad, frequently recurring regularities of certain prominent behavior traits and motivations of a given ethnic or cultural group. He proposed that the identification of such a Nazi personality would assist "future Allied Administrators of Germany ... to distinguish Nazis from non-Nazis without recourse to the very crude and fallacious criteria of reference to formal membership of the Party." He concluded in his research of German POWs that Nazism was distributed normally in the German population (i.e., in the form of a Gaussian distribution) and that 36% were "hard active" or "near Nazis" (something Dicks referred to as active carriers of this ideology). Dicks reported that the "average" member of the *Wehrmacht* could be described as tense, earnest, industrious, meticulous, overrespectful to authority, and anxious to impress. Indeed, one is left to wonder if Dicks' description of the "German character" does not, in fact, fit the military personnel of most nations. Dicks himself never attempted to use a control group to explore this, however, excluding all subjects from his study that were foreign born and not German.

If there is not a uniform German national character, perhaps the rank-and-file Nazis and the Nazi elite shared a common, homogeneous personality style. A theoretical psychological foundation, specifically for the acceptance of a Nazi ideology among the general population, was proposed by Adorno and his colleagues (Adorno, Frankel-Brunswick, Levinson, & Sanford, 1950; Greenstein, 1969). Adorno suggested the presence of an Authoritarian personality in which individuals score high on the F scale or Fascist scale. The F scale includes nine personality cluster dimensions that together yield the concept of authoritarianism as the definite antidemocratic personality syndrome: an exploitative power orientation, a moralistic condemnation of others, a distrustful–suspicious attitude, pseudomasculinity (for men), diffuse and depersonalized aggression, externalized conscience or moral authority, rigid thinking, intolerance of ambiguity, and a preoccupation with toughness. Adorno concluded that the Nazi leaders shared not only a common political ideology with their followers, but also a similar fascist personality structure as well.

The myth of the homogeneous Nazi type, believed by some to be psychopathic or fascist and by many others to be mad and German, is still popular today among the casual observers of the Third Reich. The "mad Nazi" theory only serves to comfort those who endorse it because it is perceived to have little or no relationship to the rest of us and cannot be duplicated in non-Germans or in individuals with seemingly normal human capacities. In fact, the use of the word *Nazi* implies the existence of a cohesive Nazi personality. Many Germans who supported many or most policies of the regime as they understood them were not Nazis; indeed, many non- and even anti-Nazi Germans supported some of the regime's policies. In the context of the present text the label Nazi is used for those who were working in institutions of the Party and State.

To the objective observer acquainted with history, it should become quite clear then, that the German conduct as such is not enigmatic or related to a national character. In this sense, no contemporary historian of Nazi Germany would argue today for the existence of a psychopathic Nazi personality. Historical and psychologically informed inquiries have reached this conclusion on vast and solid evidential foundations. Most historians agree that the leaders of Nazi Germany were for the most part extremely able, intelligent, high-functioning people. One piece of historical literature by the German journalist Joachim Fest (1970) does attempt to define a more or less coherent set of personality traits characteristic of the Nazi leadership, although Fest does not argue for the existence of a psychopathic Nazi mind per se. Rather, in *The Face of the Third Reich* he suggested that the behavior of Germans during the Third Reich was "too undeniably a symptom and consequence of specific faulty developments in our German history" (p. 306), which was conveniently forgotten with Hitler's death. Thus, Fest suggested that National Socialism was, to some degree, a German situational phenomenon. Kater (1989), in *Doctors under Hitler,* suggested that today's German medical establishment views the Nazi medical malefactors as nothing more than atypical, extraneous intruders, not in any way part of the hallowed German medical tradition that has rebound to its prior international heights. Kater concluded that a great majority of post-1945 German physicians have exonerated themselves and German medicine "since the premier medical criminals have been caught and sentenced, all uncomfortable questions that might have lingered have been answered and therefore things are back to business as usual" (p. 222).

THE BANALITY OF EVIL

Ritzler saw his first Rorschach inkblot record of a Nazi in 1970 when he was a postdoctoral fellow in psychology at the Yale Psychiatric Institute. At the Institute, Ritzler participated in weekly psychodiagnostic seminars taught by Brooks Brenneis who gave his students an unidentified Rorschach inkblot protocol with the instructions that it belonged to a famous person who had attained a high position in his profession. The Rorschach technique is a psychological test in which 10 plates containing bi-symmetrical inkblots are presented in a prescribed sequence to a subject who is asked "What might this be?" Responses are categorized and scored and a final evaluation of the personality as a whole is offered.[10] The students in the seminar were asked to interpret the Rorschach protocol and to guess the identity of the subject's profession.

The protocol was rather simple and easy to interpret. Ritzler and his colleagues saw a socially distant, intellectually pretentious person lacking in depth of character. No doubt, the group concluded, this psychological profile belonged to a simple man. Although there was somewhat limited depth of character there seemed to be no evidence of psychopathology in the record. Because the students knew that the subject had been successful in his profession, they speculated that he attained this success by being a good organization man, doing what he was told to do and not making waves. Although the group of students came up with this nearly unanimous interpretation, the guesses of the subject's identity showed little consistency. It seemed as if the protocol must have belonged to an individual from the field of entertainment, politics, or the media. No one suggested a person from academia, clergy, or the arts. Presumably the lack of depth in the protocol and the youthful bias of the group precluded that such a shallow personality could not be concerned about "higher" forms of human endeavor. The experience of learning the subject's identity has been unforgettable. The psychological protocol belonged to Adolf Eichmann!

Eichmann, a German SS colonel, was head of the "Jewish Desk" (*Judenreferat*) in the Reich Security Main Office (*Reichssicherheitshauptamt*), which was charged with assembling Europe's Jews under German control. There he organized the deportation of Jews to extermination camps located in Poland (Hilberg, 1971). After the war, he escaped to Argentina, where he was captured by the Israeli secret service in 1960 and taken to Tel Aviv, Israel, to stand trial. He was judged by a special ad hoc tribunal in two successive trials and condemned to death on December 15, 1961. He was executed in June 1962, cremated, and his ashes thrown into the sea.

During his trial, Eichmann was portrayed in the media as a depraved killer responsible for the deaths of millions. But the Rorschach protocol did not fit. Where was the depravity? Or, perhaps, an overwhelming sense of guilt? Sadism? Bigotry? Hatred? None of these seemed apparent in the psychological test profile. Just the opposite, the psychological protocol seemed to indicate an ordinary, rather untroubled person who, although likely to be somewhat distant and inflexible in interpersonal relationships, was not bent on the destruction of whole populations of human beings.

The Eichmann Rorschach begins to make more sense when examining the work of Arendt (1958, 1963), the noted political philosopher. Arendt, who had been assigned by *The New Yorker* to cover the Eichmann trial, was among the spectators in the converted auditorium of Jerusalem's municipal cultural center. After observing the trial of Eichmann and drawing from interview information (including some

---

[10]A more detailed description of the Rorschach test is presented in chapter 5.

Adolf Eichmann listening to Judge Landau reading the sentence (Jerusalem, Israel, December 15, 1961). National Archives, courtesy of U.S. Holocaust Memorial Museum.

knowledge of the psychological test data collected during the trial), she proposed that the actions of Eichmann and of other Nazis were not related to significant psychological derangement in those men, but were a result of a lack of personality substance, that is, banality. Arendt argued that Eichmann was not a sadist or even an aggressive individual intent on doing harm to others for depraved satisfaction, but just an ordinary, conscientious, moderately ambitious bureaucrat who was more interested in simply obeying orders than he was in sending millions of people to their deaths in the camps. Thus, Eichmann was nothing more than an "organization man" who facilitated the deaths of millions by keeping the concentration camp trains running on time.

Arendt concluded that the key to Eichmann's evil—the quality (or lack of it) in his personality that kept him from having compunction or even second thoughts about his "job"—was the banality of his character; that is, the lack of depth that was found so apparent in his Rorschach protocol. Arendt's controversial thesis simply implies that many of the Nazis were banal, morally indifferent, mundane, and without a feeling of hatred or any ideological malice toward their victims; in fact, she concluded that they were quite ordinary. Arendt's proposition seems neat and simple. Most Nazis, she suggested, were not the swaggering sadists of the "B" movie genre, but stultifyingly ordinary men who were just doing their jobs or "following orders" as they claimed in their war crimes trials' defenses.

The concept of "banality of evil" has great merit, because it implies that ordinary men in the right circumstances can perform evil deeds. But it also assumes the presence of a relatively homogeneous personality prototype that others before have argued to be sinister and vicious, not ordinary. Each of these hypotheses, the "evil Nazi personality" and "the banality of evil," start with a divergent bias concerning the behavior of Nazis. Both assume a relatively homogeneous personality type, one vicious, sadistic, and antisocial, the other obedient, indifferent, and mundane. Both have naturally stirred much debate and controversy.

Arendt's theory, however, differs from those endorsing the "mad Nazi" hypothesis in a very important way, for she suggests that the potential for behaving like a Nazi exists in each of us. If Asch, Milgram, Zimbardo, and Arendt are correct, it may be that law-abiding men and women with conventional virtues are indeed capable of committing Nazilike crimes, once the command is given and appropriate social mechanisms are set in motion.

Zillmer repeated the informal blind interpretation exercise reported earlier. Instead of handing out the psychological protocol of Eichmann, however, the Rorschach inkblot record belonging to Hans Frank was distributed to doctoral psychology graduate students studying advanced personality assessment at Drexel University.

Frank, a feisty, dapper young Nazi lawyer, was Minister without Portfolio and the head of the "Academy of German Law." From 1939 to 1945 he was Governor-General of that part of occupied central Poland that was left after the Germans had annexed western Poland and the Soviets' eastern Poland. He was given this post by Hitler who was grateful for the legal services Frank had provided the Nazi party in earlier years. Frank's diary revealed his ruthlessly brutal actions in Poland, including his participation in mass extermination of Jews at Auschwitz and the establishment of Polish ghettos. After the war, Frank, the "Butcher of Poland," attempted suicide when captured by the Allied Armed Forces. Although Frank was not one of the truly powerful men in the hierarchy of the Third Reich, he was nevertheless chiefly responsible for the bloody German reign of terror in Poland for which he was condemned to death at the International Military Tribunal in Nuremberg and hanged (Klessmann, 1993).

The graduate students in clinical psychology were asked to interpret the Frank record without knowing the identity of the subject, and similar to the Eichmann record they would respond in an almost unanimous fashion. In contrast to the Eichmann protocol, however, the students did not see a shallow, banal individual, but rather a complex, cynical, disturbed person who was most likely to be antisocial. Perhaps a prisoner or a mass murderer they added. Also in contrast to the Eichmann record, the students were not surprised to find out that the record, in fact, belonged to a Nazi war criminal.

How is this possible? Eichmann and Frank were two men who were both convicted of violent crimes on a scale that defies human imagination. Yet one is the epitome of banality, the other one cold brutality. It would seem, then, that on

Hans Frank takes the witness stand on his own behalf at the International Military Tribunal in
Nuremberg, Germany. National Archives, courtesy of U.S. Holocaust Memorial Museum.

the surface, Arendt's hypothesis of the banal Nazi does not apply to all Nazis. To
be sure, many Nazis do fit Arendt's hypothesis of the banal Nazi personality. The
psychological test profiles of Ernst Kaltenbrunner (last chief of the Reich Security
Main Office), Joachim von Ribbentrop (Minister of Foreign Affairs), and Fritz
Sauckel (General Plenipotentiary for the Mobilization of Labor), all seemed quite
ordinary, just as Arendt suggested. In contrast with Arendt's hypothesis, the
Rorschach record of Rudolf Hess was particularly disturbed and impoverished.
Hess demonstrated marked systematized paranoid delusions involving bizarre plots
on his life while in captivity in England. When Hess was confronted with the
indictment during the Nuremberg war crimes trial, he could only respond "I can't
remember." In fact, the possibility of insanity was considered for Hess by the
International Military Tribunal, but later rejected. Thus, many involved in the Third
Reich, including Hess and Frank, may have been, in fact, deranged psychopaths or
otherwise psychologically disturbed. To them, the developments of the Third Reich
may have served as a perfect vehicle to vent their impulses in more violent yet, at
that time, socially acceptable forms.

THE PSYCHOLOGICAL STUDY OF NAZI
WAR CRIMINALS

The end of World War II in Europe revealed to the world the extent and scope of the many atrocities committed by the Third Reich. These included unprovoked aggression, slave labor, and death camps. The magnitude of these and other crimes against peace and humanity seem to defy explanation and comprehension by the logical mind. Millions of innocent people were driven into forced labor, tortured in concentration camps, massacred, gassed, or deliberately starved to death, their remains burned and buried to hide the traces. This sad chapter in world history would be unbelievable were it not fully documented by many of the victims as well as by the perpetrators themselves.

When the facts of World War II atrocities became known, most people distanced themselves from the Nazi experience by regarding all perpetrators as inherently evil, psychopathic killers. To members of younger generations, the terror of Nazi Germany during the Third Reich may seem very remote and distant. Indeed, many of these individuals take comfort in their belief that the German Nazi state was a unique event. Similar crimes cannot happen again, particularly in a democracy, they surmise. It is very difficult for them to believe that the Nazis were anything else but abnormal or insane. Given the nature of the monstrous crimes committed they could not have been anything but monsters themselves. Nevertheless, when confronted with the extent of World War II atrocities many have questioned how so many individuals could have conspired in antisocial, destructive, and inhumane acts. One is also forced to wonder whether such crimes against humanity could be repeated, or, in fact, are presently occurring, albeit in a different context (Porpora, 1990).

Some would argue that rather than studying Nazi evil, it should simply be recognized for what it is and condemned. Any efforts at understanding the causes of the Third Reich only serve to explain such actions, thus making them seemingly understandable and perhaps even excusable or justifiable. Many of those who emphasize this viewpoint also take relief in the abstract concept of Nazi evil. They simplistically suggest the presence of a specific homicidal and clinically morbid Nazi personality, impossible of recurring. It is all too tempting and reassuring to portray the Nazis as madmen. One argues that because of their high degree of psychological disturbance, as well as certain unique characteristics that made such group behavior possible, the Nazi phenomenon is unlikely to happen again. Thus, if it takes a clique of madmen in power to launch a Holocaust, the danger of another historic horror of this magnitude recedes (Rubenstein, 1976).

If one is to search for a Nazi personality, whether evil or ordinary, one has to define *personality*. Unfortunately, few scholars agree on a precise definition, but some of the most influential personality theorists have defined personality as follows: a person's unique pattern of traits (Guilford, 1959); the most adequate conceptualization of a person's behavior in all its detail (McClelland, 1951); the individual's effort to adjust to his environment; or, the dynamic organization within the individual of those psychophysical systems that determine his characteristic behavior and thought (Allport, 1961).

To most psychologists, however, personality is simply an individual's most striking or dominant characteristics, those that are relatively consistent over time and across different situations. Personality embraces variables that exist widely in the population and have lawful relations to one another. Personality is the readiness for behavior rather than the behavior itself. The Nazi allegation that "natural biological traits" decide the total being of a person would not have been such a successful political device, had it not been possible to point to numerous instances of relative stability in human behavior and to challenge those who thought to explain them on any basis other than a biological one (Adorno et al., 1950). Of course, the Nazis erred in that they attributed personality exclusively to biological factors, rather than recognizing the contributing environmental and social influences that also shape and determine behavior.

To convert personality theory from speculation about Nazi personality into descriptors that can be studied scientifically, one must put one's theories into testable terms and then study them empirically. This is what differentiates science from the simple assertion of opinions and beliefs. Thus, this text investigates the psychological traits of more than 200 Nazis, traits that are taken to be quantifiable and scalable. It is assumed that individuals differ from each other more or less enduringly in the degree or amount to which they possess each of these attributes. It is also assumed that at least some traits are common in this Nazi sample. In fact, based purely on averages and probabilities of modern personality theory it would be highly unlikely that all Nazis shared one common personality, but highly likely that some traits were common to subgroups of Nazis. The Nazis were hardly a random sample of individuals from the varieties of human nature. That is not to say that many Nazis of a particular order or rank did not have specific traits in common, or were more likely to exhibit a particular personality trait than non-Nazis. But to bluntly suggest that all Nazis had a homogeneous personality and to reduce the behavior of many individuals to global and common descriptors using one or two adjectives, is an obvious oversimplification, one that has, however, been engaged in repeatedly in describing the developments of the Third Reich.

In this volume, the study of personality is therefore concerned with universal human tendencies that many of the Nazis, both rank-and-file and members of the elite, may have had in common, as well as with a description and analysis of individual differences that may make them different and unique. This is not to say that an analysis of Nazi Germany should not deal with group dynamics, social relationships, or social controls. After all, Durkheim (1982), the great French sociologist, suggested that social facts must be explained by social facts. But, do social groups and classes of society have a personality of the same structure as does the personality of an individual? In the Third Reich, the ultimate decisions were made by single humans and the war trials posed legal questions that were investigated on the individual level. Although an understanding of the social processes of aggressive behavior among groups of humans are undoubtedly helpful in understanding the Nazi phenomenon, it is both the individual context and specific group characteristics in which Nazi behavior occurred. These individual and group factors are the focus of this psychological investigation.

There has naturally been an extraordinary amount of work dedicated to documenting and analyzing the Nazi movement, both in terms of the survivors and the perpetrators. Writings have described the Third Reich from philosophical, economical, biographical, historical, criminal, and psychological perspectives. Sociologists, for example, have focused on the social complexity of modern life and the depersonalization of individuals during war, whereas anthropologists have proposed theories of cultural relativism. Behavioral and social scientists may agree that history does not repeat itself exactly, but a general replication appears possible, even though the specific cultural, social, political, and personal factors that led to the Third Reich may themselves have been unique and unrepeatable.

The casual observer of the Third Reich has a more stereotyped knowledge of the Nazi phenomenon based in large part on popular work without the benefit of empirical facts or scholarly presentation of theoretical work. Because of the scope and impact of Nazi Germany on human life and nations, numerous nonacademics have adopted and developed some theories of these sciences and many more have written about the "German mind" or the "German national character."

Many of these works that were provoked by Nazi atrocities have hardly produced compelling answers, but rather constitute mainly superficial explanations derived from inadequate methodology. Most have relied on "armchair speculation" with little if any supporting facts. Predictably, most of these efforts suggested that the actions of those involved in the Third Reich were related to their suffering from particular destructive forms of psychopathology and an overly simplistic personality organization.

The majority of manuscripts on Nazi psychology generally fall into two categories: First, Nazi research with a political agenda; that is, armchair speculations emphasizing the notion of the German (a.k.a. Prussian) national character as monsters with little, if any, data to support the speculations; and a second more sophisticated approach to Nazi research, including thoughtful and often compelling interpretations of interview information gleaned from a small number of ex-Nazis, Nazi victims who survived the Holocaust, children of Nazi perpetrators, "impartial" non-Nazi observers, or witnesses of the Holocaust.

Although this second approach is preferable to armchair speculations, it is not standardized, all data are retrospective personal anecdotes, the subjects never constitute a representative sample of Nazis, and quantitative data analysis methods were not used. Consequently, the interpretations relied heavily on personal opinion. There are many exceptions to the unsatisfactory Nazi personality literature:[11]

---

[11]The interested reader should also consult Browning's (1992) *Ordinary Men: Reserve Battalion 101 and the Final Solution in Poland* (described in chap. 9); Klee, Dressen, and Riess' (1988) *"The Good Old Days" The Holocaust as Seen by its Perpetrators and Bystanders;* Langer's (1972) *The Mind of Adolf Hitler;* Paskuly's (1992) *Death Dealer: The Memoirs of the SS Kommandant at Auschwitz;* Steiner's (1976) *Power Politics and Social Change in National Socialist Germany;* and Waite's (1977) *The Psychopathic God Adolf Hitler.*

Those include Kater's (1983) *The Nazi Party, A Social Profile of its Members and Leaders 1919–1945.* Kater examined in detail the social composition of the Nazi party's general membership and its leadership corps. He concluded that, on a superficial level, there were no significant differences between the "general membership and the functionaries with regard to their motivation for joining the party" and " ... no discernible differences in social makeup between the rank-and-file and the functionaries" (pp. 234–235). However, a detailed examination of the party revealed several important differences. First, the party elite never included a single female member; in contrast the rank-and-file were made up of a small proportion of women; second, the functionaries were much older than the ordinary members, above and beyond what one might expect related to the requirements of the office commensurate with maturity; and third, there were differences in social stratification, with the working class being clearly underrepresented and the social elite being overrepresented in the cadres.

A further study that is noteworthy was done by Merkl (1975), who provided some insight into the attitudes and beliefs of NSDAP members. Merkl published an analysis of 581 autobiographical essays taken from early Nazis who had joined the Party. The essays were collected by Abel (1938, 1965), a noted Columbia University sociology professor. In the summer of 1934, Abel announced in the sociology department of Columbia University an essay contest for "the best personal life history of an adherent to the Hitler movement." This announcement, which was given widespread publicity in Germany by officials of the Nazi party and distributed to all local Nazi offices, resulted in 683 entries ranging in length from 1 to 80 pages. Half of the essays (337) were written by members of the SA or SS (Merkl, 1975, 1980). In 1951 these *vitae* were confiscated by the FBI, possibly for use in pending de-Nazification trials. One-hundred-and-two essays were never returned and were presumably lost, as were about 3,000 additional *vitae* obtained through a second contest in 1939. Merkl's re-analyses, *Violence under the Swastika: 581 Early Nazis* was a monumental effort. These essays offered at least some degree of standardization as well as a sample large and representative enough to include several factions of the Nazi organization. To some extent, Merkl actually used quantitative methods of analysis to determine that the degree of violence perpetrated by an individual was related to certain demographic characteristics (e.g., age, socioeconomic status, and education), the individual's role in the party (storm trooper vs. other) and the date of entry into the party. Merkl (1975) analyzed the essays and concluded that the "collection still includes cases that any prudent censor would have wanted to remove because of their patent prejudice, the violent or hateful behavior they report, or the obvious lack of mental balance" with the earliest joiners showing the most evidence of violence. Merkl further commented that "the impression made by the Abel *vitae* is not exactly flattering to the NSDAP" (pp. 6–7). Thus, there is evidence among these essays that some Nazis who joined the Party in its early years did manifest an antisocial and hostile attitude, although many of the essays were benign in their content. However, we should be cautious in classifying all Party members as psychologically deranged based on this biased sample. Surely any Nazi volunteering to participate in such a contest must have been among the most enthusiastic followers and supporters of Hitler.

Another study of scientific elegance was by Lifton (1986), a psychiatrist by training who analyzed the personalities of Nazi physicians as well as their role in the Nazi genocide. Lifton's research goal was to uncover psychological conditions conducive to evil and focused on the personalities of Nazi doctors by evaluating extensive interviews of 29 ex-Nazi doctors, 12 former Nazi nonmedical professionals, and 80 concentration camp survivors who had frequent association with Nazi doctors during their concentration camp experiences (e.g., Jewish doctors working on medical blocks). Although Lifton's interviews were not standardized and his sample biased, he had much more information than the typical Nazi researcher. Most importantly perhaps, Lifton did not fall into the trap of equating demonic behavior with demonic personalities. Lifton essentially described the Nazi doctors as complex, rather than banal, personalities who, he argued, were able to commit atrocities while leading lives of model citizens, husbands, and fathers by a psychological process he referred to as *doubling.* This capacity allowed many of the Nazi doctors to compartmentalize one area of function, that is the brutal "research" and outright extermination of prisoners, from the remainder of the individual's life, which often included the conscientious medical treatment of the same prisoners later tortured or exterminated. Unlike the work of numerous other less scientific minded authors, Lifton's research revealed the often complex human operations that could be attributed to many of the Nazi doctors. As disturbing as it may seem, participation in mass murder need not require emotions as extreme or demonic as would seem appropriate for such a malignant project. Ordinary people can commit demonic acts, Lifton concluded.

The study of human history is the examination of what people did, that is, their behaviors and actions. This volume is not, however, exclusively a historical one. It does provide historical insight via the examination of new documents, including recently released correspondence from those responsible for administering the psychological test data at the International Military Tribunal in Nuremberg that has led to long delays in the publication of the Nazi Rorschachs. This account traces the conflict between a psychiatrist and a psychologist who, because of personal reasons, greed, and academic ambitions, developed a feud that resulted in many of the Nazi Rorschachs never having been published or interpreted, which could have resulted in an earlier, more objective and timely analysis of the Nazis in postwar years.

To understand history is to understand why people did what they did, that is, their motivations, needs, and drives. In some respects the current study is related to psychohistory, the science of historical motivation, a relatively new interdisciplinary field that emphasizes the need to explore beyond traditional historical causation. The aim of the psychohistorical approach is to employ the methods and findings of psychology, in conjunction with typical historical factors, in order to gain added insight into past motivations of individuals and groups having historical significance (Prisco, 1980). This text differs, however, from

traditional work in psychohistory that has almost uniformly employed psychoanalytic concepts in an effort to explain individual and group behavior. [12] This volume
is also not intended as yet another book providing comprehensive insight into
the creation of Nazi Germany, although the motivations of individuals who played
major as well as minor roles in it are closely examined using contemporary methods
of psychological analyses.

The present volume differs from other studies on the functioning of Nazis,
especially in its methodology. This volume examines these issues from a psychological perspective, one specifically related to the detailed study of psychological
test protocols of more than 200 Nazis who were involved to different degrees in
the Nazi regime. The first goal is to describe the nature of the personalities of the
Nazi elite and the rank-and-file by application of objective scoring and interpretation procedures to individual psychological protocols. This approach removes the
understanding of the Nazi phenomenon from highly subjective grounds. It may
offer a clearer picture of the motivation and personality characteristics of both the
Nazi leader and Nazi follower by integrating the findings with contemporary
personality research (e.g., the 20th-century search for the addictive, authoritarian,
criminal, or fascist personality). Relevant social and clinical research studies that
have been used in explaining the antisocial actions of the Third Reich are reviewed
and integrated with the current findings. By providing a fresh perspective to
understanding the causes that created such antisocial behavior, implications on
current and future political events are offered.

Although the Rorschach inkblot technique has been used and researched for
more than 70 years, it has been recently summarized and systematized by Exner
(1974, 1978a, 1986, 1993) in a compelling effort to make the Rorschach technique
more objective and empirical. The resulting Rorschach Comprehensive System has
been enthusiastically accepted by the psychological community (Piotrowski,
Sherry, & Keller, 1985) represents a significant and progressive step forward in
standardizing and validating administration, scoring, and interpretation of Rorschach responses. Given the publication of Exner's (1990) normative data for
groups including schizophrenics, outpatient character disorders, and normals, it
seems important to re-evaluate and examine the Rorschach records of Nazi leaders
as well as those individuals who "just followed orders." This volume sets out to
quantify the analyses of Nazi Rorschach records by utilizing this most recent form
of scoring and interpretation in an effort to establish a more accurate understanding
about the personalities of Nazis and their behavior.

A second goal of this text is to examine the serendipitous process by which
information bearing on the quest for a Nazi personality slowly came out. Thus, this

[12]Such an example of an overly theoretical and psychoanalytic "description" of Nazis was provided
by Dicks (1950). He suggested, that "Nazis were likely to be men of markedly pregenital or immature
personality structure in which libido organization followed sadomasochistic pattern, based on a
repression of the tender tie with the mother and resulting typically in a homo-sexual paranoid
(extra-punitive) relation to a harsh and ambivalently loved and hated father figure, with its attendant
sadism towards symbols of the displaced bad portion of this figure" (pp. 113–114).

book examines in detail the political events that led to the Nuremberg trials and the psychological climate in the postwar years that may have influenced and shaped our understanding of the Nazi phenomenon. It examines the context in which the psychological evaluations of the prisoners at Nuremberg were carried out, the defendants' reaction to the testing, and the preliminary findings of the data. It also explores the feud between the psychiatrist and psychologist that developed over the Nuremberg psychological test data that resulted in many of the defendant's Rorschachs never having been published or interpreted. Many of these bizarre events that unfolded during the Nuremberg trials and in the postwar years are now being presented because of the availability of previously unreleased personal letters between the Nuremberg trial psychologist and psychiatrist, and other key figures. It is proposed, that, in part, these political and personal forces shaped the quest for a Nazi personality.

SUMMARY

As long as the serious crimes that were committed at Bergen-Belsen, Dachau, and Auschwitz are kept in memory, the question will be asked why so much misery, death, and sorrow had taken place. This volume represents a highly detailed, thoroughly documented and collaborative study of the Rorschach protocols that were administered to Nazi war criminals, their interpretations, and their long delay in publication. It brings together the previous work, as well as new studies, of the authors into a single manuscript by examining the personality structure of a group of Nazi leaders as well as Nazi followers. It is intended for those readers who have an interest in the psychology of Nazi war criminals, the causes of the Holocaust, Nazi genocide, the history of Rorschach testing, or just those who wish to further their understanding of antisocial human behavior. It appears that now, nearly 50 years after the collapse of the Nazi regime, a more objective and professionally responsible examination of the psychological tests on the leaders and followers of the Third Reich can be offered. The present monograph may not seem a particularly pleasant journey to embark upon, but one, we believe, that deserves more scholarly examination as well as a broader public understanding.

Chapter 2

Historical and Psychological Perspectives on the Nuremberg Trials

The victor will always be the judge, and the vanquished the accused.
—Winston S. Churchill (also used by Göring
in his defense at the Nuremberg trials)

WAR CRIMINAL, NAZI, OR GERMAN CITIZEN?

The first assessment of how the Allied forces should deal with the crimes that were committed during the Third Reich was a legal one and not a moral or psychological one. The initial deliberations centered around who was a war criminal, what constituted a war crime, and how war criminals should be brought to justice. As we see here, the forces shaping the question of legal responsibility would have a significant impact on the issue of moral responsibility for Nazism as well. The legal deliberations set the tone for the Nuremberg trials and served as a directory for how the general public would perceive the participants of the Third Reich for decades to come.

The legal discussions, which began during the war and lasted for several years, were filled with controversy regarding precisely how to proceed once the Third Reich was defeated and those responsible captured. Each country participating in the Allied assault on Germany proposed a different solution or strategy. The initial stages on how to deal with Nazi Germany after the war were first shaped while the war was still being fought. During that period, the U.S. media portrayed the Nazis as a group of uniquely sinister, sadistic, and deranged psychopaths. It was popular to view all Nazis, if not all Germans, as representing a homogeneous group of individuals who had more in common with each other than with any other group of people. This perception resulted in the terms *Nazi* and *war criminal* becoming blurred, if not interchangeable.

Originally the term *Nazi* was an abbreviation used in Germany to describe a member of the *Nationalsozialistische Deutsche Arbeiterpartei* (NSDAP). That party membership did not imply war criminal status was confirmed during the Nuremberg trials, where the NSDAP was not considered a criminal organization, although certain organizations of the Party were (e.g., the leadership corps of the Nazi party, the *Sturmabteilungen* or SA, the *Schutzstaffeln* or SS; and the *Sicherheitsdienst* or SS, which was part of the SS). Clearly, all high-ranking members of the Third Reich as well as some military officers were Party members, as was virtually every member of the Gestapo, but they were all charged as individuals for specific war crimes violations and did not stand trial on the basis of NSDAP membership alone. Thus, being a member of the Party did not necessarily confer war criminal status. The term *Nazi,* however, served the media and the public in quickly, although often inaccurately, summarizing the crimes of the Third Reich, the right-wing political beliefs of the NSDAP, or the German people in general, with one acronym. One has to point out that such a characterization of many people was understandable in view of the magnitude of the crimes committed. Nevertheless, although many Nazis were involved in war crimes, many Holocaust perpetrators, police and auxiliary police for example, were not Party members. Likewise, although the Abel (1945) essays suggested a core of Nazis that had particular strong feelings of prejudice and hostility, not all Nazis were necessarily supportive of Third Reich atrocities.

Still, media treatment made no distinction between a Nazi, a war criminal, and a German citizen; in fact, Party membership was sufficient grounds to deny an entry visa to the United States. Consequently, the term *Nazi* became synonymous with *German,* with coldblooded murderers, and with individuals who were thought to be most likely psychologically disturbed. Such a concept was promoted by the media and was embraced by the U.S. public. The oversimplification of the Nazi evil served, of course, as a defense for the purpose of convincing oneself that the atrocities of the Third Reich could not be duplicated in the United States or anywhere else. It also assured the public, as an anxiety reducing mechanism, that "normal" or "ordinary" people would not engage in Nazilike behavior.

THE LEGALITY OF WAR TRIALS: HISTORICAL PERSPECTIVES

The complex moral question of how so many individuals could have acted in such a destructive and antisocial fashion was initially sidestepped. Also rejected was the notion that seemingly normal and ordinary people could have gotten involved and may have actually played major roles in the atrocities of Nazi Germany. Faced with the death and destruction on a scale the world had never witnessed before, people were outraged and insisted: "This must never happen again." Was it possible to get international legal agreement to establish laws against those who waged an unprovoked war of aggression? The intent was to establish acceptable and effective international laws that may prohibit future wars (Tusa & Tusa, 1983).

By 1945, and working under pressure due to the impending end of the war, it was finally agreed upon by the Allied governments that an international tribunal should convene to apply justice over captured German Nazis for crimes dating as far back as 1933 and crimes wherever committed, whether in Germany or an occupied country. Further, the trials did not have to have their legal basis in allegations that defendants had violated either established norms of war or established international law, but rather that the defendants had committed crimes against humanity. On May 7, 1945, General Alfred Jodl signed the unconditional surrender of all German forces in the presence of representatives of the Allied forces. A prosecution staff was quickly assembled to collect evidence for a post-war trial or series of trials. Still to be debated by the Allied delegations was the precise definition of war crimes to be adopted for the trials, particularly the definitions surrounding aggressive warfare and the definition of a war criminal as one who persecutes on the basis of political beliefs. Consensus was not reached easily and at one point a frustrated Chief Justice Robert Jackson (Roosevelt's long-time attorney general who was to head the prosecution team for the U.S. delegation) suggested that it might be easier for each nation to convict those captives that it held themselves. On August 8, 1945, the London Agreement was signed by all 4 nations involved and was acceded to by the 19 countries that comprised the United Nations War Crimes Commission. The agreement established a very broad definition of acts that could and would be considered a war crime and remained the basis for prosecuting those accused of committing atrocities during World War II. A war criminal could be charged with "crimes against peace," "war crimes," "crimes against humanity," as well as the "conspiracy to commit one of these acts." Specifically, Article 6 of the Charter of the International Military Tribunal (i.e., II. Jurisdiction and General Principles) stated:

> The following acts, or any of them, are crimes coming within the jurisdiction of the Tribunal for which there shall be individual responsibility:
> (a) Crimes against peace: Namely, planning, preparation, initiation or waging of a war of aggression, or a war in violation of international treaties, agreements or assurances, or participation in a common plan or conspiracy for the accomplishment of any of the foregoing;
> (b) War Crimes: Namely, violations of the laws or customs of war. Such violations shall include, but not be limited to, murder, ill-treatment or deportation, slave labor or for any other purpose of the civilian population of or in occupied territory, murder or ill-treatment of prisoners of war or persons on the seas, killing of hostages, plunder of public or private property, wanton destruction of cities, towns or villages, or devastation not justified by military necessity; and,
> (c) Crimes against humanity: Namely, murder, extermination, enslavement, deportation, and other inhumane acts committed against any civilian population, before or during the war, or persecution on political, racial or religious grounds in execution of or in connection with any crime within the jurisdiction of the Tribunal, whether or

not in violation of the domestic law of the country where perpetrated. Leaders, organizers, instigators and accomplices participating in the formulation or execution of a common plan or conspiracy to commit any of the foregoing crimes are responsible for all acts performed by any persons in execution of such plan.

Nuremberg was chosen as the site of the "Trial of the Century" in part because of that city's close association with Nazi rallies and Nazi ideology, but also because the Palace of Justice and the accompanying jail had escaped any significant bomb damage. Prosecutors assembled a list of more than 5,000 potential defendants, and by mutual agreement, 24 of them were chosen to stand in the dock at the first trial including the following:

Martin Bormann (Head of the Party Chancery)
Karl Dönitz (Naval Admiral and Hitler's actual successor)
Hans Frank (Party Lawyer and Governor-General of Poland)
Wilhelm Frick (Interior Minister)
Hans Fritzsche (Radio Minister in the Propaganda Ministry)
Walther Funk (Head of the Reichsbank and Economics Minister)
Hermann Göring (Creator of the Gestapo and concentration camps Commander-in-Chief of the Luftwaffe, and Successor-Designate to Hitler)
Rudolf Hess (Hitler's Deputy)
Alfred Jodl (Head of Planning for the High Command)
Ernst Kaltenbrunner (Last Chief of Reich Security Main Office)
Wilhelm Keitel (Chief of the High Command of the German Armed Forces)
Gustav Krupp (Industrialist)
Robert Ley (Labor Front Boss)
Constantin von Neurath (Reich Protector of Czechoslovakia and former Foreign Minister)
Franz von Papen (Vice Chancellor)
Erich Raeder (Navy Commander-in-Chief)
Joachim von Ribbentrop (Minister of Foreign Affairs)
Alfred Rosenberg (Chief Nazi philosopher and Reich Minister for the Eastern Occupied Territories)
Fritz Sauckel (General Plenipotentiary for the Mobilization of Labor)
Hjalmar Schacht (Finance Minister)
Baldur von Schirach (Hitler Youth Leader)
Arthur Seyss-Inquart (Governor to Occupied Poland, Austria, and the Netherlands)
Albert Speer (Hitler's Architect and Munitions Minister)
Julius Streicher (Newspaper editor of *Der Stürmer* and propagandist, Gauleiter of Franconia)

Although many wanted to believe that these "high-ranking Nazis" lumped together for the first trial at Nuremberg represented Hitler's henchmen and were equally knowing and responsible perpetrators of atrocities, the reality was far from

The 21 defendants in the dock at the Nuremberg International Military Tribunal. National Archives.

that. In fact, among the defendants in particular, the degree of knowing complicity or compliance in the atrocities varied greatly and, as we see here, so did the sentences on this heterogeneous group of men judged by the Tribunal.

Of the 24 Nazis selected for the trial, 23 were physically present for the indictment on October 20, 1945. Bormann was never to be seen alive again after a mass breakout from Hitler's Berlin bunker.[1] At Nuremberg he was tried *in absentia* and prosecuted. Of the remaining 23 defendants, only 21 completed the trial. Ley committed suicide and Krupp was considered too infirm to stand trial.

The deaths of the most influential leaders of the Nazi regime Hitler, Goebbels, and Himmler, as well as the disappearance of Bormann, still left a long list of 21 Nazi leaders with the most prominent one being Göring. All subjects were indicted on the four counts agreed upon by the International Military Tribunal. Nazi organizations were also to be accused because by then many had come to believe that Nazi institutions, as well as individuals, were guilty of crimes. They included:

Die Reichsregierung (the Reichs Cabinet)
Das Korps der Politischen Leiter der Nationalsozialistischen Deutschen Arbeiterpartei (the leadership of the party)
Die Schutzstaffeln der Nationalsozialistischen Deutschen Arbeiterpartei (commonly known as the SS)
Der Sicherheitsdienst (also known as the SD)
Die Geheime Staatspolizei (the secret state police also known as the Gestapo)
Die Sturmabteilung der NSDAP (also know as the SA)
The General staff and the high command of the German armed forces

The first trial opened on November 20, 1945 and ended on October 1, 1946. The defense of all the major war criminals—except Speer, who entered a partial plea of guilty—was based on the principle of state sovereignty and the absolute and binding validity of the orders derived from its supreme authority, Hitler. This is the "act-of-state" plea according to which immunity for acts committed on behalf of the state. The problem with this defense was ultimately based on the contention that the Third Reich was personified by one man whose every order, decree, instruction, directive, and regulation—whether written or oral—had the validity and binding power of law (Bailey, 1991).

The International Military Tribunal rejected the act-of-state plea (Davidson, 1966). The acceptance of it would have made prosecution impossible because the former agents of the state could not have been held responsible because they acted on behalf of the state and the state would have remained immune—except for fines and reparations—by virtue of its sovereignty. On judgment day, with the world listening on the radio, Britain's Lord Justice Geoffrey Lawrence read the various sentences. Eleven defendants were sentenced to death by hanging, 3 received life sentences, 4 were given sentences ranging from 10 to 20 years, and 3 were

---

[1] In January 1974 it was confirmed by dental analyses that Bormann died May 1945 while trying to escape through Russian defenses.

acquitted.[2] Organizations that were declared to be illegal and criminal conspiracies under the terms of Article 6, included the Gestapo, the SS, the SD, and the SA. However, the judges held that no member of these organizations could be considered a war criminal per se by reason of membership in these groups. On October 16, 1946, the Allied Control Council in Berlin announced that the sentences of death passed by the International Military Tribunal were carried out this day. Göring had cheated the hangman by taking his own life on the night of October 15, 1946, the eve of his execution day. The ashes of the war criminals were disposed of secretly after the court-ordered cremation.

Of course the most stunning discovery of the trial was the deliberate, cataclysmic destruction of millions of Jews. The oppression of German Jews began as early as 1933, many years before the invasion of Poland or the declaration of war. The Holocaust, the conspiracy against the Jewish people, is well documented (e.g., Hilberg, 1971, 1992; Jäckel & Rohwer, 1985) and not outlined here. The extent of the atrocities committed against the Jews was, however, not known until after the war had ended when the world was informed that more than 6 million Jews had been murdered. Nobody could believe that the prisoners in the dock at Nuremberg had not known at least something of this incredible slaughter.

Further prosecution of war criminals became more difficult due largely to the increasing costs and time requirements of the trials as well as the fact that the United Soviet Socialist Republic, with the beginning of the Cold War, became an enemy of the United States, making further collaboration between the superpowers increasingly difficult. Shortly after the International Military Tribunal had rendered its judgment in the autumn of 1946, 12 additional war crimes cases were carried out in Nuremberg (Taylor, 1992). Three trials were concerned with members of the SS, three with generals of the German armed forces, three with industrialists, one with physicians, one with high-ranking members of the Ministry of Justice, and one with assorted members of the Foreign Office, various branches of the Civil Service, and industrialists. The subsequent 12 Nuremberg trials differed in the lessening degree of public attention that they attracted. But the United States played a much larger role in these trials as reflected in the number of judges provided as well as in the paying of the expenses. There are no reports that psychological tests were given to any of the defendants in these subsequent trials as was the case for the initial International Military Tribunal.

When it was all over in April 1949, the longest (1,194 days) and most time-consuming trials ever had generated 135,731 typewritten pages recording the trial of 177 persons after having heard 1,355 witnesses. Hundreds of thousands of documents were individually scrutinized to prepare the cases of the prosecution. By means of simultaneous translation and a system of headphones, each lawyer or witness was able to speak in his or her native language. In principle, the trial rested

---

[2]Death by hanging—Rosenberg, Göring, Ribbentrop, Jodl, Keitel, Kaltenbrunner, Streicher, Frank, Frick, Seyss-Inquart, and Saukel. Prison terms—Hess life, Raeder life, Funk life, Speer 20 years, Schirach 20 years, Neurath 15 years, and Dönitz 10 years. Acquitted—Fritzsche, Papen, and Schacht.

on established law; its novelty lay in the fact that it was the first time in history that legal proceedings had been instituted against leaders of an enemy nation.

In Germany, Allied military tribunals continued to judge numerous war criminals. U.S., British, and French courts, working from 1947 to 1953, tried 10,400 people, pronounced 5,025 sentences, and executed 806 prisoners. After 1956, the Federal Republic of Germany continued the search for Nazi criminals. In 1958, a central office for seizure and classification of evidence was created in Ludwigsburg. It set up a dossier of more than 200,000 names, prosecuted almost 13,000 and obtained 6,000 convictions. Officials of the German Democratic Republic brought 12,821 war criminals to trial. The figures for the Soviet Union are unavailable, but it is thought that a total of at least 30,000 Nazis were tried.

German State Courts continued to prosecute lesser offenders. The crimes committed by many of the defendants at the Nuremberg trial spoke for themselves. But the legality of proceeding against rank-and-file Nazis was altogether a more difficult matter because it presented different degrees of involvement. Were the guards at Auschwitz war criminals? What about those individuals who built gas ovens or war machinery or those who operated the trains that brought millions of Jews to the death camps? Under Article 6 of the Charter of the International Military Tribunal all of them could be considered war criminals because they may have taken part in an overall conspiracy. As one would progress further down the line of command the responsibility for participating in atrocities becomes diffused and the debate over whether defendants were actually culpable and responsible for crimes committed during the Third Reich increased in intensity.

There were additional Nazi war crimes trials held in other countries including Denmark, Poland, Czechoslovakia, and Yugoslavia. In Denmark the trials focused mainly on trying defendants for conspiracy and treason, rather than crimes against humanity because no atrocities were committed there. Nazi trials were not held in the United States because it did not have jurisdiction over crimes committed in distant lands. Large-scale war crime trials were, however, held in Japan. At the request of the Americans and British, a Far East military tribunal was organized to try war criminals active in the Pacific theater of operations. In 1946, the International Military Tribunal for the Far East charged 28 Japanese war criminals (e.g., Itagaki, Dohihara, Matsui, Tojo, among others) on 55 counts of crimes against peace, murder, and war crimes. Those included the Rape of Nanking, the Bataan Death March, the treatment of POWs, and other slave laborers building the Siam-Burma Death Railway, including the bridge of the River Kwai.

The trials, conducted in Tokyo, were the Japanese counterpart of the Nuremberg court (i.e., "The Other Nuremberg"), but there was little sense that a group of uniquely demonic characters, comparable to the Nazis, had seized control. Although Tojo and six others were hanged by their Allied captors, no single madman or criminal, no Adolf Hitler, Saddam Hussein, or Pol Pot, drove Japan onto the path that resulted in the country's first occupation by a foreign power and its first major military defeat. The Tokyo war crimes trials themselves were generally seen by the Japanese as punishment to their country, for having lost, rather than for extraordinary sins. There is no evidence that suggests that any of the Japanese defendants received psychological testing of any kind as occurred at the Nuremberg trial. The names of the war criminals and the Japanese atrocities committed during World War II are for the most part forgotten, even though the magnitude of the crimes, including Holocaustlike events in China, were similar to those committed by Nazi Germany (Brackman, 1987). Unlike Germany, the Japanese government conducted no war crimes trials of its own.

THE VIEW OF THE U.S. PUBLIC:
PSYCHOLOGICAL PERSPECTIVES

The Nuremberg trials comprised a complex legal proceeding that was difficult for the average American to follow and comprehend. To the U.S. public, it was widely anticipated that the Nuremberg trials would not only demonstrate to the world the guilt of the Nazi elite in war crimes, but also expose them as manifesting a high degree of psychological disturbance. It was assumed that the Nazi regime was a unique event that would stand in isolation in history. It was above all the crime of mass murder that was being tried at Nuremberg, and the persons believed to be implicated in it were not only the men in the dock but millions of their countrymen outside the walls of the Palace of Justice—"the trial therefore was the trials of the Germans" (Davidson, 1966, p. 584). The popular view of Nuremberg is worthy of investigation because it illustrates a frame of reference in which Americans view this event of 1946 and has revealed some of the fundamental concepts, presuppositions, and values that have also influenced current thinking (Bosch, 1970).

The attitude of the U.S. people toward the trial and punishment of the leaders of World War II crystalized early during the initial years of the conflict. Particularly the assault by Japanese forces on Pearl Harbor and the atrocities committed during the Holocaust enraged many ordinary citizens and confirmed for many that those responsible must be punished. Although many Americans favored swifter punishment for the Nazi leaders, the International Military Tribunal was supported by a vast majority of Americans, particularly after the U.S. public was informed that the Tribunal was proclaimed as a U.S. policy. Without doubt, the U.S. public agreed that the accused Nazis were guilty, that the enemy leaders deserved death rather than life imprisonment, and that, in fact, the court may have been too lenient.

Many Americans furthermore believed that a larger number of Nazis should have been prosecuted. In a 1946 survey by the U.S. Information Policy Organization, a clear majority of U.S. citizens (61%) responded with "imprisonment" when asked what to do with members of the Nazi party who defended themselves by claiming that they committed crimes under orders from their superiors. The coverage of the Nuremberg trials and the immediate postwar German scene was hate-ridden, calculating, and merely opportunist. The same characterization is true of the book literature on the Nazi period that appeared during the first few years after the war. There was the same impulse to rush into print on the basis of scanty evidence and unsound premises. Clearly, to the U.S. public and media, Nuremberg became the Allied acceptance and confirmation of the "Nazi devil theory," suggesting the presence of a homogeneous evil conspiracy among all Nazis. In the eyes of the world, the Germans were fair game (Bailey, 1991).

The Nuremberg Tribunal found itself in an impossible situation. The world was prepared to have the court validate that the Nazi war criminals were deranged psychopaths. On the other hand, it could not allow the Nazis to be legally declared insane, for then there would be no one to hold responsible for the crimes. If, for example, the defendants did not to know right from wrong at the time of the crime, were not in control of their intellectual faculties, and could not appreciate the illegal nature of their crimes, then, under international law, they could not be held responsible for their crimes. In this sense the court engaged in a difficult balancing act. On the one hand, the public, the media, and the Tribunal wanted to perceive the Nazis as a group of "crazy" men, but not too crazy, because that would allow them to avoid responsibility for their behavior. Avoided was the fact that some of this heterogeneous group of Nazis assembled at Nuremberg may actually have been psychiatrically disturbed, and that a majority of them may in fact have been quite ordinary. The question of insanity was never addressed, but the issue of competency to stand trial was; it came up in the case of Hess, who asserted that he could not remember anything; Streicher, [3] whose defense counsel thought he had a "diseased mind," and Dr. Robert Ley, who claimed to be emotionally unstable.

THE CASE OF ROBERT LEY

The need for the U.S. public and the medical community to perceive the Nazis as "damaged," can be well demonstrated in the case of Ley. After the Nazi election victory of 1933, Ley[4] (1890–1945), a chemist by profession, suppressed the labor unions and replaced them with the German Labor Front (i.e., *die Deutsche Arbeits front*). He confiscated union funds and started the *Kraft durch Freude* (Strength through Joy) movement. During the war he organized the recruitment of laborers from territories occupied by the Reich, at first on a voluntary basis and then by force. At Nuremberg, Ley was accused of promoting the Nazi conspiracy's accession to power and their consolidation of control over Germany, as well as with authorizing, directing, and participating in war crimes and crimes against humanity, specifically related to labor abuse. When confronted with the charges Ley responded, "Well, they were all working, weren't they?" ("No Geniuses," 1946). Ley was one of three Nazis at the Nuremberg trials who underwent psychiatric examination to evaluate whether he was competent to stand trial. Competency to stand trial determines whether a defendant is psychologically stable, has the necessary intellectual or cognitive resources to comprehend the charges levied against him or her, and can actively participate in his or her own defense. It has no bearing on the determination of guilt. On October 26, 1945, Kelley, then Nuremberg prison psychiatrist, submitted the following report on Ley's mental status to his commanding officer:[5]

---

[3]See chapter 8 for a detailed analysis of Streicher.

[4]For a comprehensive historical profile on Ley, see Smelser (1988).

[5]All correspondence regarding the medical and psychiatric examination of Ley are from the files of Harrower.

Subject: Mental Examination of Prisoner

To: Commanding Officer, Headquarters 6850th Internal Security Detachment, International Military Tribunal, APO 403, U.S. Army

1. Prisoner Robert Ley, 31G 350028, has been observed daily for the past six weeks.

2. Mental examination of Ley reveals normal psychomotor reactions and normal attitudes and behavior. Mood is normal, but affect … is extremely labile. Ley is easily excited and demonstrates marked emotional instability. … Insight is good and judgment is fair. Rorschach examination reveals emotional instability and evidence of frontal lobe damage manifested by color and shading responses, confused form and inadequate construction of responses.

3. Ley gives a history of head injury in an airplane crash on July 29, 1917. He was unconscious for a short time and since this accident has a stammer from time to time. This speech impediment was reduced by alcohol, a common finding in organic brain damage. Ley also drank to excess and possibly further increased the frontal lobe damage.

4. Examination on October 1945 revealed also the usual emotional instability. Ley has been depressed since the Indictment, but has been planning his defense and presented no evidence of suicidal intention. He has always been one of the most potentially suicidal prisoners due to his extreme instability secondary to his old head injury.

5. Ley at all times must be considered competent, to know the difference between right and wrong and to be sane and responsible. His frontal lobe damage contributed to his emotional instability, euphoria and poor judgment, but is not extensive enough to produce psychotic reactions.

[Signed] D.M. Kelley, Major, MC

Ley's case is of interest because the Allied doctors suggested that his aberrant behavior was in all likelihood related to brain damage, although Kelley indicated that Ley would be competent to stand trial and that he knew right from wrong. Kelley reported in his examination of Ley that he was unable to carry on a coherent conversation, that his memory seemed quite good, except for recent occurrences, and, most importantly, that his judgment was very poor. Kelley (1947) argued that Ley's frontal lobes were deteriorating related to "spontaneous degeneration, possibly accelerated by alcohol, and perhaps influenced by his old head injury" [6](pp. 153–154). Kelley further suggested that Ley's medical and psychological examination, particularly the Rorschach inkblot test, confirmed his impression:

> The over-all picture of Robert Ley's Rorschach record is definitely that of an individual suffering from damage to his frontal lobes. Without doubt, Robert Ley's inability to control his emotions and his colossally bad judgment were due to actual

---

[6]On July 29, 1917, Ley was shot down during World War I operations as a flight officer and sustained a head injury. Ley was reportedly unconscious for several hours and unable to speak for nearly a week (Kelley, 1947). Related to this injury he developed a stammer that characterized his speech for the rest of his life. After the war, he returned to Germany and earned a doctoral degree in chemistry. He then became an assistant at the University of Münster and found a lucrative position as chemist at the pharmaceutical company Bayer-Leverkusen, before dedicating himself politically to Hitler.

brain damage ... [and a] direct manifestation of the imperfect functioning of his brain ... [since] the inhibitory centers of his brain had ceased to function. (p. 157)

When Ley was captured by the U.S. Army, he had already engaged in three suicidal gestures, and while at Nuremberg he insisted that he not be tried as a criminal but shot as a German (Gilbert, 1947). Then, on October 25, 1945, he was found dead in his Nuremberg prison cell as a result of strangulation.[7] Ley's suicide presented the U.S. doctors with an opportunity to examine his brain[8] for the presence of neuropathology. If the initial diagnosis of brain damage was correct, what better way to demonstrate to the world that the criminal and aberrant behavior of Ley was related to brain damage—similar behavior cannot occur in individuals with intact brains. Thus, a postmortem autopsy of the brain was ordered to verify Kelley's initial diagnosis. In 1946, Kelley reported on this autopsy:

Since Ley kindly made his brain available for postmortem examination, we were presented with the rare chance to verify our clinical and Rorschach findings. Gross examination demonstrated, as was expected, obvious frontal lobe damage. Microscopic studies have as yet not been completed but are being carried out by Dr. Webb Haymaker, and when finished will be incorporated in a complete clinical, Rorschach and pathological study of this individual. (1946b pp. 46–47)

After Ley's corpse underwent an autopsy his brain was flown to the United States for pathological examinations (Smelser, 1988). Later, the official report of the U.S. Army pathologists was announced ("Dr. Robert Ley's Brain," 1946):

The brain of Dr. Robert Ley, Nazi leader, which was shipped by air to the United States in November of last year for gross examination and microscopic study by Army pathologists shows a "long-standing degenerative process of the frontal lobes," according to Major General Norman T. Kirk, Surgeon General of the Army. Degeneration of the brain of Dr. Ley, he continued, was sufficient to account for the unusual behavior of the former German labor leader. Reports on the results of the neuropathological study of the brain, which was made at the Army Institute of Pathology under the direction of Colonel J.E. Ash, stated that photographs showed considerable thickening of the brain covering over the frontal lobes of both sides. The underlying convolutions as well as some of the blood vessels were hidden from view by this thickening. However, the rest of the brain had a normal appearance, in that it was delicate and transparent. Slight atrophy was indicated by the prominent condition of the grooves between the convolutions of the frontal lobes, and the examination of the frontal lobes under the microscope disclosed a longstanding degenerative process, which is called chronic encephalopathy. This disease process could not be ascribed to the airplane accident Dr. Ley suffered in 1917, because the damage was symmetrical,

---

[7]The details of Ley's suicide are particularly gruesome and demonstrate his desire to succeed at any cost. Neave (1978) reported that Ley had looped the zipper of his GI jacket to the water-tank lever of the toilet and twisted the hem of a towel soaked in water, in a noose about his neck. He then tore up his underpants and stuffed them in his mouth to stop the noise of strangulation as he sat down.

[8]Today, the remains of Ley's brain are kept at the U.S. Army Institute of Pathology, Washington, DC.

according to the Army pathologists. They also added that there was no evidence of preexisting meningitis. Dr. Ley's type of degeneration, the report pointed out, was sometimes seen in those addicted to alcohol, but proof that alcohol was in itself a causative factor was completely lacking. It was pointed out that the degeneration was of sufficient duration and degree to have impaired Dr. Ley's mental and emotional faculties and could well account for his alleged aberrations in conduct and feelings. (p. 188)

The fact that Ley did suffer a head injury and was by most accounts a habitual drunkard, certainly could have contributed to his often erratic and bizarre behavior including violent anti-Semitism and ostentatious vulgarism. What we now know from psychological and neuropsychological studies (Diamond, Barth, & Zillmer, 1988; Levin, Benton, & Grossman, 1982) is that even mild forms of head injury can result in some impairment of judgment and emotional lability.[9] Prolonged use of alcohol has also been associated with memory dysfunction and mental instability. Nevertheless, Ley was able to complete a doctoral degree in chemistry after his head injury and serve in a leadership position under Hitler. There are, of course, thousands of Americans with similar medical histories who have not become Nazis or political fanatics.

The announcement that one Nazi's brain did show neuropathology was extraordinary and apparently confirmed the notion that many actions of Ley, and that of other Nazis perhaps as well, may have been related to "brain damage" or other abnormal, diagnosable conditions. The neuropathological evidence of Ley's brain later turned out to be very weak and undoubtedly distorted by the significant external pressure to find "something wrong" with the Nazis at Nuremberg. On March 31, 1947, Major Haymaker, who at the time was in charge of the U.S. Army Institute of Pathology, received a second opinion of the Ley brain biopsy made by the Department of Mental Hygiene of the Langley Porter Clinic in San Francisco. It stated:

Under separate cover I am sending you a duplicate set of Nissl and a few Van Gieson preparations in the case R.L. As I warned you beforehand, I am not impressed with any definite pathology in this case, at least such as would lead one to suspect a clinical organic condition. The findings are either difficult to evaluate because of post-mortem or fixation artifact, but if real, the changes are not too significant. One would have to know more about the clinical picture and history of the case before drawing any conclusions.

This report as well as his own analysis led Haymaker to write to Kelley in a letter dated December 15, 1947:

As regards Ley, ... I have gone over the case very carefully and found changes, but they were of a lesser scope than we had at first believed. Personally, I think maybe we had better let the whole thing lie buried, as the degree of change could be subject to a difference of opinion.

---

[9] For a detailed discussion of the complex issues involved in the differential assessment of functional and organic etiologies see Golden, Zillmer, and Spiers (1992).

The fact that the U.S. Army and the U.S. public had an investment in the pathology of Ley's brain is ironic, particularly because it was the Nazis themselves who went through much effort to demonstrate through "pseudo-medical research" that "undesirable groups" such as the Jews and Gypsies were similarly biologically damaged. In a morbid display of unethical medicine, Nazi doctors at concentration camps would routinely send postmortem specimen of their targeted groups (i.e., *Untermenschen*) to Berlin for purposes of exhibiting and demonstrating their biological inferiority (Lifton, 1986). Although the Nazi views were racially based, the U.S. public and media were similarly invested in viewing the Nuremberg "gang" as biologically and psychologically abnormal. For example, British and U.S. psychiatrists went so far as to suggest that in *The Case of Rudolf* (Rees, 1948), specific anatomical features of Hess, including an extremely primitive skull formation and the misshapen ears, may serve as possible warning signals in spotting future Nazis.

Thus, it was with great anticipation and some relief that Ley's brain was initially found by experts to be impaired and that his political career in the Third Reich seemed to be in part related to brain dysfunction. The public, as well as many experts, extrapolated erroneously from Ley's abnormal behavior to the case of Ley's abnormal brain. Surely, no one with a "normal" or healthy brain would be able to engage in such atrocities against humanity. The initial diagnosis, however, did not withstand closer examination. A second, not widely circulated opinion of Ley's brain proved to be inconclusive. Ley's brain was not as abnormal as most people had made it out to be, or had wished it to be. Interestingly, after the execution of the 11 Nazi leaders at Nuremberg a request was made to perform additional autopsies, particularly histological studies of their brains. This request was denied, however, because the bodies of the Nazis were to be cremated at the Dachau concentration camp and the ashes disposed of secretly.

SUMMARY

Unquestionably, the men sentenced at Nuremberg had committed crimes of the gravest nature. But the popular belief that the Nuremberg men shared a common sadistic, psychopathic, and deranged personality shifted the burden of guilt and accountability of the Third Reich onto a few. But was the Nazi leadership solely and entirely responsible for the Third Reich? Does the German nation break down into a small percentage of sinister con men and a vast multitude of innocent dupes (Bailey, 1991)? The idea that some, if not many, of the Nazi leaders may have been psychologically normal, ordinary, or healthy individuals and that similar occurrences can happen in our own neighborhood were thoughts that most people were certainly not considering.

There are several popular attitudes toward postwar policy that the Nuremberg trials created. One is that of a legalism of the U.S. mind regarding foreign affairs, the popular American belief to find through law solutions to their problems.[10] Another popular belief was that of adopting a simplistic view of complex international affairs, specifically the Nazi regime. There was a general lack of appreciation for the complexity of the situation. Simple views of good and evil were favored. In fact, the ordinary U.S. citizen frequently seemed more convinced about the causes and blame of the Third Reich, than did many experts.

This oversimplification included the people's belief that a few wicked men (i.e., the defendants at Nuremberg or "Hitler's Henchmen") had caused all this suffering. Thus, it served this purpose to group those 21 men into very simplistic common characteristics, as naturally cruel and brutal if not blood-thirsty monsters. Those 21 German warmongers had destroyed the peace by aggressive war, but through Nuremberg the Nazi leaders had been brought to justice. Therefore, the simple conclusion was that the peace of the world was once more intact. In the postwar years little consideration was given that such atrocities may not have been unique to Nazi Germany, that the 21 men at Nuremberg may not have been a homogeneous group of psychologically disturbed individuals, or that such events could recur.

The Nuremberg trial had to take place for "political and psychological reasons" (Davidson, 1966, p. 586). In this sense, the Nuremberg judgment was congruent with the idealistic, moralistic, simplistic, and legalistic assumptions of the U.S. people. In fact, as a consequence of the Nuremberg and Tokyo trials, the development of the law of individual criminal responsibility for war crimes is now contained almost entirely in the opinions of these two court trials (Shanor & Terrell, 1980). The road to the Nuremberg trials was uncharted and may have been controversial, but the U.S. chief prosecutor, Telford Taylor (1992) suggested that there was a need to introduce the tribunal and the subsequent international laws to hold individuals responsible for war crimes against humanity. They should serve as a warning of personal accountability to prevent atrocities in the name of tribalism or nationalism, crimes that are still being committed against civilians.

In the scientific community the intensity and nature of human dynamics revealed by Nazi atrocities impelled behavioral scientists to study the psychology of war crimes. Nuremberg served as an event to study the prototype of aggressive action, totalitarian leaders' appeal to the masses, and psychological theories of destruction. The issue whether high ranking Nazis as well as those of the rank-and-file were legally responsible was, of course, important and provocative. The following chapters, however, explore an equally important question related to the psychological study of these men. Were they psychiatrically disturbed? Were they the monsters the media and public made them out to be? Did they have anything in

---

[10]This notion recently became evident during the 1991 Gulf War during which direct comparisons were made between Hussein and Hitler and a new call for "Nuremberg style" war trials. Furthermore, Sergei Akhromeyev, military advisor to Soviet President Gorbachev and former armed forces chief of staff accused democratic forces within the Soviet Union of preparing "a Nuremberg trial for the Communist Party." Akhromeyev committed suicide shortly after the failed coup by communist hardliners in August 1991.

common that would permit one to identify these characteristics in advance and thereby provide a safer leadership? Is there, in fact, a Nazi personality?

For no one was it more important than for psychologists, psychiatrists, and psychoanalysts, who were refining their disciplines and extending their clinical and scientific expertise into wider social realms, to understand the nature of Nazism. Many of them were Jewish or of German decent, or both, and many had fled fascist regimes in the 1930s (Hoffman, 1992). However, most wartime and postwartime behavioral research was narrowly focused, and much of it repeated standard stereotypes of a German national character—a belief also supported by a majority of the U.S. public.

The Nuremberg trials raised gigantic problems while providing only partial or cryptic answers that were too often misleading. These are important issues, because the answers to them may help clarify whether we are likely to see such crimes again. These questions, of course, have been asked before by many capable and thoughtful individuals. Some of their findings have been reviewed here and are further studied in subsequent chapters. This text approaches this issue by examining psychological records, the context under which these psychological tests were given to many Nazi war criminals, and the long delay in interpreting those psychological protocols.

Chapter 3

Evaluating the Prisoners at Nuremberg

There is no historical precedent for the Nazi Rorschach materials.
—Robert S. McCully (1980)

THE NUREMBERG JAIL

The Nuremberg jail was run by Colonel Andrus, a professional warden. The 22 major defendants to be tried in the International Military Tribunal were in solitary confinement. Cells were small, 9 x 13 feet, and amenities were kept to a minimum. General Eisenhower ordered that all internees were to be treated as declassified prisoners of war of equal rank. They were to be addressed only as "Mister," with no military rank, official title, or exchange of salutes. Those who still had uniforms were required to remove all insignia of rank and all decorations. Once a day, two prisoners at a time, a 15-minute walk was permitted in the prison yard. One prisoner walked up and down one side of the wall, a second prisoner on the other. No talking was permitted. Daily rations were those prescribed by the Geneva Convention for all prisoners of war, 1,600 calories per day. Some of the defendants complained over the quality and quantity of the food, but prison commander Colonel Andrus reminded them about the victims in the concentration camps. Schacht for one replied, "Don't tell me about concentration camps. I have spent many years there and have fared better than here" (Schirach, 1967, p. 322). Papen (1952) described the Nuremberg jail as damp, smelly, and icy, comparing it to Dante's hell. Lt. Dolibois (1989), who was assigned to Nuremberg as an interrogator reported that at other Allied prisons in Germany, "life was pretty grim and rigid for the declassified Nazi leaders. But that was luxury compared to the war criminals wing in Nuremberg" (p. 148). Schacht (1955) agreed, "The Nuremberg jail was the worst ... we were all treated like convicted criminals" (p. 568).

Aerial view of the Nuremberg Palace of Justice, the scene of the International Military Tribunal. In the rear of the Palace and surrounded by a wall is the prison area that housed the war crime defendants. National Archives, courtesy of U.S. Holocaust Memorial Museum.

By most accounts, Nuremberg was thought to be a strict jail, but the medical needs of the defendants were looked after carefully. For example, during the pretrial and trial period there was a medical staff, including physicians, nurses, psychiatrists, and dentists whose responsibility was that of making sure the prisoners were properly cared for healthwise. Under the direction of U.S. medical doctors, a surgery room, a dental surgery room, and a physiotherapy room were erected for purposes of keeping the Nazis healthy for the upcoming trial. As a result, Göring's hands were no longer shaking in reaction to the deprivation of paracodeine that he was addicted to when he was captured, and he no longer experienced acute stabs of pain (Tusa & Tusa, 1983). U.S. physicians had weaned him away from drugs, and persuaded him to cut down his weight. Göring originally weighed 280 pounds, but lost more than 80 pounds by the time the trial started (Neave, 1978). In the case of Göring, the absence of drugs helped him to be a healthier man than he had been during the war, in full control of his faculties. Other medical progress at Nuremberg was noted on Frank, who since his suicide attempt (he slashed his left wrist and throat) recovered some use of range of motion in his hand. Also, Ribbentrop's neuralgia[1] was responding to heat treatment, Jodl's lumbago[2] had abated, Keitel's flat feet began to respond to exercise, and Seyss-Inquart's stiff knee showed improvement. All this was due to good medical care, mostly by U.S. doctors.

The prisoners's spiritual and mental health needs were equally looked after. There were two chaplains, one Protestant the other Catholic, a contingent of psychiatrists (including Dr. Douglas Kelley, William Dunn, Richard Worthington, and Leon Goldensohn), and one psychologist Dr. Gustave Gilbert. Specifically, Kelley and Gilbert were to be involved in the administration of psychological tests to the defendants at Nuremberg.

MAJOR DOUGLAS KELLEY, MD, PRISON PSYCHIATRIST

Dr. Kelley was a distinguished and experienced psychiatrist—a graduate of the College of Physicians and Surgeons at Columbia, a Rockefeller Fellow, and a faculty member at the University of California Medical School. Before he entered the Army, he was director of the San Francisco City and County Psychopathic Hospital. In mid-1944 Kelley was appointed as Chief of Psychiatry for the European Theater of Operations and arrived at the Nuremberg jail before the start of the trials. The official reason why Kelley was at Nuremberg was "to guard the health of men facing trial for war crimes" (Kelley, 1947). He was also asked to study the prisoners and assist in making decisions about their mental status. Kelley had extensive experience in clinical psychiatry as well as training in the Rorschach inkblot technique. While a Rockefeller Fellow at the New York State Psychiatric Institute, he had co-authored a major text with psychologist Bruno Klopfer on Rorschach interpretation entitled *The Rorschach Technique* (Klopfer & Kelley, 1942). Kelley's interest toward the field of Rorschach testing can be seen in Klopfer's acknowledgment of his co-author's contribution, "Many psychiatrists, by their vital interest and participation, showed a most generous attitude to the invader from a neighboring field. I appreciate especially that my friend Douglas Kelley could find the time to prepare the clinical part of this book" (p. iv). In the introduction of the same text, Dr. Nolan D. C. Lewis, director of the Psychiatric Institute, characterized Kelley as an expert in Rorschach assessment and theory. He wrote that, "Doctors Klopfer and Kelley have had extensive experience in Rorschach work and are recognized experts in the field" (p. x).

In the 1940s it was much more common than it is in the 1990s, for psychiatrists to collaborate with psychologists in the use of the Rorschach. For example, most of the students who attended Klopfer's early seminars were psychiatrists and similarly, numerous fellows from psychiatry were quite close to Rorschach expert

---

[1]Reoccurring pain extending along the course of one or more nerves.

[2]Pain in the lower back due to vascular insufficiency.

Samuel Beck (J. E. Exner, personal communication, October 8, 1993). This may have been related to the fact that the two most widely used personality tests were conceived by psychiatrists, namely, Herman Rorschach, the founder of the Rorschach inkblot technique and Henry Murray, the creator of the Thematic Apperception Test (TAT). Today, however, both the Rorschach and the TAT are diagnostic tools that are almost exclusively used by clinical psychologists. This is related to the fact that the field of psychological testing, particularly test development, test standardization, and test theory were advanced primarily by psychologists.

Thus, Kelley came with considerable clinical knowledge to Nuremberg and was regarded by many as an expert in both clinical psychiatry and Rorschach theory. In the early and mid-1940s he served as one of two associate editors (the other one being Zygmunt Piotrowski, PhD, a Rorschach pioneer) on the *Rorschach Research Exchange,*[3] and in New York was chairman of the training committee of the Rorschach Institute. Although Kelley may have not favored the Rorschach technique as his predominant evaluation tool, he knew the Rorschach well enough, that he would, as part of his clinical examinations, administer it to the defendants at Nuremberg. Kelley could not, however, speak German and while at Nuremberg had to rely mostly on interpreters to assist him in his interviews and psychiatric examinations of prisoners who did not speak English. He left Nuremberg at the beginning of February 1946 for the United States, 2 months after the trial had started and 10 months prior to the conclusion of the International Tribunal. Upon his departure he began work on his book entitled *Twenty-Two Cells in Nuremberg* which was to be published 2 years later, in 1947.

LIEUTENANT GUSTAVE GILBERT PhD, PRISON PSYCHOLOGIST

Gilbert arrived at Nuremberg on October 20, 1945, three months after Kelley. Gilbert replaced Dolibois, the prison commandant's "morale officer" whose role was to look after the prisoners' attitude and moods as well as gather intelligence information that would be of use in the trials and for historical purposes. Gilbert's function was to be the same as Dolibois. And like Dolibois, Gilbert spoke fluent German, thus he was also to assist Kelley with the administration of the Rorschach inkblot test.

Dolibois (1989) said, "I met Gilbert, my long-awaited replacement. Gilbert was a psychologist by profession and could hardly wait to get to work on the Nazis. Later in the afternoon, I made rounds with Gilbert and introduced him to the prisoners as my replacement" (p. 187). The fact that Gilbert was a professional psychologist seems to have been a coincidence. There is no record that Gilbert was officially appointed prison psychologist, but that he suggested this title himself which was easy to do, since there was no official organization chart, no firm line

---

[3]Later to be renamed *The Journal of Personality Assessment.*

of authority, and most everyone could do pretty much what they wanted. Further-more, the prison commandant Col. Andrus, was a professional warden and was trained in supervising a military prison camp. Dolibois reported, "with all due respect, Andrus would not have known a psychologist from a bootmaker. Gilbert had pretty much a free hand and his book was foremost in his mind from the day he arrived. I assure you, I was not much more than a stooge for Col. Andrus, and Gilbert came as my replacement, not as the Prison Psychologist" (Dolibois,[4] personal communication, October, 1991). Persico (1994), in *Nuremberg: Infamy on Trial,* reported that Gilbert quickly saw the potential for a major book on the psychopathology of the Nazis. When Andrus took him aside and asked him whether he would be willing to report back to the prison commander any intelligence he may pick up among the defendants, Gilbert suggested that he had a better chance of succeeding if, instead of being a simple interpreter, he be designated prison psychologist. Andrus agreed, if it was okay with Kelley. Persico (1994), reported that "Kelley did not instantly embrace the idea of Gilbert alone getting access to the courtroom and the new title" (p. 104), but he conceded.

Gilbert (1947) himself reported that his principal duty at Nuremberg was to "maintain close daily contact with the prisoners in order to keep the prison commandant, Col. Andrus, aware of the state of their morale, and to help in any way possible to assure their standing trial with orderly discipline" (p. 7). In addition, Gilbert served as counsel to the prisoners and interpreter to Kelley. In fact, he made a point of almost daily visits to the prisoners, chatting to them about whatever concerned them, questioning them about their attitudes to the past, the indictments, the trial, each other, and making very detailed records of their conversations in his diary which he later published as the *Nuremberg Diary* (1947). Although Gilbert was assigned to the Nuremberg prison, he was not officially part of the medical corps but was a Counterintelligence Corps (CIC) officer and as such reported directly to Andrus, the prison commander. Gilbert stayed throughout the first trial and left Nuremberg in late October 1946.

In 1945, the field of clinical psychology was not as developed or organized as it is in the 1990s. It was not uncommon for psychologists to consult on clinical cases or practice clinical psychology having initially received their doctoral train-ing in a nonclinical specialization such as experimental or social psychology. This was the case with Gilbert who was educated as a social or theoretical psychologist with a degree from Columbia University in 1939. Gilbert was well known for his work on the social psychology of leadership, but was not specifically trained for a clinical setting. His presence at the Nuremberg trials was related in part to Professor Hadley Cantril from Princeton University. Cantril, a social psychologist, was in military government in Germany at the end of the war and stressed the importance of having a psychologist assigned to the prison staff "in order to probe the minds of Nazi leaders before it was too late" (Gilbert, cited in Miale & Selzer, 1975, p.

[4]After Nuremberg, Dolibois moved on to become the U.S. ambassador to Luxembourg 1981–1985, and vice president at Miami University.

xi). Besides having the right connections and an expertise in the study of leadership, Gilbert also knew the German language well, which may have served him in being placed in the Nuremberg prison. Although Gilbert did fancy himself as an expert in German he never made any pretensions about being as knowledgeable a clinician as did Kelley. In fact, he felt relatively uncomfortable with the clinical examinations of the criminals and left this primarily to Kelley. Gilbert, on the other hand, would most often meet with the Nazis for casual conversation and record their dialogues and monologues in his diary.

Gilbert learned to administer the Rorschach as part of a testing course at Columbia in the 1930s, but admitted that he was not very interested in it (J. E. Exner, personal communication, April 15, 1994). Nevertheless, Gilbert did understand the benefits of collecting psychological testing data on the defendants using standardized psychological tests. While at Nuremberg, he administered intelligence and Rorschach tests to the internees. Compared with Kelley, however, he was particularly uncomfortable with the interpretation of the Rorschach technique which would later become an obstacle for him to base any detailed interpretations of the Nazis specifically on the Rorschach data he collected.

THE PSYCHOLOGICAL EXAMINATION
OF THE DEFENDANTS

Naturally, the Nazis were heavily guarded. No one was allowed into their cells except the military police, the chaplains, the psychiatrists, and the psychologist. Security was particularly tight after Ley committed suicide on October 25, 1945. Until then, one guard was assigned to watch four prisoners. After the Ley incident, there was one guard stationed in front of each cell for continued one-on-one surveillance. The guards were under the strictest orders not to talk with the Nazi leaders. Given those circumstances, it was somewhat peculiar that Kelley and Gilbert had almost unrestricted and daily access to the defendants, communicating and interacting with them at their pleasure. Even during the serving of the indictments representatives from psychiatry and psychology were present to record the reactions of the defendants.

Neave (1978), a junior British officer assigned to Nuremberg, reported that the psychiatrists and psychologist were essential to the U.S. way of life at Nuremberg. The constant interviewing of the prisoners by them, however, disturbed both the prosecution and the defense. Neave admitted that they may have been necessary for understanding the "Nazi mind" and suggested that, within this context, much useful information was obtained from the prisoners. To the other three Allied countries this must have seemed somewhat odd, because psychiatry and psychology were hardly as integrated into the military and did not enjoy the same growth and popularity as it did in the United States. Thus, the jargon of Kelley and Gilbert may not have been understood by many, but as Neave pointed out, "it fit the deranged atmosphere of Nuremberg" (p. 59).

Prison psychologist Dr. G. M. Gilbert (right) with defendants (left to right) Speer, Neurath, Funk, Fritzsche, and Schacht. National Archives.

Main section of prisoners' cell block in the Nuremberg jail. Each defendant is watched by an individual guard who is constantly posted at his door. National Archives, courtesy of U.S. Holocaust Memorial Museum.

Some of the Nuremberg defendants enjoyed Kelley's and Gilbert's visits whereas others did not. Those who disliked Gilbert usually responded warmly to Kelley. In particular, Göring and Kelley got along well with each other (Tusa & Tusa, 1983) and Neave (1978) reported that Göring talked "endlessly to Dr. Gilbert by night" (p. 267). Some of the Nazis themselves commented on the friendly rapport they established with Gilbert and Kelley. For example, Speer (1977) thought that Gilbert, "who was Jewish ... helped all of us ... including Streicher" (p. 13), and Schacht (1955) found his talks with Gilbert "in part exhilarating" (p. 579). Papen (1952), on the other hand, complained about visits "by gentlemen who called themselves psychiatrists. It was their duty, apparently, to determine our sanity, though few of them gave impressions of having any genuine scientific qualifications. If they had, people like Göring and Ribbentrop would certainly have been fascinating subjects" (p. 546).

The acceptance of the psychiatric staff by many of the defendants was undoubt-edly related to providing some relief from the dull prison routine and the solitary confinement in which the prisoners had been placed. The Nazis were eager to talk to Gilbert and Kelley because they were virtually held incommunicado. The guards were ordered to maintain a stony silence except to correct them harshly for some breach of discipline. Even the waiters who brought the food were forbidden to return greetings.

Particularly favoring Gilbert's interactions with the defendants was the chronic lack of German speakers among the Allied prison staff. His almost fluent command of the German language facilitated the rapport he established with many of the defendants. Gilbert (1947) reported, "Indeed, for the most part, they were more than eager to express themselves to a psychologist and the only American officer on the prison staff who could speak German" (p. 4). Kelley shared Gilbert's experience that the defendants talked almost without probing or prompting. Kelley reported spending 80 or 90 hours with each defendant, often sitting on the edge of the prisoner's cot and talking to the them for 3 or 4 hours at a stretch. Solitary confinement, Kelley (1947) reported, tended to make them speak freely, "when I came to Nuremberg, I found a group of 'patients' eager to talk. Seldom have I found psychiatric interviews so easy as were most of these" (p. 12).

INTELLIGENCE TEST ADMINISTRATIONS

Most of the defendants were administered IQ tests to estimate their mental abilities in addition to the Rorschach inkblot technique. These tests were given by Gilbert and were adopted for use with German-speaking individuals from the U.S. version of the Wechsler–Bellevue Intelligence Test, Adult Form-I (Wechsler, 1944). In 1945–1946, the Wechsler IQ scales had been used by psychologists for approxi-mately 7 years. The Wechsler scales have since been revised[5] and are the most frequently used psychological test in the United States with adolescents (Archer,

_____
[5]Since the Wechsler–Bellevue Form I there have been three revisions (the Bellevue Form II, the Wechsler Adult Intelligence Scale [WAIS], and the current WAIS-Revised).

Marush, Inhof, & Piotrowski, 1991) and adults (Lubin, Larsen, Matarazzo, & Seever, 1985; Zillmer & Ball, 1987). At the time of the trials, the Wechsler Intelligence scales were certainly the best standardized and normed psychological test available, providing both age-corrected norms and corresponding percentile scores. The specific norms Gilbert used were composed of a 1944 U.S. sample of 1,081 individuals (Wechsler, 1944).

Standing watch at the Nuremberg prison. After Ley's suicide, a guard was assigned to each cell for constant "one-on-one" surveillance. Surprisingly, the prison psychiatrist and prison psychologist had almost unrestricted access to the defendants. National Archives, courtesy of U.S. Holocaust Memorial Museum.

The Wechsler–Bellevue is, like many other standardized psychological tests, an actuarial measure and has to be interpreted in terms of averages and probabilities. In the case of IQ tests, the measure is given to a large number of people and the scores are then sorted and tallied in a distribution that shows how many individuals earned each possible score. In the normal distribution, which is a particular mathematical form that often closely approximates actual score distributions (e.g., height, weight, as well as intelligence), about 66% of the scores deviate less than 1 standard deviation from the mean and about 95% of the scores are within 2 standard deviations. Thus, IQ scores are expressed as deviation units away from the norm. Each of the three Wechsler IQs (verbal, performance, and full scale IQ) have a mean of 100 and a standard deviation of 15. Table 3.1 presents a set of often used classifications of Wechsler IQ scores together with corresponding numerical limits in terms of IQs and percentages. For example, only 2.2 % of the population scores above 128, or in the very superior range, on the Wechsler IQ.

Estimating intelligence has, of course, little in common with the determination of a personality style—certainly intelligence cannot be equated with morality. Rather, IQ estimates serve the purpose of describing an individual's level of cognitive abilities and are highly correlated with academic success. The precise definition of *intelligence,* however, has remained elusive and is still debated. Wechsler (1944) suggested that intelligence be defined as the "aggregate or global capacity involving an individual's ability to act purposefully, to think rationally, and to deal effectively with their environment" (p. 3). Although there are more than 100 different tests of intelligence, the scales developed by Wechsler have become widely used throughout the world and typically include a variety of scales measuring verbal-comprehension skills and tests tapping perceptual-organization abilities.

Given the cultural difference between Germans and Americans in the 1940s as well as the difficulty in providing exact translations for each specific test item, Gilbert wisely decided to eliminate some of the scales to reduce cultural bias.

TABLE 3.1
Intelligence Classification According to IQ Scales of 1944 Including Percentages for the U.S. Standardization Sample for Each IQ category

Classification	IQ Limits	Percent Included
Very superior	128	2.2
Superior	120–127	6.7
Bright normal	111–119	16.1
Average	91–110	50.0
Dull normal	80–90	16.1
Borderline	66–79	6.7
Defective[a]	<65	2.2

[a]The current classification system has also changed from the one used in the 1940s, in part, to avoid stereotypical labeling of individuals with low IQs. Thus, the current terms High Average, Low Average, and Mentally Deficient correspond to the 1944 classifications Bright Normal, Dull Normal, and Mental Defective, respectively.

Because of the difficulty in adequately providing equivalent test items in the German language, scales tapping factual general knowledge, vocabulary, and social comprehension (i.e., information, picture arrangement, and vocabulary subtests) were not administered. Thus, only 8 of the 11 subtests were given. In fact, it would have been invalid to have administered items that inquire about general factual information of U.S. life to assess the IQ of German war criminals. For example, items included in the 1944 version of the information subscale were: How many pints make a quart? How tall is the average American woman? When is Labor Day? Incidentally, all of these items have been changed in the current version of the Wechsler scales, in part, to make the test more culturally fair to immigrants and others.

Thus, the eight subtests that Gilbert administered required relatively little verbal comprehension other than understanding the instruction of the task, which Gilbert could provide in German. They included digit span, reciting single digits both forward and backward; arithmetic, requiring mental calculations; comprehension, which includes items tapping social judgment; similarities, a test requiring verbal concept formation and abstract reasoning; picture completion, a measure tapping the ability to identify important details that have been deleted in a picture; object assembly, a test requiring constructional abilities of familiar objects; block design, a measure of visuospatial abilities; and digit symbol, a measure requiring hand speed, memory, and mental flexibility. After the administration of these scales Gilbert prorated age-corrected IQs for all the Nazis. Gilbert's test results can be examined in Table 3.2.

The mean IQ for the 21 Nazi defendants was 128 falling in the superior to very superior range of intellectual abilities. For purposes of comparison, the mean WAIS-R Full-Scale IQ of a heterogeneous psychiatric inpatient population is approximately 85—low average (Zillmer, Fowler, Newman, & Archer, 1988; Zillmer, Ball Fowler, Newman, Stutts, 1991); that of stroke patients is 87—low average (Zillmer, Fowler, Waechtler, Harris, & Khan, 1992); that of college graduates is 118—high average; and that of doctoral students is 125—superior (Kole & Matarazzo, 1965). In fact, some of the Nazis held doctoral degrees including Frank, who held a law degree (IQ = 130), Schacht an economics degree (IQ = 143), and Ley a degree in chemistry (Ley was not administered the test because he committed suicide the day after Gilbert's arrival at Nuremberg).

The Nazis responded quite differently to the request by Gilbert for IQ testing. Papen (1952) was particularly irritated, "We were called upon to undergo intelligence tests. This was above my head and I asked to be excused" (p. 547). Papen, did admit, however, that the IQ tests did provide for some lighter moments at the Nuremberg jail, "when our marks were added up and announced ... I was third,"[6] a placement that he seemed to be pleased with (p. 547). Fritzsche (1953) reported that he, along with Göring, Speer, Ribbentrop, Rosenberg, Saukel, and Hess, actually enjoyed the testing. Schacht was, however, initially skeptical of the psychometric testing. In his biography he commented on his experience:

---

[6]Papen actually came in fifth.

Ei kiuh, is not a Chinese name, but in fact the English pronunciation for IQ, which is the abbreviation of Intelligence Quotient. It seems that this mental number is important in the United States since it determines an individual's occupational talents. For better or worse, it has developed into a science in the U.S. In the Nuremberg jail, the defendants were constantly visited by physicians and non-physicians alike, who were specifically trained in the field of psychology. They had conversations with each of the prisoners to determine the mental state, and what effect the trial and incarceration had on the defendants. A sad occupation. Since I claimed complete innocence, I was a relatively undesirable object of study. Abnormalities were not to be found in me. I did enjoy the intelligence testing, however. There were several types of tests, for example, the examiner would say: 8257936; which then had to be repeated from memory. The more numbers one could remember the better the IQ. This experiment would be administered forwards and backwards. Furthermore, there were puzzles of blocks and figures and all tests were timed. Using the scores from these tests an index was calculated with the average being 100. Those who score lower than 100 are below average in talent, those who score above 100 are said to be gifted. In calculating the IQ, the age of the respondent is considered, since a child and an elderly person would not have the same mental abilities as an adult person who is in complete control of their faculties. From all the defendants I had the highest IQ. (Schacht, 1955, pp. 579–580)

Keitel became increasingly impressed and fascinated with the objectivity of the test during administration, and remarked how much "better it was than the silly nonsense that German psychologists resorted to in the Wehrmacht testing stations"

TABLE 3.2
Ranking of the Nuremberg Defendants on the Wechsler–Bellevue
Intelligence Scales

Defendant	IQ	Percentile	Classification 1944
Schacht	143	99.8	Very superior
Seyss-Inquart	140	99.6	Very superior
Göring	138	99	Very superior
Dönitz	138	99	Very superior
Papen	134	99	Very superior
Raeder	134	99	Very superior
Frank	130	98	Very superior
Fritzsche	130	98	Very superior
Schirach	130	98	Very superior
Ribbentrop	129	97	Very superior
Keitel	129	97	Very superior
Speer	128	97	Very superior
Jodl	127	96	Superior
Rosenberg	127	96	Superior
Neurath	125	95	Superior
Funk	124	95	Superior
Frick	124	95	Superior
Hess	120	91	Superior
Saukel	118	88	Bright normal
Kaltenbrunner	113	81	Bright normal
Streicher	106	66	Average

(Gilbert, 1947, p. 27). Kelley reported finding out later that Keitel had ordered all intelligence testing stopped after his son flunked one while applying for officer-candidate school ("No Geniuses," 1946).

The advent of Hitler in 1933 had, as in almost all realms of German life, a dramatic effect on the field of psychology. The most obvious consequence of the Nazi seizure was the exodus of psychiatrists and psychologists who were Jewish or simply opponents of the new regime. The Berlin Psychoanalytic Institute, the first of its kind, disappeared in 1936, and with the German annexation of Austria in 1938 came the destruction of the Vienna Psychoanalytic Society and Institute. Freud himself was exiled to one last year of life in London. Thus, "Jewish" psychoanalysis was quickly eliminated and substituted with an intellectually shallow affirmation of professional loyalty to National Socialism and a dedication to the creation of a "new German psychotherapy" (*neue deutsche Seelenheilkunde*; Cocks, 1985).

Psychotherapists responded by forming the German General Medical Society for Psychotherapy in 1933. Its leader Matthias Heinrich Göring was a cousin of Hermann Göring and thus the professional organization was approved without incident by the National Socialist party and the state medical bureaucracy (Cocks, 1985). As a result, the Göring led group established in 1936 the German Institute for Psychological Research and Psychotherapy,[7] often referred to as the Göring Institute. The institute, which in 1942 came under the direction of Hermann Göring, was situated in Berlin with branches in other major cities and had four aims: the creation of a "German" psychotherapy and psychology through the unification of the existing schools of thought; the maintenance of outpatient clinics; the establishment of advisory boards; and, the training of medical and nonmedical psychotherapists. Perhaps it was because Göring felt familiar with the profession of psychology that he is said to have loved the psychological tests administered to him and was delighted with his results. He behaved like a "bright egotistical schoolboy, anxious to show off before the teacher." When told that he was doing well, he praised U.S. methods as being "much better than the stuff our psychologists were fooling around with." Gilbert (1947) reported that Göring "chuckled with glee as he showed surprise at [Göring's] accomplishments" (p. 15). Göring became impatient, however, when he failed on the digit span subtest of nine numbers forward and seven numbers backward, and pleaded with Gilbert for further trials, "*Ach*, come on, give me another crack at it; I can do it!" (p. 15). Given this pattern of rapport there was little encouragement Gilbert needed to offer Göring to participate in the testing and try his best. But Göring was furious to discover that

---

[7]Incidentally, psychological testing was not emphasized because an important feature of the Nazi program was the defamation of everything that tended to make the individual more aware of themselves and their problems. Aptitude testing was the only kind of testing that was allowed during the Third Reich and was sponsored by the wealthy German Labor front which was interested in the industrial applications of psychology. For a more detailed description of Nazi medical psychology see *Psychotherapy in the Third Reich: The Göring Institute* (Cocks, 1985).

Schacht had beaten him, as had Seyss-Inquart, subsequently scorning the un-reliability of the test[8] (Gilbert, 1947, 1950).

Papen was not surprised by Schacht's high score nor by Streicher's bottom place. He described Streicher's position in the Third Reich as one that "could have been occupied by almost any of the other Gauleiter" (Papen, 1952, p. 547). Gilbert reported having to wait patiently while Streicher struggled to work out how much change he would get from 1 Mark if he bought 72 Pfennig worth of stamps. Streicher was sure the answer was 26 Pfennig; given a second try he stuck to his answer.[9] Furthermore, Gilbert was amazed at Schacht's inability to do mental arithmetic; he had expected great things from a financial wizard, although Schacht in his own defense concluded that any financial wizard who is good at arithmetic is probably a swindler. Gilbert (1947) concluded from the intelligence tests admin-istered that all defendants were intelligent enough to have known better.

Kelley (1947) characterized Göring's intellectual acumen as nothing less than brilliant. In fact, 11 of the defendants obtained IQ scores that were in the very superior range. If they had achieved similar scores as children in the United States in the 1990s, they may have qualified for school placement for the "mentally gifted." Furthermore, IQ scores over 130 would have made them eligible for acceptance to Mensa, an international fellowship organization for people with IQ's in the top 2% of the general population. The highest score that can be obtained on the Wechsler IQ test is approximately 150, that is if all items were to be answered correctly. Thus, Schacht's score of 143 comes close to being perfect, although he received some credit for his advanced age. Although the concept of *genius* typically involves a capacity for creative and original thought, it has also been defined as a person having an extraordinarily high intelligence rating on a psychological test (viz., IQ above 140). Thus, a few of these Nuremberg defendants could have been described as "geniuses" and many were certainly intellectually superior. The unpopular notion of Nazi geniuses may be perhaps more digestible, if one would add that this exceptional capacity of intellect was manifested morbidly in the leadership dedicated to performing destruction and warfare.

On other occasions, Kelley suggested that he did not find any "geniuses" among the Nuremberg defendants, "Göring, for example, came through with an IQ of a 138—he's pretty good, but no wizard—and Streicher was under college average" ("No Geniuses," 1946). A little known fact is that Kelley himself took part in a

---

[8]Göring actually scored the second highest on the IQ tests, behind Seyss-Inquart, if one does not take into account adjustments made for Schacht's advanced age. Göring was, however, never informed of this. The fact, that the defendants were told their precise IQ scores is peculiar and not standard practice in the 1990s because the score is a complex composite of a number of subscales and can be misleading, particularly to the layman.

[9]The fact that Streicher was unable to calculate the difference between 100 and 72 seems question-able. After all, Streicher was once an elementary school teacher and may have attempted to fool Gilbert, who was Jewish, into questioning his intelligence. Streicher's teacher certificate, obtained as an 18-year-old in 1903, showed satisfactory and good grades in mathematics and physics, respectively. Ironically, Streicher's only A (*Sehr Gut*) was in religion and church duty, quite a contrast to his open anti-Catholicism and anti-Semitism in later years (Bytwerk, 1983).

Dr. Nancy Bayley (right), one of Dr. Terman's researchers, visits the home of Dr. Douglas Kelley to interview the former head psychiatrist at Nuremberg and former child prodigy. Courtesy of Dr. Padraic Burns.

longitudinal study of "geniuses." In a landmark study, the Stanford psychologist Lewis M. Terman identified school children in California with an IQ higher than 140. Of the 250,000 eleven-year old children screened, Terman found 1,524 who fell into the bracket of "genius." Interestingly, Kelley was one of them. Because of his participation in this study Kelley may have felt particularly compelled to suggest that the high-ranking Nazis had, on a cognitive level, little in common with "his" group. However, Terman's sample of geniuses also included criminals, alcoholics, and prostitutes. Similarly, serial killers Ted Bundy and Jeffrey Dahmer have tested with an IQ of 122 and 121, respectively (i.e., in the superior range of cognitive abilities). It should be obvious to the reader that intelligence and morality are completely unrelated.

IQ testing revealed that the Nazi elite assembled at Nuremberg had at least average, and in most cases superior, intellectual skills. These findings were not widely reported. It may have suited public opinion better if the case could have been made that the defendants were in some way mentally deficient and that the crimes committed by them were related to their impoverished cognitive state. For example, prison chief Andrus (1969) did not trust the accuracy of Gilbert's findings. He questioned the intellectual acumen of the Nazis and announced that not one of these supermen would be intelligent enough to make a buck sergeant in his outfit.

Were these psychological tests valid? Would one not expect the defendants to have been extremely cautious in their interactions with mental health personnel from the United States? Surely they must have known that they were on trial for their lives and understood that Kelley and Gilbert were U.S. officers and that information collected by them could actually be used against the defendants in the courtroom.[10] However, the defendants seemed to have been relatively bored with their isolation in the Nuremberg jail and may have enjoyed company, albeit in the form of a U.S. officer. Furthermore, it appears that many of them were not only complying subjects, but were actually trying to outdo each other or genuinely attempting to impress the Allied occupiers of their psychological superiority. Many of them viewed themselves as a member of the master race (*Herrenrasse*) and wanted to demonstrate to their conquerors their intellectual prowess. After all, they had been living through many years of being told, and spreading the word, of their racial supremacy. For example, Speer (1970) commented that not only did the Nazi prisoners take the tests without resistance, but that they went to great pains to see that their abilities were confirmed, "Who, for example, in his days as a Reichs Marshal or Field Marshal, as a Grand Admiral, minister, or Reichsleiter, would have thought that he would ever submit to intelligence testing by an American military psychologist? And yet this test was not resisted, everyone in fact strove to do the best he could on it and see his abilities confirmed" (p. 509).

RORSCHACH INKBLOT ADMINISTRATIONS

During his 5-month stay at Nuremberg, Kelley administered the Rorschach inkblot test to Hess, Göring, Frank, Rosenberg, Dönitz, Ley, and Streicher. Gilbert, who was stationed at Nuremberg for 1 year (October 1945 to October 1946) administered Rorschachs to Frank, Fritzsche, Funk, Göring, Hess, Kaltenbrunner, Keitel, Neurath, Papen, Ribbentrop, Rosenberg, Saukel, Schacht, Schirach, Seyss-Inquart, and Speer.

A brief glimpse into the Rorschach administrations at Nuremberg was provided by Dolibois (1989), who served as the official interpreter for Kelley's psychological testing. He reported:

---

[10]Gilbert did consult with U.S. prosecutor Jackson about the defendants (Taylor, 1992).

After Hess' last memory test and a few minutes before he is due to take the stand, Dr. G. M. Gilbert (left) informs Hess' attorney that he will not be able to take the stand in his own defense. National Archives.

Kelley, the prison psychiatrist, specialized in the Rorschach Test, the well-known and highly useful method of personality study. The Rorschach is a projective test of personality.[11] The subject is asked to interpret ten standard abstract designs - 'ink blots'. His interpretation is then analyzed as a measure of emotional and intellectual functioning and integration. Kelley could not speak German and had to rely on interpreters to assist him in interviews of prisoners who did not know English. Dr. Kelley showed Rosenberg the design and asked what it represented to him, 'What do you see here?' I was the translator. The doctor timed the response, observed facial expressions, bodily movements, and analyzed the answer or answers. A lot can be discovered by use of this method. (p. 171)

In other cases, Kelley communicated directly in English with the defendants. Hess, for example, spoke perfect English, but Kelley asked Dolibois to sit through the Rorschach anyway, just in case an interpreter was needed. When Gilbert, Dolibois' replacement, arrived in Nuremberg he also served as an interpreter for Kelley on some of the Rorschach records. Kelley (1947) himself reported, "my assistant, Dr. Gustave Gilbert ... was also assigned to my office as an interpreter and, at my direction, made records of many of the conversations which I had with these prisoners" (p. viii).

The defendants reacted differently to the Rorschach testing. Papen (1952) referred to the Rorschach as silly problems in which one is asked to respond to "certain abstract splodges of ink" (p. 547). He suggested that if the Tribunal was interested in assessing his sanity he was "prepared to answer any question in the spheres of history, geography, politics, or economics, but apparently this was a type of conversation for which they were less prepared" (p. 547). Streicher thought "we were all wet," Kelley reported. "Doctor," Streicher said, "to determine what type of men we are, just bring a woman into each cell and see how each person acts" ("No Geniuses," 1946).

Schacht thoroughly enjoyed the Rorschach inkblot tests because he could find an astonishing number of pictures and shapes. In fact, Schacht (1955) thought of the inkblot test as a "game that, if I remember correctly, had been used by Justinus Kerner. Ink is spilled onto a piece of paper. Next, the paper is folded in the middle so that the ink is distributed evenly and symmetrically on both sides. Through this process many bizarre forms are created which are to be detected. In our case this task was made even more enjoyable since inks of different colors were used on the same card" (pp. 579–580). Indeed, Schacht had 38 responses[12] in his protocol (the average number of responses for an adult protocol is approximately 23) and McCully (1980) suggested that Schacht's Rorschach (as well as the records of Frank and Schirach) were particularly rich and would pique the curiosity of any

---

[11]See chapter 5 for a more detailed description of the basics in administration, scoring, and interpretation of the Rorschach test.

[12]The number of responses in a Rorschach protocol is an important index in assessing protocol validity. Within the Comprehensive System, records with fewer than 14 responses are thought to be invalid and unreliable, due to scarce number of material available to base an interpretation on.

experienced Rorschach analyst, "The spontaneity and rich variety of imagery in these three records alone argue against the Nazi prisoners as a group of guarded, depressed individuals, unwilling to reveal themselves due to having been on trial for their lives" (p. 312). Surprisingly, despite the expectations of a possible imminent death sentence, both Schacht and Schirach shared with the examiner, through the medium of the test, their inner resources. Hess was also quite cooperative as Dolibois (1989) reported: "Kelley had explained the procedure, and [Hess] was curious. He took his time studying each card and telling us what he thought it was" (p. 174). Although the Rorschach protocols of many of the defendants were rich with clinical material, others were clearly guarded (e.g., Speer's). This was most likely related to the circumstances surrounding the upcoming trial, although all psychological testing was virtually completed before the beginning of the trial so that the validity of the tests was not influenced directly by the stress of the courtroom proceedings.

Considering the underdeveloped state of clinical psychology and the dominance of psychiatry over psychology, particularly in the military hierarchy of the 1940s, it comes perhaps as no surprise that the examinations by Kelley and Gilbert were not well coordinated and turf issues began to surface. For example, both of them would administer the Rorschach inkblot technique to the same defendant, even though the Rorschach is most useful if the respondent reacts to it in a naive fashion. Both Gilbert and Kelley were undoubtedly aware of the enormous potential and richness of the data that they were collecting, but as is seen here, they did not necessarily share their data with each other. This was the beginning of a "tempest in a tea pot" between the two that would become, in part, responsible for delaying the interpretation of the Rorschach data. This quarrel also resulted in an unfortunate series of events that obstructed what could have resulted in a clearer understanding in the post-war years of the key personalities involved in the Third Reich.

Persico (1994), basing his reports on the personal papers of the prison warden as well as those of Gilbert, provided an interesting account of Gilbert's and Kelley's ambition to write a book while at Nuremberg. Persico suggested that Kelley first approached Gilbert about collaborating on a joint project. But upon Kelley's departure during the trial, Gilbert seemed surprised about Kelley's commitment, particularly when Gilbert discovered that "Kelley had taken all the handwritten originals of the autobiographies they had asked the defendants to write" (p. 240) as well as copy of Gilbert's notes of his cell visits. Furthermore, Kelley had departed without leaving an address where he could be reached. Gilbert was stunned when he then received a letter from Kelley in March 1946 informing him that Kelley was going ahead with a book of his own, in addition to their joint project.

This developing controversy was complicated by the specifics of the roles held by Kelley and Gilbert. Gilbert, a member of the Counterintelligence Corps, was not officially part of the medical corps. This meant that Gilbert was not a direct subordinate of Kelley in terms of line authority. Nevertheless, Kelley held the rank of major and was senior psychiatrist at Nuremberg and as such outranked Gilbert who held the rank of lieutenant. In fact, Kelley would in subsequent years often refer to Gilbert as his "assistant."

In an attempt to devalue the Nazi Rorschach protocols of Kelley, Gilbert would later accuse Kelley of not having appropriately administered the Rorschach records. Although Kelley may have been a better clinician than Gilbert he was hampered by his inability to speak the German language.[13] Thus, Gilbert suggested that Kelley's records were spoiled (because they were for the most part given through an interpreter), doctored (although he never produced evidence for what he meant by this), and referred to them as a "premature attempt" (Gilbert, cited in Miale & Selzer, 1975, p. xiv).

Kelley, on the other hand, may have been somewhat envious of the rapport that Gilbert established with many of the defendants given his command of the German language. Gilbert had almost daily access to the prisoners and recorded extensive conversations with the Nazi leaders in his diary before and during the trials. Kelley would later refer to the Rorschach records that he administered as the "originals" because many of them were given before Gilbert's arrival at Nuremberg. He would also on occasion refer to the Gilbert records as the "subsequent ones" (perhaps related to the 12 "subsequent" Nuremberg trials that were judged by many to be not as prolific and important as the initial International Military Tribunal).

It is unclear who, if anybody, ordered the administration of specific psychological testing to be performed on the defendants. Dolibois (personal communication, October 1991), reported that Kelley pretty much acted on his own. Andrus, the prison commander, seemed not to have ordered the psychological examinations; in fact, he made it no secret that he not only disliked the defendants under his care ("bunch of Krauts"), but also those experts[14] whose job it was to interrogate or otherwise examine them (Andrus, 1969). Thus, the court officials were primarily interested in the issue of whether the Nazi leaders were competent to stand trial, and Kelley's function was to make such personality studies, by whatever method he chose. In this case Kelley decided to rely on the Rorschach inkblots in part because he was knowledgeable of that assessment technique.

The fact that there was little coordination between the efforts of Kelley and Gilbert in their administration of the tests also suggests that the Military Tribunal had very little official interest in the psychological evaluations themselves. Indeed, " ... the administration of the Rorschach inkblot method to leading Nazi war criminals was the farthest thing from the minds of the military and civilian authorities setting up the trials" (Gilbert, cited in Miale & Selzer, 1975). The psychological testing protocols themselves were never used in the trials and

---

[13]There is evidence that Kelley knew some German but not enough to test the defendants in German.

[14]In fact, Andrus' contempt for Kelley led him to file a misconduct charge with the public relations officer of the War Department in Washington DC, on September 6, 1946, because of a "breach of trust" and violation of security regulations. This charge was related to Kelley, although separated from the service, offering interviews to the media even though the Tribunal was still in progress. For example, Andrus suggested in a complaint to Lord Justice Lawrence, that Kelley left Nuremberg under a cloud as the impression had been gained that he was subordinating all of his professional duties to an effort to gather information to publicize later for personal gain, and that he had even gone so far as to misappropriate in part official files.

therefore were not mentioned in the official proceedings. This further suggests that Kelley and Gilbert were not ordered to administer selected psychological assessment instruments, but rather administered the tests, with permission of the prison commander, for two purposes: First, to assist in the determination of any issues the Tribunal might raise pertaining to competency to stand trial; and second, to satisfy personal interests that Kelley and Gilbert had regarding the mental and emotional state of the Nazi defendants. Surely, Kelley and Gilbert[15] were aware that history was being made.

SUMMARY

The circumstances surrounding the psychological examination of the Nazi prisoners at Nuremberg can be described as nothing less than highly unusual if not bizarre. Nevertheless, here for the first time in recorded history was an opportunity to examine standardized mental ability and personality data collected on a group of individuals who played, by most accounts, a major role in the history of the Third Reich and World War II. There was a frenzied excitement surrounding the anticipated publication of the psychological data. For the most part, psychiatrists, psychologists, sociologists, and members of the mental health profession at large were delighted to hear that an army psychiatrist and psychologist had given psychiatric and psychological examinations to each of the prisoners on trial. Naturally, psychologists were particularly interested in the actual responses to the Rorschach inkblot test of those men who had become household symbols of horror during the war years.

---

[15]Gilbert would later refer to the Rorschach protocols as a "gold mine" (J. E. Exner, personal communication, April 15, 1994) and Kelley referred to them as a "psychological treasure" (Persico, 1994, p. 91).

Chapter 4

Delays in the Publication of the Nazi Rorschach Records

This competition or conflict within the profession is stupid.
—Kelley on Gilbert

Heaven protect me from future dependence on temperamental psychiatrists!
—Gilbert on Kelley

To understand the excitement that accrued to the news that Rorschach tests were administered to the Nuremberg war criminals and were to become available, one must remember that the Nuremberg trials had kept alive the seething emotions and understandable hatred of the Nazi regime generated during and after World War II. In terms of the degree of suspense that the Nazi Rorschachs stirred up there is nothing quite like that today. Perhaps one might catch a little of the flavor if one could imagine an announcement, at the height of the Watergate scandal, that Nixon and "all his men" had been psychologically assessed and these test results would be publicly released. This chapter attempts to deal with the perplexing fact, that the psychological Nazi records were not published until three decades after the close of the war, and then only partially.

THE LONDON CONFERENCE

In 1947, plans were being made to hold the first International Congress of the World Federation of Mental Health in London the next year. The purpose of the Congress was to promote among all people and all nations good human relations and a high level of mental health in its broadest biological, educational, and social aspects. The Congress planners hoped to bring together in one organization professional societies throughout the world that were concerned with the treatment of the mentally sick and the promotion of good mental health. In this way, associations of psychiatrists, psychologists, anthropologists, social workers, nurses, and educational specialists would become involved in the organization.

Harrower, like many other professionals in the field, waited eagerly for information as to what was actually going to be made available to specialists. As events developed, she would come to play an important role as a consultant and mediator in the initial efforts of disseminating the Nazi protocols. For example, as vice-president of the executive committee, one of Harrower's duties was to serve as a liaison between the preparatory commission, which spent several months charting the conference procedures, and those individuals who hoped to form small, interdisciplined groups and present their findings at the London Congress. The preparatory commission would then assign broad topics to each country, in order to avoid unnecessary duplication, and to see that all major mental health issues were covered. One of the topics assigned to the United States was that of "war prisoners." Thus, psychiatrists, psychologists, and social scientists with particular interest in the Nuremberg prisoners had an excellent opportunity to focus their attention on the psychological test findings and to have these findings presented before an international audience.

Harrower and Gilbert were members of this group, and Gilbert brought with him, for the group to work with, the test protocols that he had administered at the Nuremberg trials. The first decision, then, agreed upon unanimously by this small, multidisciplinary group was to make available Gilbert's protocols to acknowledged experts at that time. These 11 Rorschach experts[1] were invited to react to the protocols and to submit their reactions to the group. They were assured that their comments would be included in a report to be presented at the upcoming London Congress.

Harrower's directions to this group of experts was as follows:[2]

> As perhaps you may have heard the World Federation for Mental Health is planning to hold an International Congress in London in August 1948. To this end discussion groups are being set up in this and other countries for the consideration of problems and special material relevant to mental health. ... One such commission has been set up to study the psychiatric and psychological material which was obtained in Nuremberg. Dr. Gilbert, the prison psychologist at Nuremberg who is a member of this particular commission, has suggested that I invite you, along with several experts in the field, to make comments on the Rorschach records of the Nazi war criminals which he obtained in Nuremberg, and which are herewith mailed to you for consideration. These actual records, together with comments which we will obtain from

---

[1]The experts were: Dr. Samuel Beck, Dr. Florence Halpern, Dr. Marguerite Hertz, Dr. Bruno Klopfer, Dr. Morris Krugman, Dr. Florence Miale (a student of Klopfer's), Dr. Ruth Munroe, Dr. Zygmunt Piotrowski, Dr. David Rapaport, Dr. Ernst Schachtel, and Dr. David Wechsler. Dr. Oberholzer was also considered but was ill at the time and therefore not included. Harrower and Gilbert, of course, already had the records in their possession. Dr. Kelley's records were not included, and Kelley himself was not a member of the group.

[2]All correspondence released in this chapter are from Harrower's files. All her correspondence and records will, at a future date, be deposited with the Archives of the History of American Psychology located at the University of Akron, Ohio.

other psychologists, will then be published in monograph form under the title of "Clinical Data from the Nuremberg Jail." We do not desire complete interpretation of any of these records from you, but rather would want you to make such comments as would point out features that are, in your opinion, particularly significant as indications of the characteristics or personality traits of these individuals.

Since time is of essence in making these actual records available for study, we must have your comments by October 1st [1947]. If we do not hear from you by that time, we shall assume that you have not been able to contribute to this project.

The list of experts, many of whom Harrower knew personally, could have come out of a 1947 "Who's Who" in Rorschach assessment and theory. Rather than leaving the interpretation of the Rorschach records to only a few, the idea was to publish a small monograph containing the actual raw data and comments from as many experts as cared to go on record. because Harrower had just accepted the editorship of a new psychological series, *The American Lecture in Psychology,* to be published by Charles C. Thomas, the chances of early publication of the work of this Nuremberg study group seemed likely.

However, much to the surprise and disappointment of the Nuremberg study group, not one of those experts invited undertook the task of examining the Rorschach records that they had received. All experts regretted, although expressing it in many different ways, that they were not able to fit the work into their schedules. For many of the reviewers lack of time, unexpected personal involvements, and other responsibilities apparently intervened.

For example, Dr. David Rapaport from the Menninger Foundation wrote on September 25, 1947: "I am grateful that you thought of me in this connection [Nazi records]. My present commitments are so heavy, however, that I cannot see my way clear to do anything about these records for a long while. May I keep these records and communicate with you if and when I would find myself somewhat less tied up in knots?"

Dr. Klopfer excused himself with the following letter, dated September 27, 1947: "You will understand that it will be impossible for me to do anything with the material before October 1st. I am naturally interested in the project. I will appreciate it if I can hear more about it."

This unexpected and uniform noninvolvement in such a crucial task, with the opportunity for a joint presentation of the findings at an International Congress certainly appeared strange and noteworthy, even though the experts had only 4 weeks to submit their comments. Surely one possibility that needed examination, and undoubtedly contributed to the exodus of Rorschach reviewers, was the climate of opinion in 1947 that simply did not allow an assessment of the Nazi Rorschach records as scientifically, objectively, and dispassionately as possible. Thirty years later, Harrower (1976a) described this in the following way:

As experts in 1946 we operated on the assumption that a sensitive clinical tool, which the Rorschach unquestionably is, ... must also be able to demonstrate moral purpose, or lack of it, in persons of various assets and liabilities. That is, we expected the Rorschach to predict to which ends or goals a person's assets were directed. Implicit

also at that time was the belief that this test would reveal an idiosyncratic psychopathology, a uniform personality structure of a particularly repellent kind. We espoused
a concept of evil which dealt in black and white, sheep and goats. We had not been
challenged by such startling and unpopular ideas as those of Arendt and Milgram. We
tended to disbelieve the evidence of our scientific senses because our concept of evil
was such that it was ingrained in the personality and therefore must be a tangible,
scoreable, element in psychological tests. (p. 342)

Regardless of the reason, the disappointing fact remained that the Nazi Rorschach records were never presented at the International Congress in London in
1948.[3]

THE KELLEY–GILBERT CONTROVERSY

Although the London conference would not announce to the world the findings of
the Nazi Rorschach records, there was still time remaining for a possible speedy
publication of the Rorschach material. With the conclusion of the Nuremberg trials,
Kelley and Gilbert intended to publish the clinical material that they collected at
Nuremberg quickly and if possible to be the first to print the material. The
Rorschach records were of great interest to laymen and experts alike and could
potentially provide a unique, perhaps more objective, understanding of the personalities of leading Nazis. Needless to say, the publication and analysis of the clinical
material of the Nuremberg Nazis would also assure the author substantial public
exposure and academic esteem. Although Kelley (1947) had published *Twenty-two
Cells in Nuremberg* and Gilbert (1947) had released his book *Nuremberg Diary*, an
in-depth discussion and presentation of the Nazi Rorschachs were not included.
Thus, it should come as no surprise that an intensive and bitter controversy
developed between the investigators as to who had the right to publish the
psychological material first.

In terms of the military hierarchy, Kelley outranked Gilbert. Thus, Kelley
claimed the rights to the material and senior authorship. He argued that because
Gilbert worked under him at Nuremberg, all the material Gilbert collected should
be his. Kelley, who had conducted, via an interpreter, many psychiatric interviews
with the Nazis, planned a book in which the psychological tests requisitioned by
him, would be included as part of his presentation. On the other hand, Gilbert
claimed that because he had administered the majority of the tests, they were his
property. He announced his intentions of publishing them independently.

As editor of a new series of monographs in psychology, Harrower thought that
a comprehensive book on the psychological findings of the war criminals would
have been an appropriate way to start the new series. Ideally, the records should
have appeared in one co-authored volume with extensive notes and comments by

---

[3]Gilbert did present two related papers entitled "The Problem of German Authoritarianism and
Aggression" and "Nazi Authoritarianism and Aggression" (Gilbert, 1948b, 1948c).

various experts. She also cautioned against the publication of separate books on the topic, because she feared that the Rorschach data may not be presented well in different manuscripts. Harrower found herself in a situation in which she knew Kelley and Gilbert personally, because she had met with each of them on different assignments of mutual interest. After some negotiations about the publication of the records, an uneasy peace seemed to have been worked out, specifically between Kelley and Gilbert, to pave the way for two to three separate monographs on the Nazi Rorschachs. Harrower, however, insisted that it would be less confusing to present the Rorschachs in one volume, rather than two or three. She informed Kelley that she felt a single volume written by Kelley and Gilbert would be far more effective than two that are apt to be competitive and confusing. Kelley replied on September 29, 1947:

> As far as the publishing of the [Nazi] records goes, it doesn't make a great deal of difference to me how they are published. What I have done so far is to send out seven records I took which represent to me the most interesting individuals from various points of view. I sent these records to representatives of different schools of thought and to people in foreign countries simply to get a broad interpretative viewpoint. I then plan to edit this material so as to get as accurate a personality pattern as possible from the material. It seemed to me that if we pooled ideas from such widely divergent opinions as [Rorschach experts] Beck, Hertz and Klopfer, we might get an assortment of ideas which would be more interesting than if you or I or Piotrowski worked on them since we three seem to favor ideas taken from a wider base. ...

> Frankly, the only difficulty I can see would be in getting cooperation from Gilbert who seems extremely eager to burst into print. ...

> At any rate he continually startles me by his apparent neglect of basic ethics. For example, he writes that he agrees to the basic premise of a letter I wrote on August 29 [1947], stating that he is willing to wait until my book is ready for publication before he publishes his. His last letter, according to my lawyers, constitutes a flat written contract on this point whether he realizes it or not but in a letter I just got he states in a casual sort of way that he plans to send his to the publisher November 1st. In view of his written statements to me, of course, I am a little surprised at such behavior and it is this sort of thing that makes me wonder whether we can get together. Since as a result of his writing to me, I have sent him my protocols which he has accepted and I am told that I have a perfect right to block his publication through a legal injunction on the publisher until I am ready to publish. ...

> I agree with both you and [publisher] Thomas that this makes much better sense, and my only requirement would be that I was maintained as senior author. I feel that this demand is reasonable since if it had not been for my marked activity Gus [Gilbert] would never have had any material of any type whatsoever to publish.

In 1947, Gilbert was in an academic track at Princeton and perhaps more eager to complete scholarly work than was Kelley, who held an appointment in psychiatry at the Bowman Gray School of Medicine at Wake Forest University. Gilbert was, however, slowed down in the interpretation of the Rorschachs because of his lack of training in this technique. Thus, he was particularly dependent on the reviews of Rorschach experts, if he were to go ahead and publish an analysis of the records himself. Nevertheless, by October 8, 1947, Gilbert had not received any comments from the experts and was quite anxious to print the records himself. He wrote to Harrower:

> It looks as though it will be better for me to complete my own comments without regard to the "experts", who will probably prefer to write their own papers for their own purposes. I can foresee no end of trouble if one "expert" is quoted and another is not, or any of them is not quoted sufficiently to give his authoritative opinion. ...
>
> Kelley writes that you suggested our bringing out a volume together. The only way I can envision such collaboration would be a more ambitious volume by Gilbert and Kelley, in that order, giving comprehensive clinical evaluations of each character with something of a case history. That would be a more professional enterprise to replace the superficial attempt Kelley made in "22 Cells in Nuremberg." I am willing, of course, to overlook my grievances against Kelley, the fact that he would probably contribute nothing but other people's Rorschach evaluations. ...
>
> My own suggestion would be to go ahead with our original plan and get the clinical data into print as soon as possible. Then the "experts" in every field can make of it what they will.

By the end of 1947, the Rorschach records had been mailed out to many experts, however, in part due to the Kelley–Gilbert controversy, none of the Rorschach material had yet been published or extensively analyzed. One has to realize that the Rorschach technique at this time was anything from standardized. Beck, Harrower, Hertz, Klopfer, Piotrowski, and Rapaport were all pioneers in Rorschach administration, interpretation, and theory. All of them preferred, to some degree, different nuances in the scoring and analyses of Rorschach responses, many of which are still in use today. Thus, it is unfortunate that a detailed discussion of the same Rorschach records from different perspectives never made it to print. If it had, it would have undoubtedly shed some light on the personality make-up of the individuals concerned. The Kelley–Gilbert feud, however, was by no means over and appeared to have little concern for the inherent historical value of the material to be presented. To complicate matters further, some of the Rorschach experts (Levy and Beck, in particular) were working under the assumption that their comments were still to be integrated in Gilbert's book on the Nazi Rorschachs. They were unaware that Gilbert, in midstream, decided to complete the monograph himself. On October 17, 1947, Harrower, in her role as editor, reminded Gilbert: "I forgot to give you the only two letters of the group [of experts] which are really relevant, Levy's which shows the kind of criticism you ought to be aware of, and Beck's, which seems to me quite important in that he has obviously put in a great deal of work in regard to these records. Frankly, I don't think that you can tell him now that you won't use them."

By then, Gilbert's manuscript was sufficiently far enough along for him having obtained a contract with Charles C. Thomas for its publication in the *American Lecture Series in Psychology,* under the title *Clinical Material from the Nuremberg Jail.* From then on, however, Gilbert became increasingly anxious at what he felt were unnecessary delays in publication, although Harrower assured him that it had gone forward in a routine way. Gilbert wrote to Harrower (October 21, 1947):

> I trust to you to get as prompt publication on this over-due collection of data as possible. There is just one thing I must insist on, however, and that is that you will not be intimidated by Kelley's threats into curtailing or delaying the publication in any way. I will take full responsibility for my right to publish what I give you and for going to press when I submit the material. I will even give you a specific signed statement to that effect to protect the publisher, but I will not put up with anymore of Kelley's nonsense beyond the specific concessions I have already made, and I will be the judge of that.

Harrower responding to Gilbert (October 27, 1947):

> I wish to state at this point, however, that I somewhat dislike your suggestion that I would either be intimidated by Kelley or in any way not see that your publication got through in the routine fashion. To take the first point, if Kelley states that he will have his lawyer take action if certain material appears in print, it does not constitute "intimidation" to notify the publisher that such action may occur and that he must be the judge of whether he wishes to be involved in a possible legal rumpus. The statement from you that you take full responsibility does not in any way seem to me to be a solution. I do think you will have to have a clear and written statement from Kelley that he does not intend to fight any part of it before you can submit it to me or I, in good conscience, to the publisher.

Gilbert responding to Harrower (October 28, 1947):

> I am really quite amazed at your suggestion that I should get a written statement from Kelley that he does not intend to fight any part of my material. Kelley and I have already arrived at an agreement in writing, and you must surely have enough confidence in my professional integrity to know that I would not submit anything that could properly be the subject of legal action. … From my previous experience … rest assured that I have no interest in Kelley's pathetic little "autobiographies," although none of us recognizes his exclusive right to use them. As a matter of fact, I still think he was just bluffing to bargain for co-authorship and may never publish a clinical monograph. I suspect that even Klopfer is not cooperating with him, because the letter I received from Klopfer today states that he is not keen on the idea of Rorschach interpretation on these men out of context. Evidently it is up to me.

As the editor of the *American Lecture Series,* Harrower saw part of her responsibilities in assuring the publisher that there were no legal implications if and when the manuscript would be turned over to the publisher. To this extent the publisher, after being informed by Harrower that there may be copyright issues involved in the preparation of the manuscript, decided to take out a bond in the shape of a letter showing a recent understanding with Kelley, before the publication of the manuscript. Correspondence from Gilbert to the editor (December 30, 1947):

I have finally heard from Kelley. He says he still has not gotten the replies from his consultants, in other words, hasn't even started his project, as we suspected all along. He therefore proposes that we call off the agreement and I go ahead without using his material. That is OK with me. ... I am much happier about this arrangement particularly since I suspected Kelley of "doctoring" his records, and perhaps he was jittery about that too.

After Gilbert had decided not to use the interpretations provided by Beck, he put less emphasis on the Rorschach data in his manuscript. This decision to place less emphasis on the Nazi Rorschachs was undoubtedly related to the fact, that it was becoming increasingly more difficult to secure comments from experts, as well as Gilbert feeling particularly uncomfortable, due to his lack of Rorschach expertise, to present a monograph on the interpretations alone. Thus, it comes as no surprise that Gilbert only wanted to include about half of the Rorschach material relegating the test data to an appendix to prevent "the tail wagging the dog." However, the decision not to include any of Beck's blind interpretations on the Nazis angered Beck. He wrote to Harrower (January 9, 1948):

I do confess to some irritation following receipt of Doctor Gilbert's letter; but it was very minor, and of short duration. This was, as you have surmised, in reaction to the time and effort I put into that material. However, I am not really taking any of this seriously; and I am so heavily committed now that I certainly would not plan to publish this separately.

Regarding the Kelley–Gilbert controversy, you must recall that psychologists are human beings. In fact that is the whole problem namely, that human beings are human beings. I am fortunate in having a slight reserve of philosophical attitude. I think it may have something to do with my survival.

Apparently, Gilbert's anxiety about the publication date and the type of book (hardcover vs. paperback) caused him to deviate from the generally accepted standards of author–publisher agreement, for in the hopes of a speedier publication he approached another publisher (i.e., Norton) in March 1948 with the same manuscript. By one of those delightful twists of fate, Harrower was selected as the outside reader for Norton and was suddenly faced with the reading of the very same manuscript for which she held a contract as an editor for Thomas.

Norton to Harrower (March 19, 1948): "I hope that you will be good enough to give us a confidential professional read on a manuscript just in from Professor G.M. Gilbert of the Department of Psychology in Princeton entitled Studies in Dictatorship. This request is not only urgent on my part but ... we really need your help."

Naturally, Harrower informed Norton that Gilbert at that time still had a contract with Thomas. She corresponded (March 22, 1948):

I am absolutely dumbfounded at your request, as I have in my files a copy of a contract for the American Lecture Series for Professor Gilbert's "Studies in Dictatorship" and the contract was signed, with witnesses to all parties, July 22, 1947. ... There is a really insane jealousy at the present time among the people who were working at Nuremberg in a desperate effort to get their material to the public as the one and only book on the subject. ...

I cannot refrain from wondering what would happen if, in acknowledging the manuscript, you said you had turned it over to your reader, Dr. Molly Harrower!

It is understandable that in view of this and other threats, together with the confusion arising from Gilbert turning his manuscript over to Norton, the contract Gilbert held with Thomas was terminated. Thomas informed Gilbert that he may plan to go ahead with the manuscript material in any way which he might see fit. Gilbert did publish with another publisher, Ronald Press, in 1950 under the title *Studies in Dictatorship.* After all the *Sturm und Drang* it did not include the Rorschach test data after all!

The bad blood between Gilbert and Kelley, however, remained and was in no small part responsible for the reasons that the Rorschach records never were published until much later in 1975 by Miale and Selzer in *The Nuremberg Mind,* which featured the 16 Gilbert records. Gilbert himself never published the raw data or any detailed interpretations of the protocols, due in part to his lack of training in the Rorschach technique. As mentioned earlier, Kelley was a well-known expert on Rorschach testing. Clearly, Kelley had the clinical knowledge of presenting interpretations on the clinical material for the records that he administered, and to which he referred to as the "originals." For reasons unknown, he never did publish the Rorschach protocols with the exception of a brief report in 1947 and the Kelley records never made it to print and have remained unobtainable until now.[4] As to how the other experts interpreted the material, no comments were ever put into print. Clearly, some of those experts had to know about the degree of ownership that Gilbert and Kelley laid claim to and had little interest in getting involved.

The extent to which this animosity between Kelley and Gilbert persisted can be seen from a letter Kelley later wrote to Harrower on September 13, 1948:

I am somewhat concerned over a recent letter I received from a colleague abroad who had written me concerning the Nazi Rorschachs. He wrote requesting a set and before I could get them mailed, wrote again stating that he had received a set from Gilbert. The interpretations he sent me of the records indicate that he apparently believes he has the original records and I have no way of knowing whether Gilbert indicated that the ones he sent were retakes or whether Gilbert simply sent along copies of the seven originals which I gave him when we were considering publishing the book together with you as editor.

In view of his attitude at that time, I see no reason why I should permit him to use any of my material and have determined through our board of trustees and legal advisors to bring an injunction and suit against him and his publisher if such material appears. ...

I have simply turned the whole thing en masse to our legal staff. They point out that permanent prevention of such unethical publication would probably be difficult since the material is not copyrighted but feel that an injunction would blast the whole thing into the public eye with sufficient publicity to require the Ethics Committee of the APA to hold a formal hearing. ... I would like to stress that I have no argument with

---

[4]Two of the Kelley records (i.e., those of Dönitz and Streicher) are reviewed in chapter 8.

[publisher] Thomas, or whoever publishes the material, since I am quite certain they probably do not realize they are publishing stolen goods.

Gilbert must have felt that Kelley had him in a legal bind from which he could not extricate himself. His lack of expertise with the Rorschach test itself certainly did not facilitate his efforts for publication. Gilbert found himself in the possession of a large cache of foreign money but did not know how to exchange it!

SUMMARY

What does this Rorschach controversy suggest? In the first place, it would seem that our culture places great emphasis on the first publication when material of a highly charged nature is concerned. The two potential authors, Kelley and Gilbert, seemed to feel that unless their book was the first, it would be of lesser importance. Rather than share or pool their stories, each taking credit and responsibility for their actual contribution, they preferred to go it alone and to outmaneuver each other when necessary, refusing to contribute presumably promised supporting material, threatening legal proceedings, and operating outside the signed contract in search of a quicker publication.

The behavior of the experts called in to contribute their evaluations for the 1948 London conference, originally eager, but then "regretting" their ability to do so, due to sundry pressure of other work is also noteworthy. The opportunity to appear jointly as a commission at an international congress, where each expert's evaluation of the criminal's character would be presented, was surely not something that people, versed and soaked in the field, would forego. There are several possible explanations for this. One is that the experts did not want to become involved in the work of Gilbert and Kelley. They may have sensed the hostility among the two that they were competing over the Nuremberg material to appear in print first. They did not want to interfere or provide interpretations that later would be published under someone else's authorship.

Another perhaps more likely reason was that the experts were baffled by what they found, questioned their own interpretations, and questioned the examiners competence in administrating the records. They preferred not to go on record with a reaction that might indicate that our stereotypes of these "uniformly" horrendous criminals, had to be modified in terms of accepting their diverse personality types and personality structures. To have gone public in 1948 during a highly visible conference and declare that, according to psychological test data, many of the Nazis may actually have been normal or even well-adjusted, would have undoubtedly raised considerable criticism against not only that Rorschach interpreter, but also the whole field of psychological testing itself. The public and the media just had too much investment into thinking that the Germans, the Third Reich and the Nazis, were a homogeneously sinister and psychologically deranged group. In 1948, however, nobody wanted to "go on record" and comment on the "emperor's new clothes."

Chapter 5

The Rorschach Inkblot Technique

But it is only an inkblot.

—John E. Exner, Jr.

Psychological testing has often been associated, even considered synonymous, with the Rorschach inkblot test. How does the Rorschach test work and how are psychologists able to turn responses to inkblots into descriptions about one's personality? This chapter provides a synopsis of the main characteristics of psychological testing and presents the elements involved in the administration, scoring, and interpretation of the Rorschach Comprehensive System (Exner, 1993). Furthermore, this chapter reviews the irregularities that occurred in the Rorschach administration of the Nazi records and that may have impacted their reliability and validity. More detailed studies of the Nazi protocols are featured in the following chapters.

PSYCHOMETRICS

Psychometrics, the science of measuring human traits or abilities, is concerned with the standardization of psychological tests. A standardized test is a task or set of tasks administered under standard conditions and designed to assess some aspect of a person's knowledge, skill, or personality. Standardized psychological tests typically yield one or more objectively obtained quantitative scores that permit systematic comparisons to be made between different groups of individuals. The Rorschach inkblot technique, which is such a standardized test, provides a consistent way of test administration and of measuring individual differences regarding some psychological concept. In the present case, comparisons can be made among the Nazis, normals, and other psychiatric diagnostic populations.

For any psychological test to be useful it must be both reliable and valid. Reliability refers to the stability or dependability of a test score as reflected in its consistency upon repeated measurement of the same individual (Zillmer & Ball, 1987). For example, in

68

the case of Göering, Rosenberg, and Frank, repeat administrations of the Rorschach were given by the prison psychologist Gilbert. All things being equal, a reliable test should have produced similar findings on each administration.

The validity of a test refers to the meaningfulness of specific inferences made from the test scores; that is, does the test really measure what it was intended to measure? If a test is unreliable, it cannot be valid because a test that does not correlate with itself will not correlate with anything else. There are several different strategies for determining validity. Briefly, *construct validity* focuses primarily on the test score as a measure of the abstract psychological characteristic or construct of interest (e.g., depression, intelligence, impulsiveness, etc.). *Content validity* pertains to the degree to which a sample of items or tasks makes conceptual sense or is representative of some defined psychological domain. For example, can one interpret the verbatim response of "chameleon" seen so frequently in Nazi Rorschach records literally? Finally, *criterion validity* demonstrates that scores are related systematically to one or more outcome criteria, such as dangerousness or sadism, either now (i.e., concurrent validity) or in the future (i.e., predictive validity).

Clinical personality assessment is specifically concerned with identifying the nature and severity of maladaptive, abnormal, and bizarre behavior patterns and phenomena, as well as understanding the conditions that have caused and/or are maintaining such behavior. Numerous tests have been designed to measure such facets of personality, and it is convenient to group these tests into two categories—objective and projective personality techniques. Objective tests typically use the questionnaire technique of measurement (e.g., true–false or multiple choice), whereas projective tests rely on relatively ambiguous, vague, and unstructured stimuli, such as inkblots. Through the presentation of ambiguous material in an unstructured testing situation, the examinee may project a good deal about his or her own conflicts, motives, coping techniques, and other aspects of his or her personality. Thus, projective tests place greater emphasis on how an individual organizes and perceives the stimuli presented to him or her. For example, any stimulus situation that is not structured to elicit a specific class of responses (as do true–false inventories and the like) may evoke the projective process. The science of standardized clinical psychological testing has evolved over the past 80 years to the point where there are literally hundreds of psychological assessment instruments in use today. The Rorschach is one of the first personality tests developed and one of the most researched and frequently used psychological techniques today.

THE RORSCHACH INKBLOT TECHNIQUE

The Rorschach inkblot test is named after the Swiss psychiatrist Herman Rorschach (1884–1922). Rorschach developed the test as an extension to earlier research using inkblots to study imagination. Since first described by Rorschach, the inkblot technique has enjoyed a rich but often controversial history regarding the precise nature of the test's administration, scoring, and interpretation. This controversy is related, in part, to the developer of the test having died at the early age of 38, just a year after the test was published, and to the subsequent loss of leadership regarding the use of the test. Since the 1970s, the Rorschach inkblot test has been summarized and systematized by Exner (1974, 1986, 1993) in an intensive effort to make the Rorschach technique more objective and empirical. The resulting Rorschach Comprehensive System has been enthusiastically accepted by the psychological community (Piotrowski et al., 1985) and represents a significant step forward in standardizing and validating the administration, scoring, and interpretation of Rorschach responses.

Exner did not necessarily view the Rorschach test solely as a projective technique, but rather as a standardized cognitive–perceptual task or problem-solving exercise in which a patient's responses are compared with those of normative groups. By relating a patient's perception against extensive empirical data, a host of probable behavioral correlates can be generated with remarkable clinical accuracy. During the often stormy history of the Rorschach inkblot technique, those who have criticized its usefulness as a test have frequently pointed to problems of establishing satisfactory evidence of reliability compared to other psychological assessment tools. Test–retest studies over a period of 1 year, however, have revealed that a majority of Rorschach indices in the Exner Comprehensive System actually exceed a respectable .80. Those correlations falling below .80 are not sufficient to support a claim of stability or consistency of the variable. However, Rorschach responses can be viewed as a sampling of problem-solving behavior they may be influenced by psychological states. Thus, Exner (1986) pointed out that those variables having retest correlations between .70 and .79 are representative of state rather than trait indices. As a result of extensive research on the test–retest consistency most psychologists would agree that the Rorschach has at least adequate reliability when used with the Exner Comprehensive System. Given the recent publication of normative data for different diagnostic groups, including schizophrenics, outpatient character disorders, and normals (Exner, 1990), the Rorschach records of the World War II Nazis can be evaluated using this most recent and modern form of scoring and interpretation.

THE NATURE OF THE RORSHACH TECHNIQUE

How can responses to 10 inkblots provide any information about an individual's personality? At first glance it does seem incredulous particularly because the Rorschach method is considerably more complex than was initially conceived. To understand the process that is involved in forming a Rorschach response one has to be aware that there are numerous cognitive–psychological operations that may occur before a single response is actually delivered. In effect, the nature of the test situation forces the subject to convert the blot into something that it is not. As a result, a problem-solving situation is created that requires some violation of reality on part of the respondent. At the same time, the subject is concerned about his or her own personal integrity. Thus, the requirement to "misidentify" the stimuli provokes a series of complex psychological operations resulting in an activity that ultimately culminates in the verbalization of responses. This situation posed by the need to misidentify the stimulus card, requires many cognitive–psychological operations including the encoding of the stimulus and its parts, the rank ordering of the many potential responses created, making decisions as to which of the answers to verbalize and which to discard, and the selection of some of the remaining responses based on state and trait influences (Exner, 1986). After these phases have occurred, a response is delivered that may be as simple a perception as "a bat" or may include the process of projection as "two people fighting." In the more common, concrete responses formulated by the contours of the blot there is no evidence of projection. Rather, the respondent perceives or "sees" the blot in a certain way (e.g., "a butterfly"). Rorschach (1921) referred to this process simply as "naming."

The more obvious projected material appears in the form of an embellishment to a response. For example, the response, "Two people attempting to lift something up ... they are straining in great pain" goes well beyond the stimulus features of the inkblot and clearly illustrates projected material, a process Rorschach identified as the interpretation of the blot. Projections often provide an important interpretative source when the content of the record is reviewed, however, not all of the responses to the Rorschach test represent projected material; in fact, the majority of on nonpatient responses contain no projections (Exner, 1986, 1989). Nevertheless, the Rorschach provokes an abundance of perceptual and cognitive operations and opens the psychological door for projection to occur. If the procedures for collecting data are employed in accordance with standard procedures, the Rorschach technique can provide personality information about habits, traits, and styles, in children as young as 5 and in adults as old as 70 and beyond. The Rorschach is not an x-ray of the mind or of the soul as is often the popular opinion, but it can project a picture of the psychology of the person, when administered, scored, and interpreted correctly.

TEST MATERIALS AND ADMINISTRATION

The Rorschach inkblot technique consists of 10 symmetrical inkblots, 5 chromatic and 5 achromatic. There is nothing "special" or "magical" about these 10 blots, (see illustration) except that they are the original ones developed by Rorschach, and have been the plates most often used for purposes of research and normative studies.

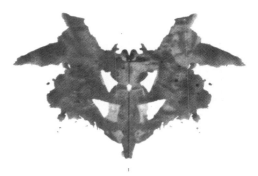

Reduced copy of Card I from the Rorschach inkblot technique (copyright, Verlag Hans Huber, Bern, Switzerland).

The Rorschach takes approximately 1 hour to administer. In the Comprehensive System, the inkblot cards are shown one at a time, always in the same order, with the instructor seated by the examinee's side—to minimize body language communication—simply asking: "What might this be?" This question sets off a series of complex cognitive operations that involve scanning, coding, classifying, comparing, discarding, and selecting. Numerous decisions occur during the process with the examinee finally articulating a selected answer which is recorded verbatim by the examiner. Typically, respondents will give more than 20 responses to the 10 cards. This initial phase of the administration is known as the *free association phase* because the examinee is asked to respond to the inkblots with a minimum of guidance or structure.

Following the presentation of all 10 cards, the examiner systematically questions the subject with regard to each response. This is referred to as the *inquiry phase*. In this phase, the responses are reviewed to clarify in each case the coding or scoring as accurately as possible. The immediate objective of the inquiry is for the examiner to understand what the subject has seen or, at the very least, to comprehend where in the blot the subject sees his or her response, and what features of the blot cause it to be seen that way (Exner, 1993). The inquiry period is neither a new test nor a time when new information is collected, but rather a delicate part of the examination, for if misunderstood by the subject or mishandled by the examiner, it can lead to many errors in scoring and to subsequent problems in the interpretation of the record.

All responses are then scored in terms of their location on the blot and for the determinants used in forming the response, the level of accuracy of the percept, the general content of the response, the degree to which organization occurs, as well as other special criteria reflecting inadequate thought process or the presence of a specific content. After all the responses have been scored, the scores are tallied and a number of specific ratios and indices are computed that make up the *structural summary*. The structural summary represents a composite of code frequencies plus many ratios, percentages, and numerical derivations that are based on the scores assigned to the subject's Rorschach responses. The scores, together with the actual content of the responses, generate data from which many important postulates concerning psychological characteristics and functioning are arrived at.

The following definitions serve as a brief discussion of the primary Rorschach elements used in scoring and interpretation (Exner, 1993; Korchin, 1976). A detailed description of Rorschach criteria are, however, beyond the scope of this chapter because of the length and complexity involved. The reader is reminded that there are some important, general interpretative hypotheses that are used regarding each scoring categories. If interpreted in isolation, they do not reflect valid descriptors of personality and are therefore routinely combined in ratios and indices. For purposes of illustration, however, an overview of the main interpretative hypotheses of the Rorschach codes are outlined here, so that the reader can follow more clearly some of the more detailed discussions on the interpretation of the Nazi case records presented later.

RORSCHACH SCORING

The scoring of Rorschach responses provides psychologists the constancy of a language that recognizes the same Rorschach characteristics in a single record or across different records. The basic rule of Rorschach scoring is that (a) the code or score should represent the cognitive operation that occurred at the time the subject gave the answer, and (b) all components that appear in the response should be included in the coding (Exner, 1993). Numerous studies have been conducted to insure adequate interscorer reliability for each variable, using a minimum standard of 80% agreement among coders.

Location. The location of a response is scored first and refers to the exact area of the inkblot that was used in formulating the response. The location score can vary from the entire or whole blot (i.e., scoring code = *W*) to the use of common details or of unusual detail (i.e., scored *D* and *Dd*, respectively). The location of an individual response is determined with the aid of diagrams that specify location designations. The area chosen generally indicates the subject's cognitive orientation; that is, whether he or she integrates or separates experiences, deals more in the abstract, is limited to conventional categories, or is drawn to the trivial and unusual. Thus, many whole responses (i.e., *W*s), if of sufficient complexity and accuracy, are usually considered to show a capacity for abstraction and integration. An abundance of detail responses (i.e., *D* and *Dd*) are the mark of conventional thought. In general, detail responses are less energy-consuming than are whole responses. Thus, they are by far the most frequent location choice made by normal adults. Overall, however, a healthy record should reflect balance among the location scores.

Determinants. After scoring the location of the subject's responses, the next scoring issue that warrants examination is related to what aspects of the blot were used in producing or determining each individual response. Determinants refer to the style or characteristic of the blot to which the examinee responds. Many specific categories and scoring conventions have been suggested for scoring determinants and it is in this realm that the clinician's judgment is most taxed. The major determinants are as follows:

1. Movement: Movement responses are of particular interest to the clinician because the blots are obviously immobile. Thus, in seeing movement in a static stimuli, the subject is going beyond the given. For these reasons, clinicians consider the presence of human movement (scored *M*; e.g., "two people talking") a measure of the capacity for fantasy and inner reflection. Rorschach research has demonstrated that high frequency *M* people are creative, imaginative, and well endowed intellectually. They are capable of delaying action and emotional expression by substituting thought and fantasy. Although *M* is associated with the ability to delay and carefully think through stressful situations, the presence of animal movement (scored *FM*; e.g., "a bear prowling") may reveal inappropriate and sometimes

impulsive behavior and appears to be much more associated with internal need states. Studies have demonstrated that inanimate forms of movement (scored m; e.g., "an explosion") are most likely linked to outside stresses, that is, situations and circumstances that are beyond one's control.

2. Shading: Variations in hue are typically scored as shading. Most clinicians would agree that the presence of pure shading (scored Y; e.g., "an x-ray") is associated with the unpleasant experience or anxiety of being helpless in dealing with stressful situations. Texture responses (scored T; e.g., "hairy fur") are associated with a need for emotional contact with others, whereas the vista determinant (scored V; e.g., "a valley stretching out before me, the darker part makes it look like it goes back in the distance") is associated with the experience, most often painful, of thinking about oneself or introspection. Research on shading responses has demonstrated that Y codes occur with greater frequency in depressed individuals than in individuals who are anxiety free. Regarding texture or T, most nonpsychiatric adults have one texture response in their record. In contrast, a variety of patient populations are characterized by either more or no texture responses, reflecting either an inordinate need for emotional contact and dependency (i.e., $T \geq 2$), or denial of any need for this sort of experience (i.e., $T = 0$). The vista response (V) occurs most frequently in Rorschachs of chronically depressed and suicidal individuals.

3. Color: Briefly, color responses (scored C) are thought to be related to the emotional life of an individual, particularly how one experiences and modulates one's mental or emotional life. The degree to which form is used in the perception of any color (also for shading responses) is indicated by the addition of a score of form (i.e., F). For example, a sunset only based on colors is scored pure C; if some form is involved, but color is more important, it is scored color–form (or CF; e.g., "a garden, it is green"). If the shape is more important than color, it is scored form–color (or FC; e.g., "the shape of a red tulip").

Normative studies indicate that children have more CF and C in their records than FC. Conversely, adults who are able to delay their responses in a problem-solving task have more FC than CF or C in their record. Achromatic color (scored C') is scored and interpreted when the gray, white, or black feature of the blot has been utilized in the percept. This code has been correlated with the constraint or the internalization of emotion, in contrast to the color (C) response, and indicates an ability to express emotions.

Form Quality.   The form quality scoring reflects how accurately each Rorschach response corresponds to the form of the inkblot, that is, does the response occur statistically more frequently in nonpsychiatric populations than in psychiatric populations. Thus, the examiner assigns a score of superior (+) or ordinary (o) for percepts in instances where appropriate form is involved and that a majority of individuals would have no difficulty seeing. Unusual (u) or minus (−) form quality reflects an unconvincing, ill-conceived, distorted, and statistically rare use of form fit. In nonpsychiatric populations, approximately 80% of all responses have good form quality (i.e., a score of + or o), whereas in psychiatric populations that percentage decreases markedly. Individuals with an abundance of poor form quality responses typically demonstrate eccentric behavior, poor reality testing, and in severe cases a psychotic adjustment.

Content. The scoring and interpretation of content responses is related to what an individual sees. Normative studies suggest that animals and humans are most frequently seen. Some responses are normatively so frequent that they are called *popular* and are scored *P*. Research on content categories has demonstrated that schizophrenics give fewer *P* responses, depressives fewer human responses, and that a group of content categories, including plant life, clouds, maps, nature, and landscape, can be associated with a distant, isolated interpersonal style. In general, however, the reliability and validity of interpreting the content of Rorschach responses has not been empirically substantiated and considerable controversy remains regarding the precise nature of the interpretation of such codes. Regarding the Nazi war criminals, this debate has centered around whether contents of military regalia or the presence of chameleon responses occur more often in the Nazi protocols than they do in normals, and whether to attach any special interpretative significance to these categories.

INTERPRETATION OF THE RORSCHACH

After the examinee's responses have been scored according to the above criteria, they are rearranged into quantitative formulas and ratios that make up the structural summary. These data reflect the proportions and comparisons for the various Rorschach factors outlined earlier. The primary interpretations are based on the quantitative formulas, not on individual characteristics of the record. Thus, the usefulness of Rorschach interpretation is realized only from the complete sum of its parts. This is a new direction in Rorschach interpretation and is related to research associating specific behavioral and diagnostic categories with the presence of specific Rorschach clusters, rather than a simplistic *pathognomonic* (Greek for "fit to give judgment") "sign" approach or a psychodynamic "symbolic" interpretation, which have contributed little to validate Rorschach theory (Meehl, 1973).

The interpretation of the Rorschach is quite complex and only a brief overview is offered here. Fundamental requirements in interpreting the Rorschach include an understanding of personality theory, expertise in psychopathology and psychodiagnostics, a grounding in psychometrics, an understanding of the test itself, and access to normative data in order to be able to reject or accept interpretative hypotheses. The interpretative process begins with the development of hypotheses using the data from the structural summary. This includes frequencies for each of the scoring codes, as well as numerous ratios, percentages, and derivations obtained from the frequencies (in total more than 100 variables). Structural summary variables appear to have the greatest reliability and much validation research has been accumulated on them. Next, the interpreter proceeds to the *sequence of scores* that affords a picture of the coding for the answers in the order in which they occurred in the record. Often the sequence of scores will provide additional important information about clustering of codes and about the manner in which the subject has approached the blots. The final step in the interpretative procedure is a careful review of the words themselves that the subject used in formulating his or her answers. The verbatim responses may reflect some of the idiosyncrasies of the subject and can be very important in enhancing previously developed propositions.

As the interpretative procedure moves from one data set to another; that is, from the structural summary through the sequence of scores and finally to the verbal material, a psychological picture of the subject gradually unfolds. The final interpretation may include a myriad of reliable and valid features about a subject's personality, such as the quality of cognitive operations, perceptual accuracy, flexibility of ideation and attitudes, modulation of affect, goal orientation, self-esteem, interest in people, and so on. Using all of the Rorschach elements discussed, the psychologist is therefore prepared to provide a comprehensive description of an individual's personality.

IRREGULARITIES OF THE NAZI RORSCHACH ADMINISTRATIONS

Several features of the Nazi records did not entirely conform to modern Rorschach administration. It is important to discuss these irregularities here because they may influence the subsequent scoring and interpretation of the Nazi material. Most of the differences are related to the fact that the Rorschachs were administered according to the older Klopfer system. Given Kelley's close association with Klopfer (Klopfer & Kelley, 1942), both Kelley and Gilbert administered the Rorschach using this system, which was the most popular one among psychologists in the 1940s. Although the Klopfer administration of the Rorschach technique included a free association and inquiry period, it differs in a number of important ways when compared with more modern administration procedures (Exner, 1993). For example, in the Klopfer system the latency of all responses is routinely timed and recorded. This recording of the reaction time to responses was subsequently proven to be a relatively inaccurate science and not related to any specific descriptors of personality. Thus, the response latency of the defendant's answers to the Rorschach technique are not included in the presentation of the Nazi records here and are not used in any modern interpretation of Nazi Rorschachs.

Furthermore, it was standard practice in the 1940s to "test the limits," a technique in which the examiner, after having administered the Rorschach, exerts pressure on the subject in a systematic and controlled way in order to provoke reactions and to cover "conspicuous omissions" on the part of the respondent. This is done to ascertain whether the subject is capable of other sorts of responses by calling attention to particular areas of the blot and hinting or, for example, asking outright "Might it also be a bat?" Gilbert criticized Kelley's administration as incomplete because he did not comply with the standard Klopfer procedures of

Rorschach administration as regards testing the limits (Miale & Selzer, 1975). It appears, however, that Kelley did employ this technique; he referred to it in the inquiry phase as " ... on testing. ... " The practice of testing the limits was, and remains, a very controversial procedure. It may render any repeat administrations of the Rorschach to the same subject invalid because the subject would no longer be naive about the Rorschach responses. Incidentally, testing the limits has fallen out of favor in contemporary Rorschach administration, in part, because of the response bias it creates for any further Rorschach testing of the same subject, and also, because empirical studies have never determined any construct validity for this procedure. Thus, information collected by this technique has not been included in modern analysis of the Rorschach data.

Further idiosyncrasies in the Kelley records presented in this text are related to his presentation of the inquiry phase, which Kelley paraphrased rather than recording it verbatim in accordance with standard procedure. His presentation of the inquiry period in summary form is probably due to the fact that he took many notes during the administrations, some of which were translated to English and then copied and summarized in his final record. In this sense, the inquiry leaves something to be desired because on some occasions we have to make due with Kelley's impressions, and this may lead to scoring differences.

Another habit peculiar to 1940s Rorschach administration is related to the examiner asking the respondent routinely, and without being prompted, "Is it alive?" to inquire for active (e.g., "flying") or passive (e.g., "hanging") forms of movement. Thus, in reviewing the Kelley records the reader will notice on many occasions that Kelley made a note whether the percept was alive or not. In the current Comprehensive System, this procedure is considered improper because it is thought to lead the respondent too much into giving a specific answer. For the current purpose of scoring and interpreting the Nazi protocols, all responses involving movement that did not spontaneously occur within the context of the record were ignored and not scored. Finally, it was common procedure in the 1940s to routinely record additional responses or spontaneous elaborations during the inquiry period and to treat these as part of the record. Again these have been discarded in more recent Nazi Rorschach research.

The protocols presented in this text, although not faithfully administered within the modern standards of Rorschach testing, are remarkable testimonies to the rich history of psychological testing, and provide intriguing opportunities to evaluate the personalities of influential Nazis as well as those of the rank-and-file.

Chapter 6
Interpreting the Nazi Rorschachs: The Nazi Elite

To see the Nazis as more or less ordinary men is neither to excuse their deeds nor minimize the threat they pose. On the contrary, it is to recognize how fragile are the bonds of civility and decency that keep any kind of human community from utter collapse.

—Rabbi Richard L. Rubenstein, Professor of Religion (1976)

The psychological records of the Nuremberg group attracted a great deal of attention during the first several years after the Nuremberg trials. Particularly for Gilbert and Kelley—who had the records in their possession and argued over the ownership of them—they were not only the key to understanding the personalities of leading Nazis, but also a sure route to fame and respect in the academic community. Thus, when Kelley's tour of duty at the Nuremberg jail expired, he returned to the United States to immediately begin working on the Nazi material he had gathered.

It needs to be remembered that the main purpose of the Nuremberg jail was to safeguard the Nazi defendants and to assure their availability to stand trial, not to perform detailed psychological testing on them. Thus, the jail was managed by professional military wardens much like a prison facility, not a psychiatric hospital. It is understandable, therefore, that the work completed by Kelley, Gilbert, and other mental health staff members went mostly unnoticed. Surely, Kelley could have stayed on at Nuremberg throughout the duration of the trial, but Kelley seemed to have been fed up with the uselessness of what he was doing at the prison. Kelley felt that he had collected enough psychological data and psychiatric notes during his 5-month stay at the Nuremberg jail for whatever professional use he might want to make of it (J.E. Dolibois, personal communication, October 2, 1991).

THE KELLEY RECORDS

On April 26, 1946—only months after Kelley (1946a) had left Nuremberg—he presented a paper entitled *Preliminary Report of Rorschach studies of Nazi War Criminals in Nuremberg* at the 17th annual meeting of the Eastern Psychological Association hosted by Fordham University in New York City. Kelley's friend, former co-author and Rorschach expert, Bruno Klopfer (then associated with City College), served as the chairman for the paper session entitled *Round Table on Projective Techniques*. The same year Kelley also read the identical paper at the 7th annual meeting of the Rorschach Institute, also in New York City.

There are no notes available that shed any light on how Kelley's presentations were received, and there are no proceedings available as to what Kelley presented. His thoughts about the Nuremberg Nazis became clearer when he published his *Preliminary Studies* in the *Rorschach Research Exchange* (Kelley, 1946b). This journal article is important, for it represents the very first publication concerning the psychological functioning of the Nazi war criminals and provides us with an initial perspective of the psychological profiles of high-ranking Nazis. Kelley's first report may also have been a more objective account of the Nazi personalities, because it was published before the verdicts of the International Military Tribunal were announced in October 1946. Thus, Kelley's paper may not have been affected as much as later reports were by the immediate posttrial publicity surrounding the execution of 11 of the Nazi prisoners. In *Preliminary Studies* Kelley argued that the Nuremberg defendants were:

> essentially sane and although in some instances somewhat deviated from normal, nevertheless knew precisely what they were doing during their years of ruthless domination. From our findings we must conclude not only that such personalities are not unique or insane, but also that they could be duplicated in any country of the world today. We must also realize that such personalities exist in this country and that there are undoubtedly certain individuals who would willingly climb over the corpses of one half of the people of the United States, if by so doing, they could thereby be given control of the other half. A realization of this fact and an understanding of the types of personality capable of such action is an important step along the path for prevention of such an occurrence. (p. 47)

During this time, Kelley was interviewed by the *New Yorker Magazine* in an article entitled "No Geniuses" (1946). Excerpts from the interview shed further light on his opinion of the top Nuremberg defendants as well as on Kelley's own persona.

> We have just had an illuminating talk with Lt. Col. Douglas M. Kelley, until recently chief psychiatrist at the Nuremberg trials, a man who had a unique opportunity to get acquainted with Göring, Ribbentrop, Hess, et al. We found him about to receive his release from active duty in the Army and inevitably, to settle down to write a book about his experiences with German leaders. He [Kelley] is a lithe, agreeable chap in his early thirties, with a shock of brown hair and an authentically sardonic smile.

"Basically," he said "my job was to determine if any of them were insane, and to predict any possibility of a breakdown during the trial. With the exception of Dr. Ley, there wasn't an insane Joe in the crowd." Dr. Kelley lighted a cigar. "That's what makes this trial important—there are twenty-one ruthless people with counterparts all over the world, none of them sufficiently deviate to be locked up by society under normal conditions. In my time, I've run across some strange birds," Dr. Kelley puffed at his cigar "but I've never met twenty-one people who considered themselves so pure and lily white." (p. 6)

Kelley's position—which was based on the Rorschach interpretation as well as on his psychiatric expertise—suggested that most of the Nazis were essentially normal. This opinion, which was opposite to the general public's consensus that the Nazis were more or less mad, did not attract much response from the media, the public, or the academic community. In fact, the issue of Nazi normalcy did not resurface until the 1960s when social theorists began to have second thoughts about demoniacal or pathological interpretations of the Nazis. Although Kelley indicated that many of the Nazis may have been psychologically "sane" he also proposed that some of the Nazis demonstrated psychopathology, such as paranoid deviations, in the case of Hess, or severe depression, in the case of Ribbentrop. But essentially many of them were not sufficiently deviant to "require custodial care according to the laws of our country" (Kelley, 1946b, p. 47). Thus, the potential to act like a Nazi may exist in many of us, Kelley suggested.

In his *Preliminary Studies* paper, Kelley concluded that:

it is our intention to prepare these records for distribution among interested Rorschach workers, since it is our definite feeling that a knowledge of the personalities of these individuals should be made public property and publicized in general. One of the most important values of human intelligence is its ability to learn from previous experience. It is imperative to our country and to the future of civilization that every intelligent American learn a lesson from the horrors of the Third Reich. The devastation of Europe, the deaths of millions of unfortunate peoples, the almost utter destruction of values of the whole world will have gone for nought if we do not derive some conclusion concerning the forces which produce such chaos. We must learn the why of the Third Reich so that we can intelligently take steps to prevent the recurrence of this evil at any future time. (p. 47)

Unfortunately, Kelley failed to provide either the verbatim responses of the records or a comprehensive analysis of the psychological data. At the time he must have believed that this initial contribution was, true to its title, just a preliminary report. A more detailed analysis, Kelley hoped, could be achieved through the distribution of the records to "outstanding Rorschach experts throughout the country." This would "produce the clearest possible picture of these individuals, the greatest group of criminals the human race has ever known" (p. 48).

Kelley (1947) provided more detailed insights into the defendant's world in *Twenty-Two Cells in Nuremberg: A Psychiatrist Examines the Nazi War Criminals*. With *Twenty-Two Cells*, Kelley intended to provide "an intelligible analysis of the personalities which were able to warp and control the actions of 80 million

Germans" (p. vii). Unfortunately, the book falls short of this goal, primarily because Kelley's insight into the Nazi leaders was not always firsthand, but was provided via interpreters, often based on observation alone, or taken from written reports when the Nazis were "at the top of the heap." In fact, Kelley even went so far as to attempt an "armchair" personality study of Hitler himself. In *Twenty-Two Cells* Kelley argued that Schirach was not a homosexual, but just good material gone wrong. Hess' amnesia he contended was not a hoax. Göring—despite all of the war propaganda—was not a fat, impotent, homosexual fool, but a capable man.

There are, however, several interesting features about Kelley's obscure book. For example, Kelley was one of the first to realize that the Nazi leaders were not unique individuals that could only be found in Nazi Germany: "No, the Nazi leaders were not spectacular types, not personalities such as appear only once in a century" (p. 239). Kelley extrapolates this to U.S. society and argued that there was "little in America today which could prevent the establishment of a Nazilike state" (p. 238). One has to realize that this was somewhat of a shocking statement to make in 1947 because it was the strong belief of the public and fueled by U.S. propaganda, that the Nazis were in fact monsters and that an American Nazi state was impossible. Kelley's position was not a popular one to take in the political postwar climate. Kelley formed this objective opinion not because of political belief, but because of his scholarly training as a psychiatrist. In arriving at his conclusions he undoubtedly analyzed data from the Nuremberg Rorschachs as well. As an expert in the Rorschach technique he was aware of the lack of severe pathology in many of the Nuremberg Nazi records. Kelley was, however, not naive about the crimes committed by the Nazi state, nor was he naive about the possibility that the structure of the Third Reich allowed many individuals who did manifest psychopathology to operate rather freely. But Kelley did suggest that Hitler was "an abnormal and mentally ill individual" (p. 235).

A curiosity of some sorts was Kelley's infatuation with Göring. In *Twenty-Two Cells,* Kelley referred to Göring as a shrewd but brilliant man. Kelley became Göring's friend and took a liking to the charming Göring, often defending his actions. For example, Kelley explained Göring's drug addiction by describing it as a habit: "Confused reports have appeared concerning the dosage Göring took at the time of his capture. Göring took the drug partly because of the addiction, of course. But he took it partly—and few persons realize this difference—because he had developed the habit. Addiction and habit are not the same. Göring was a paracodeine addict, but he also had the paracodeine pill habit, in the way that many people have the cigarette habit" (p. 57). Göring's drug addiction is well documented and it seems a bit of a reach on the part of Kelley to portray Göring as something less than an addict.

Kelley was also unusually concerned about Göring's obesity—280 pounds at the time of capture. Kelley pointed out to Göring that he "would make a better appearance in court should he lose some weight. He agreed and ate abstemiously" (p. 59). Kelley's fascination with Göring does not necessarily suggest that he was taken in or manipulated by Göring as many of his critics suggest. Kelley realized, of course, the situation that Göring was in, and he was aware of the atrocities that were being put squarely on Göring's shoulders.

One cannot help but think that Göring admired Kelley as well. For example, Göring wept unashamedly when the psychiatrist left Nuremberg for the United States. Kelley concluded his chapter on Göring with the following statement: "his [Göring's] suicide, shrouded in mystery and emphasizing the impotency of the American guards, was a skillful, even brilliant, finishing touch, completing the edifice for the Germans to admire in time to come" (p. 76). The chapter of Göring's suicide was, however, not closed. On New Year's Eve 1957 Kelley too died of his own hand. Although it is unclear what motivated his act, it is significant for the method he used was that by which Göring had killed himself, namely a potassium cyanide capsule taken from the Nuremberg prison as a souvenir. At the time, Kelley held an appointment as professor of criminology at the University of California at Berkeley.

The mysterious but similar circumstances surrounding the two suicides brought about speculations whether it was Kelley who slipped Göring the cyanide capsule that was used to evade the executioner (Swearingen, 1985), or alternatively, did Göring possibly give Kelley a suicide capsule? The fact that Kelley had access to the pills and befriended Göring make him a clear suspect. Also, a little known fact is that Kelley was deeply interested in the study of conjuring and became an outstanding authority on the psychology of misdirection and a vice-president of the Society of American Magicians. Kelley, however, left Nuremberg after the first 2 months of the trial and thus Göring would have had to hide the capsule for a considerable length of time (approximately 10 months). After all, each Nazi prisoner was subjected to one-on-one observation and to constant searches—each prisoner's cell was given a "shakedown" inspection up to four times a week. The prisoner was forced to strip and stand in a corner of his cell while military police carefully checked through his bedding, clothing, papers, and other impedimenta. Kelley reported these shakedowns to have been so thorough that it took the prisoners up to 4 hours to restore their cells to order. Thus, it appears highly unlikely that Göring received the suicide pill from Kelley and the mystery surrounding Göring's suicide remains unsolved.

Kelley's general thesis outlined in *Preliminary Studies* and expanded on in *Twenty-Two Cells* contradicted many of the U.S. wartime myths concerning Nazi leaders and was much at variance with U.S. wartime legend. As is seen here, Kelley's conclusions were in general contrary to Gilbert's sketches. Kelley argued that the modern tragedies of aggression and atrocities documented at Nuremberg were created by individuals with generally superior mental ability who were, with few exceptions, comparatively normal in the psychiatric sense. At most, some defendants may have been considered eccentric or fanatic, but not insane. Thus, Kelley provided little support for the "madman" theory.

Nevertheless, in *Twenty-Two Cells,* Kelley falls short in demonstrating to the reader the precise basis for his statements and his conclusions. His remarks, although very canny in their observations and perhaps more accurate than many other opinions that have been written about the Nazis, are not well supported—they are speculative and entirely based on expert argumentation. In this sense, Kelley gave us his diagnosis as a physician, a diagnosis that he did not seem to want to elaborate on. Had the book contained a careful analysis of the Nazi Rorschach data, together with his historical interactions in the Nuremberg jail, Kelley may have been taken more seriously.

Kelley left many questions unanswered in his two publications and he admitted that his work was hurried and incomplete. He also decided not to publish the verbatim responses of the Rorschach records, although he often commented about them. He indicated that complete studies of the personalities in his book were under way and that they would be published in the professional journals in due time. As it turns out, however, Kelley never completed that work and never published the verbatim responses of the seven Nazi Rorschachs that he administered. Little did he know that his records would not be further interpreted and that the hostile controversy with Gilbert would result in not one of his records being published. Until now that is!

RETRIEVING THE KELLEY RECORDS: THE SAMUEL J. BECK ARCHIVES

On July 18, 1947, Kelley contacted Rorschach expert Samuel J. Beck, PhD, to assist in the Nazi interpretations:

> I have finally translated the enclosed seven Rorschach records of the Nazis criminals from my rough notes. I am sending them to you in the hope that you will be able to help me with the project that I mentioned to you when I saw you in New York. I have sent several sets of these records out to other experts and I am hoping to get from everyone personality description of each individual criminal. I will edit these descriptions from a point of view of their agreements in an attempt to gain as perfect a picture as possible of the personality of each Nazi leader which would prove of considerable value to posterity.

Beck was a pioneer of the Rorschach inkblot technique who contributed greatly, both directly and indirectly, to the science of projective techniques and personality assessment. It was Beck who in 1930 was the first American to write a research report on the Rorschach test. There is little doubt that Beck was familiar with Kelley's work in the area of Rorschach research, because in the 1940s the professionals that were interested in the Rorschach technique consisted of a close and relatively small group. It was also Beck who reviewed Kelley's text he had co-authored with Klopfer, *A Manual for a Projective Method of Personality Diagnosis*, in the *Psychoanalytic Quarterly* (Beck, 1943). Beck lauded Kelley's effort, "Dr. Douglas Kelley's contribution, the final eight chapters of the book, summarize and evaluate investigations with the test. The chapters by Kelley are the most satisfying in the book. They reflect a caution born of clinical seasoning and a balanced approach to Rorschach problems, unhappily missing in most of the rest [i.e., Klopfer's contribution]" (p. 586).

When Beck received the seven Nazi records from Kelley he appeared to be pleased and replied in the following letter dated August 19, 1947:

> I have just returned from four week's absence to find the usual pile of accumulated mail. Most welcome and of course, intriguing was the material you sent to me. I certainly am going to study these records and would be happy to help you to the extent that I can. ... Do let me know what deadline you may have. If possible, I will send you the interpretations so as to meet your requirements. In any event, [I am] deep [with] gratitude for letting me have these records.

On February 6, of the same year Kelley wrote Beck once more, assuring him that he had "any amount of time" to complete the project. By 1948, Kelley had published *Preliminary Studies* and *Twenty-Two Cells*, and was not immediately ready to burst into print with a third publication on the Nazis. What happened over the years leading up to Kelley's suicide in 1958 is uncertain, other than that the Kelley records remained unpublished. Whether Kelley lost interest in the records or was somehow unable to complete his work for emotional reasons is not clear.

Beck himself had put much effort into interpreting the Gilbert records that, as we now know, were not used in any of Gilbert's publications. Thus, with the arrival of the Kelley protocols Beck was now in possession of a full set of the Nuremberg records. On February 29, 1976, Molly Harrower wrote to Beck to confirm that he was in possession of the Kelley records, because by then it seemed that nobody had a copy of them. Harrower was naturally aware of the whereabouts of the Nazi records including the Kelley protocols, given her involvement regarding the records and her acquaintance with the participants involved:

> I wonder if you would agree to my stating that you are probably the only person who has the original [Kelley] records of the Nazi prisoners? ... I think it is important for people to know that you are the only person in possession of the originals [Kelley records], even if you did not publish them.

Beck responded on March 8, 1976:

> You are entirely at liberty to state in your article that I am probably the only person who has those original Rorschach records, of the Nazi prisoners. I did not know that the records in my possession are the only ones, but you explored the field and I rest on your finding—but like yourself I am also saying "probably." You are at liberty to state, in a footnote or text, that these records are in my possession. And I do admire your scholarly caution in this.

When Harrower (1976a) published her own accounts of the Gilbert records in 1976, she mentioned in a footnote that the records administered to the major Nazi war criminals at Nuremberg by Douglas Kelley "are in the possession of Dr. Samuel Beck" (p. 345). This prompted many inquiries to Beck about the Kelley records as well as requests to obtain them given their historical importance. In one of Beck's letters (dated 1978) addressed to one of those requesting the Kelley records, it becomes clear that Beck never did share them with anyone:

> I have given careful thought to your letter regarding the [Kelley] Rorschachs of the Nazi leaders tried at Nuremberg. I do have them, [but] I have never published them, partly for technical reasons, partly because the [Nazi] descendants are still living, but more especially because of some sensitivity which it would be superfluous to go into. Yours is not the first request I have received and I am aware of the scientific interest in the make-up of these personalities. So for the present I will not release them and I am now toying with the idea of publishing [them myself].

Presumably the technical and sensitive issues that Beck eluded to were associated with the controversy between Gilbert and Kelley and related to the authorship of the records. The fact that Beck, then at age 80, wanted to publish his own accounts of Gilbert's and Kelley's records may have been due to the fact that by 1978, both Gilbert and Kelley were deceased. There was not one living person who could claim ownership of the records. From 1978 to 1980, Beck reported having written three chapters on the topic of the Nazi records, and at the time he was also pursuing a book contract with The University of Chicago Press. Beck reported that chapter 1 was entitled "The Power Set-Up in Germany in the Years of Nazi Rule"; chapter 2, "Göring"; and chapter 3 "Ribbentrop." Beck may have been well on his way to completing his project had it not been for his untimely death in 1981. Again, as had been the case for the preceding 35 years, the Kelley records failed to make it into print!

In 1992, Reneau Kennedy, a postdoctoral fellow at Harvard Medical School and Massachusetts General Hospital, was involved in a series of serendipitous events. As a psychology student, Kennedy developed a strong interest in the personality profiles of murderers. She researched this topic and not surprisingly came across research on the Nazi Rorschach records. In reading Harrower's 1976 article, she also was intrigued by the footnote that the unpublished Kelley records were in Beck's possession, although she never wrote Beck asking for them. Then, in 1991 Kennedy was working on her dissertation on the Rorschach records of male murderers, when she collaborated with James C. Beck, MD, PhD, head of the Cambridge Court Clinic, on a research project involving the assessment and treatment of violent offenders. Coincidentally, James Beck proved to be Samuel Beck's son. Although aware of his father's work on the Nazi Rorschachs during the last years of his life, James Beck was under the impression that the project had died. Nevertheless, he informed Kennedy that his mother had deposited his father's working papers with the Institute for Psychoanalysis in Chicago, and that they may include all or part of the Nazi documents. Energized by the possibility that the Kelley records may be found after all, Kennedy asked James Beck whether he was willing to write the Institute on her behalf in order to ascertain whether the records still existed. Thus, on March 31, 1992, James Beck corresponded with Dr. Arnold Goldberg, the director of the Institute, to inquire about the lost Kelley records:

I write in support of Ms. Reneau Kennedy's request to have access to the Nazi
Rorschach protocols and associated materials that are now the property of the Institute
for Psychoanalysis. I had a number of discussions with my father in the years before
his death about the Nazi Rorschach protocols. For many years my father kept these
protocols without ever working on them. I asked him about why he had let them lie
for almost 30 years. He was never able to tell me why he had, he could say only that
it had been his strong sense that he was not ready to take them out and work on them.
Knowing my father as well as I did, I speculate that the pain associated with the
memories of the war and its atrocities was too great for him to bear until that much
time had elapsed. He was not a man who would have been able to say that, either to
himself or me. My father began to work on the protocols sometime in the 1970s. It
was his intent to write a book based on his scoring and interpretation of the material.
He also intended to do some serious historical research on the men and prewar
Germany. He worked on this material for five or six years until his death. Unfortunately, he had an acute attack of shingles two years before his death. As often happens
with old people, he declined precipitously after that episode. He was never the same
again, either physically or mentally. He rarely left the house thereafter and when he
did it was on my mother's arm, and for a walk measured in feet. He sat in the front
bedroom "working" on the [Nazi] protocols.

As you know my mother was my father's devoted colleague for many years. After
my father's death, even she could not decipher the "hen scratches" he had made near
the end of his life. I thought the project died with him. I was unaware that the protocols
were among the papers my mother had given to the Institute. I thought that his long
time friend and colleague, Herman Molish, had a copy of the protocols and was
working on them. I was concerned that the project not die. I contacted Herman who
always claimed to be working on the protocols, but apparently never did. I asked him
to send me a copy, and he promised me he would. He never did. During his [Molish's]
terminal illness, my sister made efforts to contact him and his family. Those were
unsuccessful, and that trail is now a dead end. I thought the protocols were lost forever,
and I was deeply troubled. ...

I doubt that I have any legal standing in this matter. Still, I hope my opinion counts
for something. I was close to my father, both personally and professionally. He would
certainly want these protocols to be analyzed, and the results published.

On April 10, 1992, in response to James Beck's letter, Kennedy was given
permission by the director of the Institute to inquire about the records herself
firsthand. Before Kennedy traveled to the Institute to examine the material personally, she decided to first contact Harrower, the source of the Kelley–Beck connection, to inquire whether Harrower would support her effort, which she did. Next,
Kennedy contacted Zillmer to ask how to proceed and what precisely to look for
in the Beck archives.

Kennedy then telephoned the Institute but was initially told that no such Nazi
Rorschach records existed for the simple reason that psychiatrists do not engage in
that form of psychometric testing, as do clinical psychologists. Kennedy patiently
reminded the contact person on the telephone that the Rorschach was used extensively by psychiatrists many years ago and that psychologists who were using the
technique were then members of the Psychoanalytic Society (today the members
of the Society are almost exclusively psychiatrists). Luckily, Kennedy was referred

to a librarian, Heidi Rosenberg, a doctoral psychology student herself, who had a personal interest in the Holocaust and who was familiar with the Rorschach technique. Through the assistance of Rosenberg it then became clear that Beck had deposited three boxes of "papers," the contents of which were largely disorganized. Disturbingly, the boxes were also marked for removal.

Upon her arrival at the Institute, Kennedy discovered in the Beck archives detailed handwritten notes on the Nazi records, six of the seven Kelley records, and all of the Gilbert records. The papers were in no particular order and much of the material was apparently missing, including Rorschach records on Albert Einstein and Franklin D. Roosevelt. The most important findings of the Beck archives were undoubtedly the six "lost" Kelley Rorschach records. These included the first administrations of Göring, Rosenberg, and Frank as well as test data on Karl Dönitz (commander of the German Navy from 1943 to 1945 and German Chief of State for 7 days in May 1945), and the record of Julius Streicher (the violent anti-Semitic editor of the Jew-baiting weekly *Der Stürmer*). Particularly the Rorschach records of Dönitz and Streicher are of historical importance because they comprise the only personality tests available on these two subjects.[1] The other three original records of Göring, Frank, and Rosenberg are particularly useful for comparison with the subsequent second administrations conducted by Gilbert. Missing from the collection, however, was the first Rorschach administration of Hess.

The skeptic may question the authenticity of these records, given the abundance of fake Nazi paraphernalia on the market today, including the Hitler diaries that were authenticated by historians[2] from the academic community. As prominent historian Gerhard Weinberg pointed out, "too many things turn up which are not supposed to exist."[3] There is little reason, however, to suspect that the Rorschachs in the Beck archives are not genuine. Independent correspondence from Beck, Kelley, Gilbert, Harrower, and others, all point to the fact that Beck had such records in his possession. Comparison of the three initial records of Göring, Frank, and Rosenberg with the retests are also consistent with what one would expect on re-administration of the Rorschach (i.e., some responses that are similar, some that have been elaborated on, and some that are new). Furthermore, the Kelley records are consistent with reports by his interpreter Dolibois (1989), who commented on his experience in the Nuremberg jail in his biography entitled *Patterns of Circle*. Kelley himself published partial verbatim responses of the Ley record in his 1946 article that were consistent with the Ley protocol found in the Beck archives. Finally, the records of Dönitz and Streicher, among others were subsequently secured from Piotrowski's correspondence and proved to be identical to the ones found in the Beck archives. Thus, there is little reason to question that the six Rorschach records were the ones collected by Kelley during the Nuremberg trials.

---

[1] Both records are presented and discussed in detail in chapter 8.

[2] For example by well-known English historian Trevor-Roper (Harris, 1986, p. 24).

[3] Cited by Harris (1986, p. 267).

The Beck archives did not reveal any completed book chapters, but did contain many pages of notes and tabulation of Rorschach indices on the Nazi records. From these "hen scratches" it is difficult to ascertain what Beck's view of the Nazi Rorschachs exactly was. It seems as if Beck had mostly used his time scoring the Nazi Rorschachs rather than interpreting them. In some instances there are, however, brief interpretative statements; for example, Beck wrote that " ... this subject Dönitz ... stands out [and is] a lively spirit." Unfortunately, Beck, one of the greatest Rorschach experts to date, did not leave the psychological community with an integrated and comprehensive summary on the psychological functioning of the Nuremberg defendants.

The Beck archives did reveal the exact dates when the Gilbert records were administered. Interestingly, all but the re-administration of the Hess record were recorded in October, November, and December 1945 (the Hess record was administered in January 1946). This time period of the Rorschach administration is critical to the validity of later claims by Kelley, that the Gilbert administrations were directed by him (see chapter 4). The dates confirm Kelley's involvement in the Gilbert records including the assertion that Gilbert was directly supervised by him, because he stayed in Nuremberg until February 1946. However, Gilbert was free to move around the prison on his own and may have very well administered the tests without assistance or supervision.

THE GILBERT RECORDS

Similar to Kelley, Gilbert also rushed into print with his Nazi material with his 1947 publication of the *Nuremberg Diary,* which provides fascinating dialogues with the prisoners. Gilbert, who spoke German fluently, remained in Nuremberg throughout the trial and had constant access to the prisoners. Clearly, Kelley and Gilbert both intended to write several books on the Nazis. They conceptualized their first efforts as providing limited analysis and therefore proceeded to furnish much initial detail about the trials and the defendants themselves. In this respect, Gilbert's text comes across better and is the standard text referenced when quoting conversations with the Nuremberg defendants. Certainly, Gilbert's accounts, particularly the insights and dialogues that he held with the Nazis, have proven to be very interesting and rich and the *Nuremberg Diary* has been frequently cited as one of only a few texts providing an insider's view of high-ranking Nazis.

Gilbert's (1950) attempts at a psychosocial analysis of the Nazis is summarized in *The Psychology of Dictatorship*. Gilbert, however, gave only brief commentaries on the Rorschach tests and based most of his analysis on his personal impressions formed during his stay at Nuremberg. Gilbert's record of the Nuremberg defendants can hardly be described as a rigidly structured psychological study of the defendants (Snyder, 1947), but rather as a series of psychological cameos and psychiatric phrase diagnoses—Hess' reactions to the psychological tests were typical of the hysterical personality, and Streicher had an obsessive–compulsive neurosis or an organic psychosis.

Eighteen years later and in response to the Eichmann trial,[4] Gilbert (1948c, 1963) put forth a psychological explanation of the Nazis he had studied in two articles entitled *Hermann Göring, Amiable Psychopath* and *The Mentality of SS Murderous Robots*. In contrast to Kelley, who felt that the Nuremberg Nazis were for the most part not "ideally normal" but also not severely disturbed, Gilbert (1963) suggested that the Nazis, particularly the SS, had cultivated a personality type he described as

> the unfeeling, mechanical executioner of orders for destruction no matter how horrible, who goes on and on with this ghastly work as though he were a mere machine made of electrical wiring and iron instead of a heart and a mind, with no qualms of conscience or sympathy to restrain him once someone has pressed the button to put him into action with a command. (p. 36)

Furthermore, Gilbert suggested that this personality type is principally the "reflection of the disease symptoms of a sick society [and] diseased elements of the German culture ..." (p. 40). Although this personality type, lacking in empathy and constricted in affect, may make up part of the Nazis or the core SS, Gilbert simplistically suggested that forces of a mysteriously evil Germany are responsible for it.

Although the final chapter in the Gilbert–Kelley feud has yet to be written, it seems clear that Gilbert himself was an opportunistic and ambitious scholar who at times unduly magnified his clinical qualifications as well as the authenticity of his reports. Concerning the latter, there is evidence that a number of "recollections" and anecdotes in *The Nuremberg Diary* were not firsthand reports (many of the Nazis did not take kindly to Gilbert who was Jewish), that a number of log entries he reports as having occurred during his watch actually took place in Mondorf before the prisoners were moved to Nuremberg, and that he may have misquoted people. Gilbert's arrogance, however, did not go so far that he literally absconded with Kelley's protocols as some of his critics have suggested. He certainly did not give Kelley the credit he deserved for initiating and collecting the Nuremberg Rorschach records either. Surely, Kelley played a much larger role than Gilbert testifies to: "There was a psychiatrist [i.e., Kelley] on the medical staff who was unable to speak a word of German[5] and left home after the second month of the year-long-trial" (Miale & Selzer, 1975, p. xiii). By then, however, Kelley could not respond to Gilbert's comments for he had passed away 17 years earlier.

---

[4]In 1961, during the trial of Adolf Eichmann, some of Gilbert's Rorschach material on the Nuremberg Nazis was admitted as evidence (he submitted five documents that were placed in the record T/1168 to T/1172). Gilbert testified at Session 55 and the first part of Session 56 on May 26, 1961. During the Eichman trial he was asked by Attorney-General Hausner, as a witness to the prosecution, what kind of mentality did the mass murderers of Hitler's SS possess to be able to commit such horrible things? Gilbert was not allowed to answer because the question was disallowed by the Court as being irrelevant to the judicial question of Eichmann's guilt.

[5]Kelley, in fact, knew some German.

If the "First Act" of this strange drama was stormy and filled with pressures, the second act was characterized by an almost equally unusual lack of activity, in what amounts to 30 years of burying the whole issue of the Nazi Rorschach records.

MODERN NAZI RORSCHACH STUDIES
(1975 TO PRESENT)

The first to provide a comprehensive analysis of the Gilbert Nazi records was Harrower. In 1975, Harrower, then professor at the University of Florida, was asked to address the American Civilization Seminar, a faculty-organized, highly respected, academic group, composed of representatives from all university departments. She decided at that time to present some psychological findings and unexpected conclusions, which a systematic reevaluation of the Nazi Rorschach records had forced her to accept. In essence, her main findings showed that there was no single, uniform, abnormal personality that could serve to explain the unspeakable horrors of Nazi behaviors. The reception Harrower received at this presentation led to television interviews, produced a flood of newspaper comments, and reopened a topic forgotten since 1948.[6]

In preparing her presentation, Harrower realized that 30 years had elapsed since she had read through the test records of the Nuremberg Nazis. Harrower saw each prisoner's record as different from the other as any 16 test records selected at random would be. To Harrower, the test performances varied qualitatively and quantitatively when compared to a group of more than 5,000 protocols she had collected for normative purposes, including 1,500 Unitarian ministers, hundreds of medical students, psychology students, nurses, business executives, but also psychiatric outpatients, criminals from Sing-Sing prison, and juvenile offenders in the Manhattan Children's Court (Harrower, 1943, 1955a, 1955b, 1957, 1961, 1965, 1970). In all these studies, Harrower found that the outstanding feature among members of these populations, was the wide range of personality types and different degrees of mental health potential, or lack of it.

Rather than a homogeneous group, the Nuremberg defendants' personalities showed a frequently found distribution, a bell shaped curve with a cluster of scores in the center and a small percentage at each end ranging from well adjusted to impoverished. Arranged on such a scale the protocols showed far greater variation than they did uniformity. Harrower concluded that there was no common denominator reflecting some type of psychopathic personality. In fact, Harrower thought that with the exception of a few Nazis, who fell into clearly definable psychiatric types, counterparts for the others could be found in any normal population. Harrower realized in a flash the problem that had confronted her 30 years ago. She and the group of experts had most likely operated out of a solid climate of opinion,

---

[6]It may be remembered that Harrower had in 1948 been the psychologist responsible for inviting the 10 Rorschach experts at that time to submit their assessment of the Nazi Rorschach records. All the invitees had declined to accept this invitation—a big surprise.

with the expectation that the tests would show a subhuman type of monsters, and that any test that did not reflect this assumption would be instantly discounted and the interpreter discredited.

Now it became imperative for Harrower to see if well-versed Rorschach colleagues would fail to spot the Nuremberg Nazi records per se when assessed without knowing the subject's identity. In the hands of a skilled clinician, the Rorschach technique can be a sensitive diagnostic tool. But one problem with the Rorschach is that even a well-trained clinician can be influenced by what he or she expects to find. If Rorschach interpreters look for evidence of sadism in the answers of a psychopathic murderer, the chances are they will find it. To avoid such bias, Harrower suggested that the Nazis Rorschach results must be scored "blind" (i.e., without the Rorschach experts knowing the identity of who they are evaluating).

The basic aims of Harrower's experimental procedure was threefold: First, she needed to demonstrate experimentally that such a "blind analysis" was necessary in any program in which the defendant's records were to be evaluated and contrasted with controls. Second, she needed to demonstrate the necessity of Rorschach experts to have had the experience of contrasting a wide variety of populations, a realistic possibility because the development of the Group Rorschach in 1943 (Harrower & Bowers, 1987). Finally, she needed to demonstrate that regardless of whether the Rorschach record was produced by one of the Nuremberg defendants or by a control subject, it could be placed on a scale of "Mental Health Potential." Such a scale describing eight dimensions of psychological qualities is summarized here and was based on specific scores from the individual's responses to the Rorschach inkblot test. The illustration on the next page contrasts Harrower's findings of Ribbentrop (minister of foreign affairs) versus those of Schacht (finance minister).

The test findings of Ribbentrop were pathetic. The test shows that he was emotionally barren and imaginatively vacant. Schacht, in contrast, could call on an inner world of satisfying experiences to stand him in good stead in the stressful months prior to sentencing—he was duly acquitted after having been hauled out of a concentration camp into the Nuremberg prisoner's dock.

Next, Harrower presented 10 acknowledged authorities in Rorschach interpretation with eight Nazi Rorschach records (all collected by Gilbert) and eight records produced by a control group (i.e., Unitarian ministers and psychiatric outpatients). All records, those of Nuremberg prisoners and controls, that were submitted to the experts were scored by Harrower as well as independently by a colleague and Rorschach expert (i.e., Matilda Steiner) using the standard Klopfer method. The Rorschach experts, who were blind to the nature and identity of the test records, received only the location of each response as well as a summarized quantitative scoring of the records to minimize the "squabble" between various scoring systems that were used in the 1970s. The defendants and control groups were arranged for the experts in two different ways. One way was to keep together the test records that reflected the different backgrounds of the testees. Thus, two subgroups each contained only Nazi records, another only clergymen controls, and a third group, were only records of patient controls. The experts were asked to look at these groups

CHART 1

Joachim von Ribbentrop **SUMMARY OF TEST FINDINGS** Hjalmar Schacht

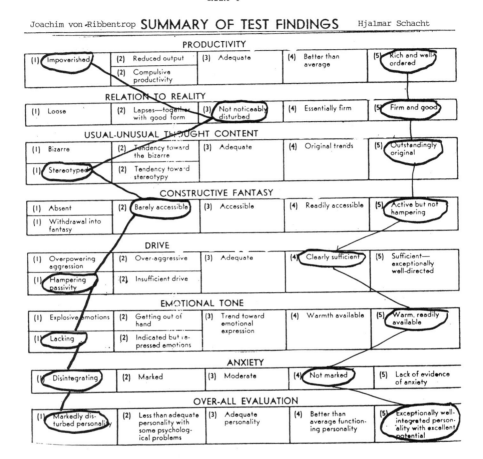

Harrower's Mental Health Potential scale.

and note any similarities that they saw within any of them. The other way of arranging the records was based on the degree of positive qualities, or lack of resources, on a scale of mental health potential. Thus, the experts were asked to arrange all records along a continuum from superior, normal, less than adequate, to deeply disturbed.

When Harrower received the results it became clear that the experts did not feel that there was a communality, or common denominator, within any of the individual groups (i.e., defendants vs. controls). Thus, they were unable to detect any group similarities or group indices of mental disturbances from the Nazi Rorschach responses. Furthermore, the experts concluded that six of the eight Nazis demonstrated no serious maladjustment and two of them (Schacht and von Schirach) were particularly well adjusted. Thus, Harrower's Mental Health Potential scale did allow the "positive" features of some Nuremberg personalities to be recognized as having some "good" psychological qualities, while other Nazi prisoners (e.g., Ribbentrop) showed inadequacies and disturbances, or a "sadistic feel."

Harrower (1976a, 1976b) concluded that psychological assets per se, do not prevent behavior from occurring that will go down in history as a crime against humanity. Göring, for example, came through on the Rorschach as a dynamic, but crude, insensitive man of action who was lacking the ability for subtle emotional experiences. Harrower characterized Göring's personality, however, as normal because she saw many of the same personality characteristics in U.S. decorated combat pilots.[7] Thus, she was forced to admit that whatever role Göring played in the atrocities of the Third Reich, one could not ascribe that role to a psychopathic personality per se. Harrower further characterized Hess as an immature, oversensitive, and suspicious individual (i.e., as a less than adequate personality), and Speer as a disturbed and impoverished personality.

From the results of her study, Harrower suggested that productive and well-integrated personalities may become involved in large-scale "horrors." She also found that the individual differences in the Nazi records greatly outweighed any similarities. Harrower (1976b) commented that "it is an oversimplified position to look for an underlying common denominator in the Rorschach records of the Nazi prisoners. The Nazis who went on trial at Nuremberg were as diverse a group as one might find in our government today, or for that matter, in the leadership of the PTA" (p. 76). She further suggested that the Nazi crimes were not related to the presence of a mental disorder or insanity, but that the Nazis were quite similar to an average group of U.S. citizens. "It can happen here," she concluded (p. 80).

At roughly the same time Harrower was re-investigating the Rorschach records, Miale and Selzer also were preparing a detailed interpretation. Miale, a student of Klopfer, was one of the 10 Rorschach experts who were consulted by Harrower about the Rorschach records in 1947, but who declined at that time to respond (see chap. 4). Miale was therefore aware, from the beginning, that the top Nazi officials were subjected to psychological testing and held the Rorschach records in her possession. In 1975, two years before Gilbert's death,[8] Miale and Selzer published *The Nuremberg Mind: The Psychology of Nazi Leaders.* The Miale and Selzer book was the first comprehensive investigation of Nazi Rorschach records featuring *verbatim* responses of the Nazi prisoners to the Rorschach records. It was by most accounts, however, a disappointing effort. Essentially the authors attempted to summarize and group all of the defendants into a highly distinctive group, a Nazi personality. From the 16 Rorschach records available to them, Miale, a psychologist and experienced Rorschach expert, and Selzer, a political scientist and author of several books on Jewish affairs, concluded that the Nazi leaders were psycho-

---

[7]Göring was one of Germany's top-scoring fighter aces during World War I.

[8]Gilbert attempted to block the publication of the book, but came to a compromise with the authors to write the foreword. Gilbert died in 1977 at the age of 65 after a long and distinguished career in psychology including 17 years as chairman of the Department of Psychology at Long Island University.

logically disordered individuals who not only shared a "common ideology with their most devoted followers, but a similar personality structure as well" (Miale & Selzer, 1975, p. 286). It appeared that the authors started with a specific bias concerning the highest ranking Nazis (Allen, 1984), namely, that they were a homogeneous group of warped psychopaths exhibiting depression and a proclivity for violence and narcissism. "The Nazis were not psychologically normal or healthy individuals" (p. 287) Miale and Selzer (1975) concluded, but bigots who experienced no real guilt for their instrumental roles in the slaughter of millions of Jews and other victims of Nazi terror.

Although many might wish to believe that the individuals responsible for the Third Reich had little in common with "normals" and were a distinct and select group of psychopathological individuals, there have been serious criticisms about Miale and Selzer's approach to the Rorschach records and of their conclusions as well. For example, their analyses and interpretations of the Nazi officers were conducted with full knowledge concerning their identities and their historical pasts, factors that could have substantially influenced their Rorschach interpretations.

This view was also reflected in Rubenstein's (1976) critique of *The Nuremberg Mind*. Rubenstein, a professor of religion, referred to the book as an "unhappy one" (p. 84) and suggested that Miale and Selzer intentionally attempted to portray the Rorschach records as exhibiting certain types of psychopathology. In support of this possibility, the Miale and Selzer content-analysis approach to interpretation was highly subjective, and an empirical basis was typically not utilized to evaluate responses. For example, on the basis of the defendant's tendency to respond to the inkblots with concepts such as helmets, caps, hats, and other headgear, Miale and Selzer claimed that the group as a whole was preoccupied with violence. Furthermore, the absence of particular contents or verbalizations in the Nazi records was frequently sufficient evidence for Miale and Selzer to suggest very specific forms of psychopathology. One example will suffice. On Rorschach Plate II Neurath responded benignly "two women—greeting each other." Miale and Selzer (1975) suggested that this response was "by default an indication of the intense conflict within the subject, and of his aggressiveness towards others. These are frequently masked by superficial politeness and courtesy" (p. 144).

To assume that the absence of a certain type of content on the Rorschach argues for the presence of a specific personality style is not very convincing to any except the most fervent Rorschach advocate. Such a method of evaluating Rorschach responses can be referred to as placing emphasis on the content of the Rorschach responses, rather than on the more formal analysis of the perceptual experiences outlined in chapter 5. Indeed, Rorschach (1921) himself was very cautious in his estimate of meaningful interpretation from such a response-by-response evaluation of verbalizations as performed by Miale and Selzer. Such an approach is used most frequently by examiners with training and experience in psychoanalysis, depth psychology, and concern with symbolism (Kovel, 1976) and bears little relationship to the science of psychology. In summary, *The Nuremberg Mind* was clearly written with an agenda. Unfortunately, we learn more about the authors' values and prejudices than we do about the Nazi leaders.

Thus, serious questions remain regarding the validity and accuracy of the Miale and Selzer conclusions (Kovel, 1976). It is understandable that survivors of the Holocaust, when confronted by any aspect of the event, often react with violent and uncritical emotion. Certainly we must remember the Holocaust, not only to honor the victims and their loved ones, but also to assure that it will not occur again. To respond with anguish as Miale and Selzer did, however, distorts the lessons that this terrible event holds for humanity's future.

In 1978 Ritzler published *The Nuremberg Mind Revisited: A Quantitative Approach to Nazi Rorschachs*. To rectify many of the criticisms leveled against Miale and Selzer, Ritzler utilized a quantitative approach in evaluating the Nazi Rorschach records. Thus, he statistically compared the 16 records collected by Gilbert to those of a control group matched for age and level of pathology (i.e., utilizing both psychiatric and normal subject records). Whereas Miale and Selzer utilized content analysis approaches to Rorschach interpretation, Ritzler, like Harrower, used a standard scoring system for Rorschach responses (i.e., Beck, Beck, Levitt, & Molish, 1961). His results indicated that the defendants' records did deviate from those of normals, but not as much as might have been expected from the discussions of Miale and Selzer.

In contrast to Miale and Selzer's assertion of uniform Nazi demons, Ritzler proposed that, as a group, the Nazi leaders were not psychotic and their responses did not resemble those of depressed and anxious nonpsychotic patients. Ritzler further commented that the Nazis may have performed like "successful psycho-paths" on the Rorschach, that is, opportunistic, but not severely dysfunctional, impulsive, or sadistic. Thus, Ritzler took the middle ground between Kelley's conclusion that the Nazis were ordinary people similar to "the man next door" and Miale and Selzer's findings that the Nazi leaders were profoundly disturbed. The Nazi Rorschachs also did not seem to fit Arendt's stereotype of the "banal"; a majority of the Nuremberg defendants Ritzler suggested were rather colorful personalities.

Miale and Selzer's conclusions were also refuted later by Zillmer, Archer, and Castino (1989; Zillmer & Archer, 1989, 1990; Zillmer, Harrower, Ritzler, & Archer, 1991) and by Resnick and Nunno (1991; Resnick, 1984). These investigators further quantified the analysis of the Gilbert Nuremberg Rorschach records by utilizing the newer Exner (1985) standardized Comprehensive Scoring System. This modern analysis of the Rorschach records, based in part on objective compu-terized interpretation, demonstrated that the Nazi war criminals could not be grouped together into one specific mental disorder capable of adequately charac-terizing such diverse individuals.

Resnick (1984) further compared the protocols of the 16 Nazis to the 9 dimen-sions of the *F* scale[9] of authoritarianism (Adorno et al., 1950). It was hypothesized that the Nazi leaders would score high on the authoritarianism scale, because a

---

[9]The dimensions include conventionalism, authoritarian aggression, authoritarian submission, anti-intraception, superstition and stereotyping, power and toughness, destructive and cynicism, pro-jectivity, and concerns with sexuality.

pro-authoritarian set of beliefs exemplifies the dogmatic or rigid mindsets that will readily comply with the commands of an authority without question or protest. The Nuremberg war criminals, however, converged upon only three of the nine dimensions of authoritarianism for corresponding Rorschach criteria. Those included, anti-intraception (i.e., opposition to subjective, tender-minded, and imaginative functions), superstition and stereotyping (i.e., cognitive rigidity and belief in the mystical determinants of fate), and projectivity (i.e., the predisposed beliefs that the world is dangerous, hostile, and evil). Resnick concluded that the F scale more accurately defines the personality characteristics of the leader of a Fascist or totalitarian regime than they relate to the personality characteristics of the underlings and henchmen who blindly follow.

Certainly, the Nazi leaders were not uniformly "normal" either, but rather, they displayed varying degrees of psychopathology as illustrated by computer analyses of individual Rorschach protocols. For example, significant deficits in reality testing and possible thought disorder were manifested by some of the defendants, with particularly striking evidence in the case of Hess. Furthermore, although these defendants appeared to be prone to difficulties in response to emotional stimulation, only a minority of the Nuremberg defendants displayed Rorschach protocols indicative of chronic impulse control problems. Thus, as a group, their actions would not appear to have been the result of a highly impulsive personality. Finally, this group was surprisingly free of symptoms of depressive processes, particularly in light of their assessments occurring immediately prior to their trials. It is notable that in the Zillmer et al. (1989) study, the majority displayed problems in terms of self-esteem involving either some damage to the view of self, or an egocentric and narcissistic overevaluation of the self. The most important overall statement regarding these defendants, however, is the degree to which each of these individual records contained idiosyncratic features, and the wide response variability in members of this group.

With the exception of the Miale and Selzer study, several independently working scientists underscored the richness of the data provided by the Gilbert records and the heterogeneous nature of the protocols that demonstrated the limitation of prior attempts to achieve an understanding of a "Nazi personality." The Nuremberg Rorschach records, however, also suggested that this group of individuals varied from normal expectations in a variety of important ways. But the use of any overall descriptors to attempt to summarize the personality functioning of this group was frustrated by the individual and complex nature of each of the subjects. Although Nuremberg revealed to the world the terrible crimes committed by Hitler's followers, the Miale and Selzer conclusion of an evil homogeneous personality style among the defendants appears unjustified.

THE NAZI ELITE

The results of the psychological findings of the Nazi elite are not surprising, given that the 21 men lumped together at Nuremberg came from different cultural, educational, political, and military backgrounds. Their psychological profiles are very much like their historical records—the Nazi leaders assembled at Nuremberg were neither thoroughly homogeneous nor extremely heterogeneous.

Of course there were are similarities among many of the Nuremberg defendant's records that may suggest some interesting insight into the Nazi phenomenon. These are not abnormalities in a psychiatric sense, but rather personality characteristics that may be present in many.

For example, one major personality characteristic to be noted is their overall problem-solving style. This is related to the defendants' score on a Rorschach score known as the *Erlebnistypus* (*EB*; German for "experience base") and supported on the basis of quantitative analysis (Resnick, 1984; Ritzler, 1978; Zillmer et al., 1989). Rorschach (1921) considered the *EB* as one of the most important characteristics of the test and proposed that it reflects the underlying preferential response style of an individual. The *EB* represents a ratio of the sum of human movement[10] responses to the Rorschach on one side and the sum of chromatic color responses on the other side. Rorschach hypothesized that when the ratio is distinctly weighed in the human movement direction the Rorschach subject is more prone to his or her inner life for basic gratification. This problem-solving approach is known as *introversive* (not to be confused with the Jungian concept of introvert, which is conceptualized as someone who is socially isolated or withdrawn).

Introversive subjects prefer to delay final decisions until they can mentally review alternatives and potential results. They rely heavily on their own ideation for decisions and direction and exert greater control over their emotions (Exner, 1986). At the opposite pole is the extratensive person whose *EB* is markedly weighed on the color side of the ratio. The extratensive is prone to manifest feelings to the world. Extratensive subjects prefer to make decisions based on their "gut feeling", that is, without delaying a final decision until they can review alternatives or ponder on the consequences of their results. In contrast to the introversive and extratensive, the ambient (i.e., the *EB* ratio contains near equal values on each side) has failed to develop a consistent preference or style in their coping behaviors, which may lead to less efficiency and more vacillation in decision-making operations.

The *EB* ratio is not necessarily a measure of psychopathology, but simply a particular preference for a psychological style that is a relatively stable psychological feature of the individual. The normative data suggests that slightly more than 75% of nonpatient adults are either introversive or extratensive and that the proportion for each is about the same (Exner, 1990). In a problem-solving study, introversives were found to perform the fewest operation before reaching the solutions, extratensives performed more operations but were able to achieve solutions to the problems in about the same time as the introversives and with the same results. Ambients, however, performed more operations than the extratensives, required significantly more time to achieve solutions than either the extratensive or introversives, and repeated more operations and made significantly more errors in those operations. This, and other studies, suggest, that the ambitent

[10]Also see chapter 7 for a discussion of this Rorschach index as it relates to the rank-and-file.

is particularly vulnerable to difficulties in coping situations than either the intro-versive or extratensive. Thus, ambitents are considered to be the least efficient and least consistent in their behavior patterns (Exner, 1986).

Among the 16 Gilbert records an unusually high number of the Nazis (i.e., 9 or 56%) were ambitent (Resnick, 1984; Zillmer et al., 1989). The ambitent style in the Nuremberg defendants may indicate the lack of a clear preference for coping with the environment and a tendency to vacillate between thinking through behav-iors and trial-and-error behaviors in responding to their surroundings (Zillmer & Archer, 1985). This predominant problem-solving style among this group of Nazi subjects suggests a preference for incorporating the styles of others around them and a tendency for vacillation when confronted with difficult tasks. Interestingly, the diagnostic group with the highest frequency of ambitents are a population of character problems or sociopaths (56%) compared to only 24% ambitents in the normal reference group (Exner, 1990).

Hess was one of four Nazis who scored with a markedly extratensive response style suggesting that he does not modulate emotional displays as much as most adults and, because of this, is prone to become very influenced by feelings. Only three of the subject's records suggested an introversive response style indicative of a preferred coping style involving "thinking through" behaviors before they are emitted. It would seem that most citizens would be most comfortable with their political leaders manifesting this particular response style, although only a minority of the Nuremberg group actually did.

The unexpected prevalence for an ambitent style was also reflected in the Rorschach records of five Nazis who gave frequent content responses of a chame-leon that did not typically appear in a comparison group protocol (Ritzler, 1978). One could characterize the chameleon as a passive, opportunistic creature that protects itself by blending in with the prevailing color scheme in the environment—much as this group of Nazis may have protected themselves by blending in with the prevailing forces of Nazi Germany. Curiously, four of the five Nazi prisoners who gave the chameleon response were either acquitted or received relatively light sentences, suggesting that even at Nuremberg they were able to "blend in" enough to prevent total destruction (Ritzler, 1978). In fact, Rorschach postulated, that the ambitent may be the most flexible of the three personality styles with regard to the use of resources for obtaining gratification. Thus, the psychological profiles of the Nazi elite differed from most people in one respect; they possessed a "cham-eleonlike" personality that allowed them to adopt the beliefs and objectives of whatever leadership was in power at that moment, rather than to base their judgments on an "internal compass." Incredibly, many leading Nazis, upon their surrender to the Allied forces, went so far as to offer their services in helping to rebuild postwar Germany. Certainly, this characteristic set many of the Nuremberg defendants apart from the majority, although perhaps more than 20% of the U.S. population operates in a similar fashion.

Although the prevalence of the ambitent style and the relative absence of the introversive style in the Nuremberg group is the most notable finding for a common denominator among the Nazi elite, there are other, less stable, personality characteristics that may also define the group as a whole. For example, one characteristic was how the top Nazis approached the Rorschach test itself. Many of the defendants rejected the responsibility for their responses significantly more often than did a comparison control group. For example, Kaltenbrunner responded to an inkblot "the general impression is of a cuttlefish" and then immediately repudiate the responsibility of his own response by adding "of course it's not a cuttlefish at all." At times the Nazis would show a related tendency by being more likely to place special emphasis on how clearly they perceived common Rorschach responses (e.g., "This looks definitely, and without doubt, like a butterfly"). This may suggest a chronic uncertainty in the Nazis who were overly enthusiastic and almost relieved when they gave responses that were almost entirely free of ambiguity.

Thus, the Nuremberg group as a whole was more likely to blame the Rorschach test itself, the testing situation, or the examiner for any uncertainty or uneasiness they felt about the quality of their responses. Although the defendants did what they were told on the Rorschach and put up a pleasant front with a high percentage of positively toned responses, when the going got tough and they became uncertain about their ideas and actions, they resorted to denying responsibility and blamed the test or the examiner, perhaps in the style of the notorious defensive plea at Nuremberg—"We were only following orders" (Ritzler, 1978, p. 353).

With the exception of the characteristics just described, however, research on the records of the Nazi elite failed to identify a homogeneous Nazi personality. In fact, the differences among the members of this group by far outweighed any similarities. Incidentally, this variability is also reflected in the sentence passed by the International Military Tribunal ranging from death, prison sentences of varying terms, to acquittal. Thus, it is important to reemphasize that the Nuremberg Nazi elite demonstrated a complex range of personalities and cannot be simply defined in strict terms. Furthermore, the records did not show the Nazis to be the impulsive-dominated, hostile sadists that Miale and Selzer made them out to be. At the same time we should not accept the conclusion that the Nazis are no different from the man next door. Although many of the Rorschach protocols differed from those of normals in a variety of important ways, they were not a random sample of human behavior either.

It is certainly possible that many of the rank-and-file Nazis were indeed highly disturbed individuals, but the Nazi leaders on trial at Nuremberg, it must be remembered, were not the concentration camp commandant, the SS killer, or the executioner. They were, for the most part, higher echelon bureaucrats, dedicated to the Nazi cause and obedient to the word of the Führer. None of them, as far as history records, ever dropped a gas pellet or manned a crematory oven. Thus, they were at considerable distance to their victims. Lifton (1986) suggested that such distancing was of considerable importance for the Nazis in alleviating the psychological problems experienced by the *Einsatzgruppen* (i.e., readiness troops) who were carrying out face-to-face shooting of Jews and prisoners of war in Eastern Europe. In interviewing psychiatrists who treated large numbers of *Einsatzgruppen* personnel, Lifton estimated that 20% of those doing the actual killing experienced these symptoms of psychological decompensation.

Thus, if the sadism and viciousness not found in the Nazi leaders assembled at Nuremberg could account for the atrocities of the Third Reich, maybe such characteristics can be found in rank-and-file Nazis. Although the Nazi leaders ordered the deaths of millions, it was the rank-and-file who carried out their orders. If we failed to detect a specific Nazi personality within the Nuremberg group, perhaps we can find one within a sample of "ordinary" Nazis sentenced to death or prison sentences for war crimes and crimes against humanity. Such research on nearly 200 Nazi war criminals, Danish collaborators, and German military occupation personnel, is presented in the next chapter.

Chapter 7

Danish Collaborators and German Occupation Personnel: A New Sample

Under conditions of tyranny, it is far easier to act than to think.
—Hannah Arendt (1958)

This chapter summarizes recent research on a sample of nearly 200 previously unpublished Rorschachs. They include German military personnel who stood trial for war crimes in Denmark with the majority of the sample qualifying as rank-and-file. A minority were high-level Danish officials who were being tried for treason for cooperating with the Nazis in matters of government administration. Of interest here are specifically the psychological protocols of those individuals who were inducted into the Nazi military and quasi-military organization, that is, those who did not hold leadership or supervisory positions.

Although the Nuremberg Rorschachs, reviewed in the previous chapter, provided fascinating glimpses of the personalities of notorious, upper echelon Nazis, they are an inadequate sample for studying psychological factors associated with the rank-and-file. Because of their high political positions, the Nuremberg subjects were not representative of rank-and-file Nazis. Indeed, the majority of the Nuremberg International Military Tribunal defendants were neither responsible for giving direct orders to commit atrocities nor for carrying out such orders—many of them were policy makers or high-level administrators who were well insulated from acts of inhumanity performed by the rank-and-file.

One problem with the Nuremberg sample, besides its heterogeneity, is its extremely small size. A sample of less than 20 subjects is insufficient for an adequate analysis of possible patterns of scores from the dozens of variables in a Rorschach scoring system such as the Comprehensive System (Zillmer & Vue, in press). Fortunately, a much larger sample of Rorschachs of rank-and-file Nazis is available for analysis. After Ritzler published the first quantitative analysis of the Nuremberg Rorschachs, he participated in a symposium on the Nuremberg Rorschachs at the 1979 convention of the American Psychological Association in New York (Ritzler, 1978, 1979). At this symposium he learned of the existence of a large sample of Nazi Rorschachs administered at the war crimes trials in Copenhagen in 1946. The Rorschach records were those of 175 Danish citizens convicted of collaborating with the Nazi occupation and of 32 German military personnel who were sentenced for war crimes committed in Denmark. The individuals charged in these cases were collaborators involved in matters other than the Holocaust.

On April 9, 1940, Denmark was invaded by the German army (*Aktion Dänemark*) and occupied within 1 day. The Danes were in a hopeless situation. Their country was incapable of defense, in part because before the war Denmark had adopted a policy of almost complete disarmament. The Danish people were taken completely by surprise and offered little resistance (Bracher, 1976). The German–Danish nonaggression pact of May 30, 1939 was rendered worthless by the German attack. The Germans claimed that the occupation was necessary in view of the threat of an Allied invasion of Norway. The goal of the German occupation forces was to "assure peace and order," to facilitate the transfer of agricultural products from Denmark to Germany, and to maintain a military presence. Many members of the prewar government resigned and some, mostly social-democrats, escaped to England. Under occupation, Denmark was allowed to keep, under close supervision, a puppet regime in place.

In 1940, Denmark was one of the European countries least resistant to the Nazi occupation (Birn, 1986). This was related to the fact that a majority of the population supported the government's policy of negotiating with the Germans as the best strategy to preserve the Danish people and their basic values. This may have been the case because the early German military regime was generally mild and accommodating. However, this is changed under the Nazi leadership of Werner von Best. In the course of time, as concessions, infringements, and encroachments increased, and none of the guarantees given by the Germans at the time of the occupation were honored, internal debate became more critical and active opposition gained in momentum. In 1943, with the tide turning against Germany and in response to increased resistance and acts of sabotage, a German police force (*Polizeiapperat*) was organized and mobilized in Denmark, which in part initiated the deportation of Danish Jews (Thomsen, 1971).

Denmark had always been a tolerant, peaceful, and democratic country, and Denmark's Jewish population was more integrated than in other countries. The Danish authorities had granted them equal rights, had preserved their freedom, their property, and their honor. In part because of the special character and moral stature of the Danish people, a successful rescue operation was launched by the population which resulted in almost all of its 6,000 to 7,000 Jews (8.2% of the population) being saved in an organized exodus across water to Sweden. The relatively small number was manageable, but the operation was nevertheless unique. It had been assembled ad hoc and in haste. There were neither Danish police on whom the

Germans could rely for help, nor were there an appreciable number of informers who were prepared to betray the undertaking (Hilberg, 1992). Undoubtedly, a considerable number of Danes took part in in the rescue operation in protest against German infringement of the law, rather than from any positive attitudes toward the Jews. Nevertheless, many Danes were married to Jews or involved with them in close business or personal relationships. The German attempt to act singlehandedly in a seizure operation was not successful and aborted. In all, only 477 Jews were deported to Theresienstadt, and only 40 to 50, mostly older people, perished. All others were safely transferred by boat to nearby, neutral Sweden (Friedman, 1957; Yahil, 1969). The Danish experience showed that it was possible to preserve cultural values in theory and in practice, and in doing so a tragedy of great proportions was prevented.

Denmark was liberated on May 5, 1945, when more than 250,000 Germans surrendered to Allied forces. A total of 14,268 citizen[1] were convicted for crimes committed as collaborators (Christiansen, 1950). During the war crimes trials in Copenhagen, a forensic clinic was established for the purpose of assessing the personality functioning of those Nazi collaborators. The assessment procedures included the Rorschach inkblot test that was administered by Dr. Nancy Bratt (later, Nancy Bratt-Oestergaard, 1950), the psychologist in the forensic clinic. Nearly three decades later, Bratt-Oestergaard gave the Rorschachs of the Danish war criminals to Michael Selzer, a political scientist and psychohistorian from Brooklyn College and co-author of *The Nuremberg Mind* (Miale & Selzer, 1975), which contains Florence Miale's assessment of the Nuremberg Rorschachs (reviewed in chapter 6). Using the support of a Ford Foundation grant, Selzer spent a sabbatical leave collecting and translating the Danish collaborators' Rorschachs. Ritzler's trip to the New York convention led him to Selzer who agreed to make the Danish protocols available, with the provision that Ritzler obtain permission from the Danish government to have access to the documents. Such permission was secured with the assistance of Bratt-Oestergaard and the quantitative assessment of the Danish Rorschachs was begun in 1980 using Exner's (1974) Comprehensive System. Several major revisions of the Comprehensive System scoring definitions (Exner, 1986, 1990) necessitated an equivalent number of revisions in the scoring of the Danish protocols. This chapter presents, for the first time, a summary of the final analysis of the Danish collaborators' Rorschach results.

SUBJECTS

There were 207 subjects in the original sample obtained from Selzer. However, 13 of the Rorschachs were not analyzed because the data were incomplete or not suitable for scoring. An additional 7 Rorschachs were eliminated because they

---

[1]In March 1943 the Danish National Socialist Workers' party (DNSAP), the main National Socialist party in the country, revceived 43,309 votes, or less than 2% of the total votes cast (Yahil, 1969). Although certainly a minority, the anti-Jewish sentiment seemed to spread in Denmark with an increase of anti-semitic propaganda by the Nazis.

contained less than 14 responses, and so were considered too brief to provide sufficient information to allow for a meaningful interpretation.

Of the remaining 187 protocols, 22 belonged to German military personnel who were being tried for war crimes in Denmark, because their wartime activities were limited to that country. Another 17 subjects were being tried for treason for their collaboration in matters of government administration. The remaining 148 subjects clearly qualify as rank-and-file collaborators. Although frequently inducted into the Nazi military and quasi-military organizations, they did not hold leadership or supervisory positions. They simply carried out orders or fulfilled implicit expectations of the Nazi military and the Danish administrative collaborators. Most of the results reported in this chapter are based on the 148 rank-and-file Rorschachs; the final paragraph also reports on the military and administrative groups.

A tabulation of the most serious crimes charged for the 148 rank-and-file subjects yielded the following results:

Multiple murders (three or more)	$n = 16$
One or two murders	$n = 39$
Torture and/or brutality (with no ensuing deaths)	$n = 34$
Sabotage and other acts of terrorism (not involving the perpetration of direct physical harm)	$n = 16$
Informing on resistance groups (14 other informers also committed more serious crimes)	$n = 20$
Simple, nonviolent collaboration (e.g., guards, clerks, chauffeurs, etc.)	$n = 18$

METHODOLOGY

The Rorschachs were scored according to the Rorschach Comprehensive System developed by Exner (1974, 1978b). Each protocol was scored at least three times: once immediately after obtaining the Rorschachs (1979–1982), again (1986–1989) after the publication of the revised edition of the Comprehensive System manual (Exner, 1986) that introduced significant changes in scoring criteria, and then again in 1990 after publication of the third edition of the workbook (Exner, 1990) that made further changes and added some important new variables to the scoring system.

Ritzler scored all of the Rorschachs during each scoring period. The same material also was scored by several carefully trained research assistants during the first and second scoring periods. Such double scoring allowed for an evaluation of the reliability of the scores. Disagreements were resolved through discussion. Because only a few variables changed with the third edition of the workbook, research assistants scored only 20% of the Rorschachs to provide a reliability check for the final scoring period. The research assistants were doctorate-level graduate students in clinical psychology; during Period 1 from the University of Southern Mississippi and during Period 2 from Fairleigh Dickinson University. In addition to having two semesters of Rorschach instruction, each assistant went through an additional training period of several weeks using the Comprehensive System workbook procedures for developing scoring proficiency. As a result, the percent agreement reliability estimates exceeded 85% on all scoring categories when Ritzler's scores were compared to those of the assistants.

Some modifications had to be made in the scoring system because of flaws in the administration of the Danish Rorschachs (some of which are addressed in chap. 5). Although the responses were recorded verbatim and their locations on the blot carefully noted according to a standardized numbering system (Beck et al., 1961), the inquiry, a vital part of the administration procedure, was omitted. In standard Comprehensive System administration the subject is initially instructed to respond to all ten cards with little prompting from the examiner. After the initial viewing of the 10 cards, the examiner takes the subject back through the responses in what is technically referred to as the "inquiry" (see chap. 5). During this phase, the examiner attempts to ask nonleading questions to clarify the location and general organization of each response and to determine which stimulus properties of the blot were used by the subject in formulating the response. These properties include the blot's shape and general form, color, the shading of the ink, and the propensity of the blots to elicit responses involving some form of movement. All of these features are represented by one or more specific scoring categories and are important in generating interpretative hypotheses.

Thus, the absence, or inadequacy of the inquiry during the collection of the Danish sample's Rorschach records poses a problem. However, this problem has already been addressed by empirical research (Ritzler & Nalesnik, 1990). Briefly, 140 complete, verbatim Rorschachs of psychiatric patients and normals were examined to determine the effect of inquiry on the Comprehensive System scoring. All Rorschachs were scored with and without inquiry. The results indicated that when the location of the response is clearly specified, inquiry has little effect on scoring categories that depend primarily on location and content—two aspects of a response adequately provided by the Danish Nazi sample. Inadequate inquiry, however, significantly decreased the identification of color and shading as important determinants of a response. Also, an important scoring category technically referred to as special scores was significantly underscored by insufficient inquiry. Special scores are features of Rorschach responses, including unusual verbalizations and other forms of unusual content and integration that have been interpreted more qualitatively in the past. The special scores most effected (i.e., underrepresented) were those identifying serious thinking disturbances. Other special scores that are based primarily on simple content, such as that provided by the subject's first communication of the response, were not seriously affected by insufficient inquiry. Such unaffected scores include measures of aggression, social cooperation, morbid–depressive attitudes, and intellectualization as a defense.

This same study also tested some methods for remediating the loss of scoring validity when inquiry was absent. Such modifications were effective in restoring over 80% of the "lost" color and shading scores. This modification simply consisted of scoring for color or shading whenever the content of a response was consistent with the quality of the blot area used and the basic nature of the response focus in everyday life. For instance, when "smoke" was given to a gray or black area of the card, the response was scored for diffuse shading. When "blood" was given to a red area, the response was scored for color. The only shading scoring not reasonably restored by such methods was that obtained when a subject used shading to give a three-dimensional quality to the response (e.g., "a tongue sticking out, the coloring makes it look thicker"). This particular use of shading is usually employed by individuals who engage in painful introspection— (i.e., critical self-evaluation). As a result, the amount of painful introspection is probably underrepresented in these analyses of the Danish Nazi data. Nevertheless, the amount of overall introspection, painful or otherwise, is probably accurately represented, because a three-dimensional quality of a response usually is expressed by the subject in the initial response period whether or not shading is mentioned. A three-dimensional quality is associated with introspection regardless of how it is determined. When shading is not mentioned in the inquiry as a determinant of the three-dimensional quality, the subject is likely to be the type of individual who frequently engages in introspection, but without the discomfort and self-criticism of the person who uses shading for the three-dimensional effect. Thus, the distinction between painful and nonpainful introspection cannot be made from this Nazi data, the presence or absence of an introspective orientation can be identified.

Although scoring modifications were tried for special scores, none was effective in restoring scoring validity. Consequently, the results concerning severe thinking disturbances are not to be trusted with the Danish sample and will not be interpreted in this chapter.[2]

RESULTS

A logical approach to analyzing the Danish Rorschach data would be to compare the results with normals derived from an appropriate sample of nonpatients. However, statistical comparisons between the rank-and-file Danish Nazi data and the Comprehensive System norms have not been computed because of discrepancies between the two samples involved. The Comprehensive System normative sample was compiled in the United States more than four decades after the Nazi sample was collected. Furthermore, the Comprehensive System normative sample has a wider range of age, socioeconomic status, and education. In contrast, the Nazi sample had no subjects older than 48; the socioeconomic status was middle to lower middle class, and the mean education was only 8 years. Consequently, the results presented in this chapter are based on general cut-off scores and simple comparisons of means. They are meant to give definition to the Nazi data, but are not

---

[2]The experienced Rorschacher may also argue that two other important scoring categories, Blends and *Lambda* (both measures of the complexity of information processing) would be seriously effected by insufficient inquiry. The previously cited empirical study of the effect of inquiry, however, showed that both categories returned to inquiry-assisted levels with the use of the scoring modifications.

intended as stringent tests of the differences between the Nazi and Comprehensive System's normative sample. If cut-off percentages and simple means were not radically different between the two samples, no speculation was made that the variable in question was a potentially defining characteristic of the rank-and-file Nazis. Where major discrepancies existed, the variable involved was considered important in understanding the Nazi personalities. Such "conclusions," however, should be regarded as descriptive and tentative, as they have not yet been substantiated by mathematical comparisons. That awaits a better comparison sample.

The Rorschach Comprehensive System allows for assessment of several psychological traits related to empirically determined variable clusters derived from quantitative test scores. These components, which also serve as a general strategy for purposes of interpreting the two case examples in chapter 8, are: control and stress tolerance, situational stress, interpersonal perception and relations, self-perception, problem-solving style, affective features, information processing, mediation, and ideation. Danish Nazi Rorschach results relevant to each component are summarized in the following sections.

Control and Stress Tolerance.   The Rorschach Comprehensive System provides an estimate of personality resources referred to as the *experience actual*. This variable consists of the sum of responses involving human movement and the "weighted" sum of responses involving chromatic color with weights assigned according to the basic importance of color in a response. The human movement score provides an estimate of cognitive resources (i.e., the potential capacity to use thinking for adaptive problem solving), whereas the weighted sum of all color responses provides an estimate of emotional resources (i.e., the capacity to use emotional feedback in the problem-solving process). Regarding the Nazi experience actual, the mean estimate of personality resources was noticeably less than the mean score from the Comprehensive System norms, primarily because the Nazis' human movement mean score of 2.72 was less than that of the Comprehensive System value obtained for normals ($M = 4.54$). This finding suggests that the Nazis as a group showed deficiencies in cognitive resources necessary for effective stress tolerance. It is apparent that many rank-and-file Nazis were not deep thinkers and may have had difficulty in making their own decisions.

In contrast to the findings on problem-solving resources, the Comprehensive System indicator of stress impinging on the individual is not significantly inflated in the protocols. Several Comprehensive System variables are associated with different subjective experiences of stress, including: (a) animal and inanimate movement (reflective of cognitive stress such as worries, intrusive preoccupations, or guilt), and (b) responses that are determined by the shading nuances of the blots (associated with emotional stress such as affective constriction, painful self-awareness, loneliness, and acute feelings of helplessness). Added together, six variables make up the derived score referred to as *experience stimulation*, an estimate of the amount of subjective stress impinging on the individual. The Nazi experience stress stimulation mean score (8.20) is practically the same as the Comprehensive System norm ($M = 8.21$). This finding suggests that, although the Nazis were not showing unusually high levels of stress as a group, they were vulnerable to becoming "stressed out" because of a reduced capacity for stress tolerance.

Another indicator of the capacity for stress tolerance is the Coping Deficit Index (CDI), which, when significant, suggests difficulty contending with the natural demands of the social world. In other words, the CDI seems to measure the sort of social skills deficits that lead to poor social outcomes and dissatisfaction with the quality of life. In the Nazi sample, 46% of the protocols show a significant CDI score (i.e., > 4) compared to only 3% in the Comprehensive System norms—another indication of a significant problem with stress tolerance and general coping for the Danish Nazis.

In summary, the Nazis as a group appear to be deficient in stress tolerance and thereby vulnerable to even typical levels of subjective stress. As a result, many of them were individuals who needed more than the usual amounts of external structure, guidance, and reassurance in managing their everyday lives. This finding is also consistent with the frequently used defense of rank-and-file Nazis that they simply were "following orders." Their submission to external demands may well have been an adaptive means to stabilize their environment and reduce their level of stress tolerance.

Situational Stress.   Now that vulnerability to stress has been demonstrated for a substantial number of Nazis, the Comprehensive System has the capability of determining if the stress is acute or chronic. Faced with the situation of the war crimes trials, the Danish Nazis were logical candidates for situational stress. Two variables in the Rorschach Comprehensive System are associated with the subjective impact of stress resulting from situational crises. These variables are inanimate movement (m; the cognitive situational stress variable) and diffuse shading (Y; the affective situational stress variable). The subjective impact of situational stress is estimated directly by making adjustments in the overall measure of subjective distress by correcting for the amounts of inanimate movement and diffuse shading in the record to yield an adjusted stress tolerance score. When the adjusted score (adjusted D; the primary indicator of situational stress in the Comprehensive System) is significantly higher than the overall "unadjusted" D score, it is very likely that the subject is experiencing situational stress.

The Nazi war criminals were on public display while being tried for infamous crimes. They had lost a war and an ideology. Many knew their lives were in the balance. Even those who did not receive the most severe sentences were aware that upon their eventual release they would be subject to many negative reactions from their countrymen. We have already surmised that these are individuals who were particularly susceptible to stress. But in spite of this susceptibility and the potential stress in their current predicament, the rank-and-file Nazis showed remarkably little indication of situational stress. Only 17 (9%) had adjusted stress tolerance scores that were higher than the unadjusted stress tolerance score, compared to 7% in the Comprehensive System norms. Apparently, the Nazis were somehow inured to situational stress in spite of their relatively low ego resources. Such an imperviousness might be the result of a defensive style that relied heavily on denial.

Interpersonal Perceptions and Relations.   The Danish rank-and-file Nazi war criminals showed deviation in four variables associated with interpersonal perception and relations. These variables have labels that clearly suggest their interpretive significance. They are the CDI, active-to-passive movement ratio, texture responses, and cooperative movement responses.

The CDI was established by Exner (1990) when he discovered that the Depression Index failed to identify a sizable group of individuals clinically diagnosed as depressed. When assessed as a group, these depressed individuals scored significantly different than normals on several variables that became the items in the CDI. As Exner (1993) suggested, people who have scores of four or more on this index are likely to have impoverished or unrewarding social relationships. As indicated earlier, the Nazis clearly showed coping deficits with 46% of the rank-and-file subjects having a significant CDI compared to only 3% of the Exner normative sample.

Concerning the active-to-passive ratio, 33% of the Nazis gave passive movement responses that exceeded the number of active responses by more than one. This compares with the Exner normals that show only 6 out of 7,000 subjects. A predominance of passive movement in Rorschach responses is associated with marked passive behavior in relationships (Exner, 1978a). Clearly, the Danish Nazis were significantly inclined toward such passivity.

In regard to another indicator of interpersonal orientation, 67% of the Nazi protocols had more than one texture response compared to 7% in the Exner normative sample. There was no difference between the Nazis (12%) and the nonpatient males (12%) for Texture = 0. This suggests that contrary to popular belief, Nazis were not avoidant of, or unresponsive to, close, supportive relationships. However, the preponderance of Texture = 1 protocols suggests that the Nazis may have been feeling deprived of such affiliations—a circumstance that is not unlikely considering that they had recently suffered a complete defeat of their major institutional support and were in prison and on trial, many for their lives. Given such acute deprivations, the basic texture data may not be sufficient as an indication of the Nazis' capacity for forming supportive affiliations. In an attempt to explore these issues, a study was done of the specific content of texture responses from various clinical samples. The main hypothesis was that the potential to connect affectively with others is associated with positively toned textures such as "fur" and "silk," whereas those who are suffering support deprivation, because of deficiencies in the capacity to affiliate, will give responses with harsh or spoiled textures. Patients and nonpatients with positive texture responses were much more likely to have ongoing supportive relationships than were subjects with negative texture responses. In the same study, the Danish Nazi protocols were compared to Rorschachs of normals, inpatients, outpatients, and prisoners from a state prison. The Nazis were the only group to show more negative than positive texture responses. This suggests that although the Nazis may have been sensitive to the need for supportive intimacy (i.e., *Kameradschaft*), their affiliations may not have been giving them the degree of comfort experienced by most individuals in intimate relationships or they may not have had the ability to accept intimacy to the same degree.

Finally, 53% of the Nazis had no cooperative movement responses (COP) and only 3% showed COP > 2. This compares to the Comprehensive System norms with COP = 0 at 23% and COP > 2 at 37%. The COP coding is assigned to any movement response involving two or more objects in which the interaction is clearly positive or cooperative (e.g., "Two men lifting something") and is associated with a tendency to perceive relationships as based on cooperative, mutual behavior and concerns. Individuals who give more than two COP responses tend to be gregarious and socially successful. Obviously, the Danish rank-and-file Nazis as a group did not show such tendencies.

In general, the data suggest that the Nazis showed signs of social skills deficits that may have been manifested in an inability to form close, supportive attachments outside the structure of the Nazi organization. It can be speculated that the Nazi affiliation of these rank-and-file collaborators may have served as a substitute for interpersonal intimacy. If so, the defeat of the Nazi movement may have been particularly painful and left many of the collaborators with nowhere to turn for support. Such a crisis could account for an acute increase in texture scores on the Danish Nazi Rorschach.

Self-Perception.   The Comprehensive System provides a measure of self-focus referred to as the *egocentricity index*. It is based on the empirical finding that responses involving symmetrical pairs, especially those conceptualized as reflections, are associated with self-esteem and self-interest, extending to narcissism when at least one reflection is produced by the subject. The *egocentricity index* is calculated by three times the number of reflections plus the number of simple pairs divided by the number of responses, that is, $3r+(2)/R$. As a group, the Danish Nazis showed a decrement in this index. Scores below a level of .33 suggest a deficit in self-esteem. Of the Nazi protocols, 75% scored in this low range compared to 13% in the Comprehensive System norms. Only 5% of the Nazis scored above .44, a level marking the beginning of potentially narcissistic overevaluation of the self, compared to 19% in the Comprehensive System norms. This finding suggests that rather than the overblown, self-important major-dodo of popular lore, the rank-and-file Nazis as a group may have been rather self-effacing and lacking in confidence. Such an interpretation is further supported by an elevation in morbid content (MOR) with 28% of the Nazis giving more than two morbid responses compared to only 4% in the Comprehensive System norms. A response is scored MOR when an object is identified as dead, destroyed, damaged, or broken (e.g., a decaying leaf) or of a clearly dysphoric feeling (e.g., a sad tree). Apparently, a substantial number of Nazis included in their low self-esteem the concept of being personally damaged or disadvantaged. This type of negative self-perception seems consistent with the frequently used defense of rank-and-file Nazis that they simply were "victims of circumstance."

Another Rorschach Comprehensive System phenomenon empirically associated with self-orientation is the projection of a three-dimensional quality to the response (i.e., answers that involve impressions of depth, distance). Several studies (Exner, 1974, 1978a, 1990) indicated that three dimensionality on the Rorschach is associated with introspection—the existential, in-depth examination of one's thoughts and feelings. The Danish Nazis appear to be much less introspective than the subjects in the Comprehensive System norms. Of the Nazis, 37% gave at least one three-dimensional response, compared to 86% in the Comprehensive System norms.

Another set of Comprehensive System self-perception indicators is associated with interest in or preoccupation with body functions and physical well-being. Anatomy and x-ray responses provided this psychosomatic variable set. The Danish Nazis tended to show more anatomy and x-ray responses than did the subjects in the Comprehensive System normative sample. The Nazi frequency for anatomy and x-ray responses was 85% compared to 36% for the Comprehensive System normals.

Perhaps the most telling discrepancy in the Nazi self-perception indicators is the low number of responses depicting whole, real human beings compared to responses involving parts of the human figure (e.g., arm, leg) or responses with mythical, fictitious, or caricatured human figures (e.g., fairy tale characters, giants, witches, devils, etc.). Empirical studies (e.g., Exner, 1993) have shown that when the number of whole, real human contents on the Rorschach is equal to or greater than the number of part- or quasi-human contents, the subject is likely to be particularly responsive to feedback from real, ongoing relationships. When all responses involving human content are added together, the Nazi average (5.27) is not markedly different than the mean from the Comprehensive System norms (5.72) suggesting that the Nazis had normal tendencies to conceptualize experience in human terms. However, the Nazis' mean for whole, real human responses was 1.62 compared to 3.40 for the Comprehensive System norms, suggesting that the Nazis were less likely to have formulated their self-awareness on the basis of feedback from real relationships. Instead, the Nazis, with their high proportion of partial- and quasi-human responses, seem to have been more likely to have a sense of self that is based on "part-object" conceptualizations in which the individual is likely to view him or herself and others as objects to be manipulated and exploited, rather than complete and complex individuals capable of shared, intimate relationships.

In summary, the Nazis appear to have had low self-esteem with a tendency to view themselves as victims of circumstances. They were not likely to have engaged in introspection, but tended to be preoccupied with physical well-being. Most importantly, they were likely to disregard feedback from real relationships in forming their self-images that may have been associated with viewing themselves and others as incomplete part-objects vulnerable to manipulation and exploitations.

Problem-Solving Style. As already discussed in chapter 6 with the Nuremberg defendants, the *EB* is an extremely stable indicator of the typical approach a subject takes toward solving problems and making decisions (Exner & Murillo, 1975). If the ratio is weighted by at least two human movement responses, compared to the weighted sum of chromatic color responses by 2.5 points, the subject's problem solving style is primarily cognitive. Such individuals are likely to first think about a problem and formulate a solution before trying it out. Emotions do not typically play a major role in this process, but rather tend to be experienced as noise or interference. The reader may recall that this particular style is referred to as *introversive* and was not predominant among the Nuremberg group.

In contrast, when the *EB* ratio favors the weighted color side, the style is called *extratensive* and refers to an affective or intuitive approach to problems in which the individual uses emotions as a guide in a predominantly trial-and-error approach in which solutions are worked out through actions rather than extensive preliminary thinking. Both the introversive and extratensive styles are remarkably stable across situations, although most individuals are able to shift to the opposite style when their usual approach is not effective for a specific problem. Some individuals, however, are unable to shift approaches and stubbornly stick to their usual style despite repeated failures. The Comprehensive System identifies these individuals with the "pervasive quotient" which is calculated by dividing the higher number of the *EB* ratio by the lower. When the quotient exceeds 2.5, the problem solving style is likely to be of the inflexible, pervasive type. Individuals with such rigid styles are referred to as *super introversives* or *super extratensives.*

When the *EB* ratio shows a difference of less than 2 between the human movement and color scores the individual is not likely to show a consistent problem-solving style. They are likely to vacillate in a haphazard way between a cognitive and an affective approach so that they have great difficulty solving problems on their own and are likely to be influenced by the opinions of others or an external structure. This fluctuating, ineffectual problem-solving style is referred to as *ambitent* and identifies individuals who essentially have "no mind of their own," a characteristic identified by the lack of clear dominance of cognitive or emotional resources in a record.

As a group the Danish rank-and-file Nazis showed a rather dramatic tendency toward the ambitent problem style (46% compared to 23% in the Exner norms). They showed fewer introversives or thinkers (19% compared to 33% for the Comprehensive System norms) and about the same proportion of extratensives (35% to 44% for the Comprehensive System norms); however, they showed double the proportion of super extratensives (24% to 12%) and about the same proportion of super introversives (14% to 8%). Consequently, the data suggest that the Nazis are more likely to be either problem solvers who ineffectually vacillate and are easily influenced by others; or they are rigid, stubborn adherents to cognitive problem solving styles which are not adaptable to different problems demands, a finding also seen in the Nuremberg group (see chap. 6). Relatively few of the Nazis (16% compared to 57%) showed well-established, but reasonably adaptable, problem-solving styles.

Affective Features. In the Comprehensive System, chromatic color responses are indicative of affective resources or the capacity for purposeful emotional expression. Furthermore, the extent to which the form or shape of the blot is integrated with color provides an estimate of the extent to which emotional expression will typically be modulated by the individual. Color responses in which form plays a dominant role (FC; e.g., a flower, red) are indicative of well-modulated emotional expression. Color responses that integrate form in a nondominant or indefinite way (CF; e.g., green leaves) indicate less well-modulated emotional expression that is typical of relatively spontaneous, partially modulated expressions of emotions. The presence of more than one amorphous color response (pure C; e.g., orange flames) in the Rorschach record, indicates the potential for unmodulated emotional expression commonly referred to as "letting off steam" or "letting it all hang out."

The ratio, FC/CF+C provides the Rorschacher with an estimate of the extent to which an individual modulates emotional expression. A ratio of approximately 4:2.5 with FC > CF + C is standard in adults. Subjects are considered to have a clear cut affect modulation style when one side of the FC/CF+C ratio exceeds the other by more than one. Correspondingly, the Danish Nazis show a greater propensity for the opposite direction, CF+C > FC+1 (24% to 6% for the Comprehensive System norms) with a corresponding decrease in the frequency of FC > CF+C+1 (21% to 77%). This predominance of CF+C over FC scores seems to be the result of a decline in FC responses ($M = 2.08$ for the Nazis compared to $M = 4.16$ for Comprehensive System norms). It is important to note, however, that the Nazis seldom gave amorphous color (pure C) responses—averaging only 0.15 per subject compared to 0.67 for the Comprehensive System norms. Consequently, the form of emotional expression typical of the Nazis as a group was that of a relatively simple, unmodulated style that, nevertheless, seldom reached the most extreme, unbridled level.

Contrasting to the availability of emotional resources as indicated by color responses is the presence of emotional stressors that impinge on the individual and are manifested as subjective emotional pain, passivity, and discontent. These stressors are assessed in the Comprehensive System by the frequency with which the subject uses the shading of the blot as a quality of the response. The impact of emotional stress is considered particularly salient when the number of shading responses (Y; indicators of "emotional" stress such as anxiety and depression) exceeds the number of animal movement (FM) and inanimate movement (m) responses (indicators of cognitive" stress such as worries and guilt). The Nazis showed a greater frequency of Sum Shading > FM+m (66% compared to 13% in the Comprehensive System norms) suggesting that the stress experienced by them was more likely to have been of an affective, rather than cognitive, nature. In other words, Nazis, with their relatively simple emotional expression, were more likely to experience anxiety or feelings of depression (i.e., emotional stress) rather than suffering from worry or other negative thoughts and preoccupations (i.e., cognitive stress).

Information Processing. The Comprehensive System provides information for the assessment of how the individual selects and organizes informational input. Distinct processing characteristics of the Danish Nazis were indicated by several variables: (a) *Lambda*, (b) the Z score, (c) obvious detail responses, (d) vaguely specified responses, and, (e) perseverated responses.

Lambda (L) is a measure of the proportion of responses with only form (or shape) as a determining factor. A high Lambda score suggests that the subject is not responsive to the nuances of experience and prefers to organize experience in a simple and straightforward manner. More than half of the Danish Nazi sample (61%) had Lambda scores greater than .99 compared to 5% in the Comprehensive System norms. Because Lambda is the ratio of form-only responses (i.e., answers that are based exclusively on the form features of the blot) to responses with other determinants, a Lambda greater than .99 means that at least half of the responses in a protocol have only form as a determinant. The mean Lambda for the Nazi sample was 1.36 compared to a 0.56 in the Comprehensive System norms.

A Z score is given to a response when the subject uses the whole blot in a definite manner or combines more than one area of the blot into a more complex Gestalt. The frequency of Z scores for the Nazi sample was low (an average of 7.88 responses per Rorschach) compared to the Comprehensive System norms (10.08 per Rorschach). This means that the Nazis showed a reduced tendency to organize responses by using the whole card or combining areas of the blot to form responses with more than one figure or element.

The Nazis also gave a higher number of responses using the obvious, well-delineated areas of the blot (referred to as "usual detail responses," - 17.57 compared to 13.19 for the Comprehensive System norms). This is consistent with the previously interpreted tendency to respond in the most simple, straightforward manner.

The Nazis also gave more vaguely specified responses in which the form of the response was left highly indefinite or given no specification at all (amorphous responses). The Nazis averaged 5.71 such responses per Rorschach compared to an average of 1.65 from the Comprehensive System norms.

Finally, the Nazis perseverated much more frequently than the Comprehensive norms (i.e., responding in an identical manner to different blots) with an average perseveration rate of .42 per Rorschach compared to .04 for the Comprehensive System norms and suggests a form of cognitive dysfunction or a marked psychological preoccupation.

To summarize, the Danish Nazis as a group tended to process information simply and without much attention to the nuances of experience. They tended to process the most obvious aspects of experience in a fashion that was rather vague and lacking in complexity. Such information processing predisposes individuals to relatively unimaginative thinking.

Mediation. The Comprehensive System allows for assessment of cognitive mediation by which processed input is translated into ideation (i.e., the process of forming ideas or thinking). In this assessment, the variable Lambda is an index of mediational complexity. As we have seen in the information-processing assessment, the Nazis tended to score high on this variable, suggesting that their mediation is relatively uncomplicated and perhaps lacking in depth.

The shallowness of the Nazi mediation should not, however, be mistaken for "common" or "ordinary." For instance, popular (P) responses in the Comprehensive System are those of nearly identical content given to the same area of a blot by at least 26% of the normative sample. The average frequency range of popular responses is four to seven per Rorschach. Compared to the Comprehensive System norms, the Nazis gave fewer popular responses overall (26% gave fewer than four and only 5% gave more than seven). In the Comprehensive System, nonpatient adult norms only one subject out of 700 gave less than four populars and 41% gave more than seven.

The popular response results, however, could be a function of the cultural and chronological differences between the samples. In other words, a popular response in the United States in the 1980s might not have been a popular in Denmark in 1946. A more telling indication of the uncommon nature of the Nazi mediation is the degree to which the content of the responses matches the general shape and configuration of the inkblots. This correspondence is referred to as "form quality" and represents an estimate of an individual's tendency to interpret the world in an accurate and/or conventional manner. Overall form quality is measured by the X+%—the higher the X+%, the more accurate and/or conventional the subject's interpretation of the blots. The "normal" range is 70%–85%. None of the Nazis had an X+% greater than 89% whereas 85% of the sample showed X+% less than 70. In the Comprehensive System norms, 5% showed X+% > 89 and only 10% showed X+% < 70.

Responses that are highly inaccurate interpretations of the inkblot represent distorted and usually problematic mediation and are measure by the X-%. Accurate, but very unconventional responses are summarized by the Xu% (u for "unusual"). The Xu% and X-% means were 27% and 17%, respectively for the Nazis compared to 14% and 7% for the Exner norms.

The typical Nazi mediational style appears to be simplistic, but unconventional. The Nazis probably were matching their perceptions to very basic and unusual schema. Such an approach is consistent with a cognitive style which draws frequently on odd (often inaccurate) stereotypes to make sense out of experience. In other words, the Nazis may have been particularly susceptible to prejudice and bigotry—not because they were inundated with sadism and aggression, but more because they assumed an overly simplistic and unconventional approach to cognitive mediation.

Ideation. Ideation refers to the final step in the cognitive cycle during which processed and mediated information is converted into conscious thoughts that are instrumental in decision-making and meaningful communication. The Comprehensive System is very effective in identifying bizarre and severely disturbed thinking. Also, the Comprehensive System can identify eccentric ideation which is indicative of less disturbed forms of unconventional thinking. One category of variables that provides such distinctions is form quality that already has been used to describe the Nazis' mediational functioning as less accurate and more eccentric than the Comprehensive System norms. Of course, less accurate interpretations of experience will often result in less conventional and effective decision-making and communication. However, Nazi form quality scores fall short of the most disturbed psychotic levels of thinking disturbance. In other words, the Nazis' ideational problems probably are best described as "eccentric" and "moderately inefficient" rather than "psychotic" or "severely disturbed."

Perhaps the best indicators of bizarre thinking are the six Special Scores categories derived from studies of schizophrenic thinking (e.g., Rapaport, Gill, & Schafer, 1968; Weiner, 1966) referred to as the "Sum 6" variables.

Even though the previously referenced study of the effects of inadequate inquiry suggests that these six special scores probably are under-represented in this Nazi sample, the thought disorder special score indices are consistent with the unusual, but not psychotic nature of their thought processes. For instance, 22% of the Nazis gave at least one of the more severe thought disorder responses compared to only 1 out of the 700 Comprehensive System normative subjects. Nevertheless, the sum total of thought disorder scores from the Nazi protocols was only slightly higher than the Comprehensive System norms. Only 5% of the Nazis gave more than six thought disorder responses (the Comprehensive System cut-off) and the overall weighted thought disorder index (WSum6) was 5.99 for the Nazis compared to 3.28 for the Comprehensive System norms and 44.69 for the Comprehensive System sample of inpatient schizophrenics.

Apparently, the Nazis showed some unusual thought patterns, but not enough to indicate grossly disturbed thinking. The unusual quality of the Nazis' ideation also extended to their thinking regarding human relationships. In addition to the eccentric quality of the Nazis' Rorschachs, there are indications of rigid and pessimistic thinking. Again, the tendency to think unusual, but not highly bizarre, thought combined with rigid and pessimistic thinking is consistent with the cognitive style of bigotry and prejudice characteristics of the Nazi propaganda.

CHAMELEONS

Although the previous sections essentially exhaust the comparisons between the Nazi rank-and-file protocols and the Comprehensive norms, a unique characteristic of the Nazi Rorschachs remains to be mentioned. The Ritzler (1978) assessment of the Nuremberg Rorschachs revealed an odd fact; namely that 5 of the 16 (31%) Nuremberg Nazis saw a chameleon in an area of Card VIII which often yields the popular response of some kind of animal (Dönitz's protocol presented in the next chapter also has a chameleon response on Card VIII). In fact, for the Nuremberg group, a chameleon was the most frequently seen animal in this area of the blot. By contrast, a computerized tally of all Rorschach responses given by 568 medical students at John Hopkins Medical School (Thomas, Ross, & Freed, 1964) showed that the chameleon response was given by only 1.7% of the subjects.

In the rank-and-file Danish sample, 36 of the 148 protocols (19%) responded with chameleons in the animal area on Card VIII. Again, the chameleon is the most frequently seen animal for the Nazis, compared to an 11% frequency for the second most frequent animal, a "rat."

The content of a chameleon presents a tempting speculation for the personality of a rank-and-file Nazi. That is, a chameleon is an animal that, for survival, subtly changes color to blend with the prevailing environment. Surely, the talents of a chameleon might be useful in the often hazardous environment of the Nazi movement. The ability to "blend in" and remain inconspicuous might assure survival when other, more assertive and flamboyant styles might encounter difficulty.

In spite of the logic of this tempting speculation, a caveat is in order. A small lizard of the chameleon family occurs in greater numbers in Europe than the chameleons seen in this country. Furthermore, the European chameleon has a pinkish hue, the same color as the "animal" area on Card VIII, compared to its greener U.S. counterpart. It may be that a European sample of Rorschachs might, indeed, have a chameleon as the most frequently seen animal on Card VIII without having the implications suggested earlier. The speculation remains tempting, however.

NAZI SADISM

The Danish Nazi Rorschachs provide an opportunity to test a popular hypothesis that the Nazis were pathologically sadistic. In an earlier analysis of the Danish results, Ritzler and Saraydarian (1986) identified two groups of 50 collaborators with contrasting levels of violence in their war crimes. One group consisted of collaborators who participated in frequent episodes of brutality and murder. The second group did not directly commit violent acts.

In order to assess the degree of sadism expressed in the two contrasting groups, Ritzler and Saraydarian used the aggressive movement (AG^3) and morbid (MOR) scores from the Comprehensive System. As hypothesized, the violent crime group gave significantly more AG and MOR responses than did the nonviolent group. A closer look at the frequency distributions of the two groups for the AG and MOR variables gave an even more striking, specific assessment of sadism as a contributing factor to war crimes. In the violent group, 17 of the 50 subjects (34%) gave at least four AG and/or MOR responses. In the nonviolent group, only 3 (6%) scored at this level. However, the remaining 33 subjects in the violent group have AG and MOR frequencies that are no different from those of the nonviolent group. Clearly, although sadism appears to be associated with violent actions, it is not sufficient to explain the violence of the majority of the violent crime group. Although our image of the Nazis tends to be that of thugs and murderers (see Lifton & Markuson, 1990), the current analysis suggests that many ordinary people became involved in atrocities who did not demonstrate any particular inclination toward violence.

ADMINISTRATORS AND GERMAN MILITARY PERSONNEL

The rank-and-file subjects have been analyzed separately from the top Danish Nazi administrator ($n = 17$) and native German *Wehrmacht* officers ($n = 22$). The following is a brief summary of the Comprehensive System results for those two groups compared to the rank-and-file.

---

[3]The AG coding is used for any movement response in which the action is clearly aggressive (e.g., two animals fighting).

Comparing some demographic characteristics of the three groups indicates that the administrators were older and better educated than the other two groups. In turn, the German military subjects were older and better educated than the rank-and-file. Finally, the rank-and-file were more likely to have been single than the other two groups. The analysis of these demographic variables suggests that the administrators and the military were more settled in their life circumstances as a result of having more time and opportunity for adult achievement. Consequently, it is not surprising that their Rorschachs reflect higher levels of functioning.

In addition to the demographic differences, the three groups differ regarding important ratios, percentages, special indices, and miscellaneous variables on the Rorschach. Although there are many similarities across groups, it is apparent that the administrators and military personnel almost never show introversive (cognitively oriented) problem-solving styles with more than half of the administrators classifying as extratensives (emotionally oriented) in their problem-solving styles. The administrators and military also are more likely to be underincorporators and somewhat less eccentric that the other two groups. They also were more likely to use intellectualization and were more responsive to the interactive nature of human experience. Surprisingly, the military were not likely to show aggression.

In general, the German military personnel did not differ much at all from the rank-and-file collaborators. On the other hand, the administrators show up as a somewhat more emotionally responsive group that may have been showing a greater sense of lost affiliation in reaction to the defeat of the Third Reich. They were less depressed, however, suggesting that they may have been using their defense of intellectualization to rationalize their collaboration. As intuitive underincorporators they also may have been more prone to "jumping on the bandwagon" when faced with the influence of the Nazi occupation.

SUMMARY

It is tempting to use the descriptive results of the analysis of the Danish Nazi Rorschachs to define a typical rank-and-file personality profile. However, the results discussed above are based on comparisons of group means and frequencies and do not apply consistently across all Nazi subjects. Indeed, it is apparent that few, if any, protocols contain all the characteristics identified here that differentiated the Nazi group from the Comprehensive System norms. The most that can be concluded is that certain personality characteristics tend to be associated with perpetration of wartime violence. For instance, vulnerability to stress and ineffective methods of independent problem solving may have made the organizational structure of the Nazi movement quite attractive to a number of the Danish collaborators. Also, the observed indications of social skills deficits and low self-esteem are consistent with the speculation that many collaborators may have achieved a sense of status and self-respect through their affiliation with the Nazis. Furthermore, the structure and dogmatic propaganda of the Nazis may have provided the kind of simple, but unconventional, interpretation of experience apparently preferred by many of the collaborators.

Perhaps the most telling characteristic differentiating the Danish rank-and-file collaborators from the Comprehensive System's normative sample is the tendency to view themselves and others as simple, incomplete, part-objects. A strong case can be made that the Nazis were not capable of perceiving themselves and other human beings as complex, integrated personalities. Such overly simplistic attitudes lend themselves to arbitrary, prejudicial beliefs about the integrity of human beings and may make it possible for individuals such as the Danish collaborators to treat others as if they were not human. Even though some Nazis, particularly those who perpetrated the worst crimes, showed increased sadistic tendencies, it is apparent that sadism alone is not sufficient to explain the inhumanity of the Nazi rank-and-file. Shallow, overly simplistic, and socially limited personality style also seems to play a part, suggesting that there may be some validity to Arendt's characterization of the "banality of evil." Even so, enough highly complex Rorschachs exist in the Danish sample to indicate that banality also is not a sufficient explanation for the Nazi phenomenon.

Consequently, while the Danish Nazi Rorschachs suggest that personality characteristics associated with perpetration of war related violence do exist, a purely psychological explanation is not enough. Obviously, political, socioeconomic, and even cultural factors are necessary for a fuller understanding. On a final note, that lack of evidence for obvious and severe psychopathology in the Danish Rorschachs once again reminds us that the Nazis can not so easily be explained away as disturbed, highly abnormal individuals. One limitation of the current sample is related to the generalization of these findings to rank-and-file perpetrators of the Holocaust, since such atrocities were not performed on Danish soil. Although at first spared, in October 1943 Danish Jews fell under the shadow of the Nazi racial laws. A "naval bridge" organized by institutions and individuals evacuated a large number of Jews to Sweden with the aid of sailors and fishermen from both countries. As a result, 7,200 of some 8,000 Danish Jews were kept out of German hands and only 50 lost their lives. Thus, the implications of the current findings on the involvement of the rank-and-file in the Holocaust must be approached with caution.

Chapter 8

Two Case Studies of Nazi War Criminals

In this chapter two case studies are presented in detail, protocols that are being published and interpreted for the first time, more than 50 years after they have been collected. Among the many Rorschach data reviewed in the preceding chapters, the psychological records collected by Dr. Kelley stand out as particularly important, because they have hitherto not been examined. This is not to assume that other psychological profiles were less interesting, but for either the specific characteristics of the Rorschach inkblot record or the historical significance of the individual taking the Rorschach, or both, the records of Karl Dönitz and Julius Streicher are presented here for close inspection.

METHODOLOGY

Initially, each Rorschach record was scored by three experts in accordance with the Exner Comprehensive System, with at least two experts having no knowledge of the identity of the subjects. There is sufficient evidence to suggest that adequately trained examiners can agree reasonably well on their scoring of Rorschach variables. In fact, the *Journal of Personality Assessment* requires authors of Rorschach studies to provide evidence of interscorer agreement. Inability to reach at least 80% agreement indicates a need for revised scoring (Weiner, 1991). In the present scoring the interscorer agreement among all the responses of the two records reviewed here exceeded 85%. Scoring disagreements were most often related to the presence of inadequate inquiry or to idiosyncrasies of the Rorschach administration (see chap. 5 for review).

Once the responses of the Rorschach records of Dönitz and Streicher were scored in accordance with the standards described here, computer-generated structural summaries and interpretive hypotheses were generated as a starting point for psychological analysis. The use of computerized Rorschach interpretations as an initial step in the interpretative process is most useful here, because it removes the subjective bias that one may, knowingly or unknowingly, have toward the Nazi Rorschach records (see Zillmer et al., 1989). The software used here, the Rorschach Interpretation Assistance Program-Version 2 (RIAP2; Exner, Cohen, & Mcguire, 1991), has been proven to be a particularly useful tool (Zillmer, 1991) because it generates interpretative hypotheses based on construct validity studies of the Rorschach Comprehensive System. The statement bank of RIAP2 contains over 370 comments that typically take into consideration multiple features of the Rorschach record and is arranged into several interpretative clusters (e.g., situational stress, self-perception, etc.), with the most salient features of the record being presented first.

KARL DÖNITZ (1891–1981): "THE LION"

The only thing that really frightened me during the war was the submarine threat.
—Winston Churchill

Early History

Although Dönitz was born inland near Berlin, he lived almost his entire life near or on the North Sea. His father was an engineer with Carl Zeiss optics, and his mother died when Dönitz was only 4 years old. Entering the German Imperial Navy in 1910, Dönitz served first as a signals officer on cruisers. In 1916 he retrained in submarine warfare becoming a U-boat commander the following year. During World War I, his U-boat was sunk in the Mediterranean in October 1918. He escaped drowning only to serve 9 months as a British prisoner of war (POW). Upon his release in June 1919 he returned to the German navy (Dönitz, 1959, 1968). Married and the father of two sons and one daughter, he was posted as advisor to the navy inspectorate's U-boat department in 1923. The Treaty of Versailles had forbidden the construction of German submarines, and so his department was officially charged with defending against them (Bird, 1977). However, the navy was already planning its future U-boats and Dönitz was seen as a rising star. In 1924 he moved to the Navy High Command in Berlin in a liaison post to the army. After further sea duty in 1929, he returned to Berlin in 1930 as a staff officer. During the first months of Hitler's chancellorship, Dönitz was absent in the far east. He returned to a National Socialist and anti-Marxist Germany that met with his approval. In 1935 he was given command of the light cruiser *Emden,* which he took on a flag-showing world cruise (Thomas, 1990).

The U-Boat Campaign

When the Anglo-German Naval Treaty removed many of the restrictions of Versailles in 1936 and permitted Germany's navy to expand, Dönitz took command of the new U-boat flotilla with the rank of captain. He was an experienced submarine officer and quickly set to training new crews and launching the new U-1

Lieutenant Karl Dönitz in the summer of 1917 as watch officer on board U-boat U-39.
Bundesarchiv Koblenz.

from a tightly guarded shed in the Kiel shipyards. Dönitz, who knew from personal experience the weaknesses of the 1918 U-boats, built the new U-1 with heavy-duty electric batteries (to stay submerged underwater for longer periods of time) and with a revolutionary torpedo design. With the conception of the U-1, Dönitz campaigned for a crash U-boat building program, suggesting that a force of 300 using his *Rudeltaktik* (i.e., wolfpack tactics) could block Britain's trade routes and force her collapse in a future war. He believed that England could be paralyzed by waging what he called a "tonnage war," that is, by sinking all merchant ships carrying cargoes to England, regardless of the flag they flew (Salewski, 1970).

Initially, however, Hitler preferred the idea of large, powerful warships (*Weltmachtflotte*) sailing into European ports where, flying the swastika, they contributed to the Third Reich's intimidating image. Moreover, the senior admirals in Berlin preferred to envision confrontation between surface ships, with enormous battleships trying to blow up their enemies into submission (L. Kennedy, 1974). Thus, Erich Raeder, then commander-in-chief of the German navy, embarked on a big ship program, while Dönitz vigorously promoted submarine warfare strategies (Salewski, 1970). In 1939, when Germany possessed only 48 submarines, Dönitz established himself as the foremost expert on German U-boat warfare publishing a book on the subject entitled *Die U-Bootswaffe*. The work was much more than a naval textbook because it showed his approval of Nazi militarism and his devotion to the brotherhood of the submarine crew. The outbreak of war, however, found the U-boat force considerably smaller than Dönitz had envisaged with only 27 U-boats suitable for Atlantic operations (Bird, 1985).

The turning point for Dönitz's U-boat program came when the U-47, commanded by 31-year-old Dönitz protégé, Lieutenant Guenther Prien, sank the British battleship H.M.S. Royal Oak as she lay at anchor in her Scottish base on October 13, 1939. It was Dönitz's audacious plan to study aerial photographs of the Scapa Flow bay and attack a British battleship at anchor in its greatest naval base. Even though more than 786 officers and men were trapped in the ship and perished, Churchill admired the submariner's achievement—what a wonderful feat of arms (G. Snyder, 1976). For years, the German navy had been the stepchild of the Third Reich and Dönitz's plea for support of a large submarine fleet had been largely ignored. But the Scapa Flow exploit was an eye-opener. Dönitz had scored a coup for his U-boats and Prien had become a national hero. Hitler was ecstatic, promoting Dönitz to rear admiral and commander-in-chief of U-boats, and decorating Prien[1] with the coveted award for heroism, the Ritterkreuz.

The Laconia Incident

One of the most controversial U-boat incidents of World War II occurred on September 12, 1942, when, in response to Dönitz's orders, a long-range U-boat sank the liner Laconia in the south Atlantic. The Laconia was a passenger ship of the "Cunard White Star Line" which had been converted to a British troopship. With 19,965 tons she was a large ship, carrying 2,732 passengers and crew, including 286 British military on vacation, 80 women and children, 1,800 Italian prisoners of war from the North African battle grounds, and 160 Poles who were guarding the Italian POWs. The Laconia was sunk by U-156 under command of Kapitänsleutnant Hartenstein in clear, calm weather. Although most of the passengers went down with the ship, more than 1,000 were able to escape into lifeboats

---

[1]Prien was killed in the Atlantic in March 1942, but not before sinking 28 ships and becoming one of the top German U-boat aces.

or jump into the shark-infested waters. Hartenstein signaled to Dönitz at his headquarters in Paris: "Sunk ... Laconia ... unfortunately with 1,500 Italian prisoners of war ... please instruct" (Davidson, 1966, p. 403). Dönitz sent one Italian and two German submarines to assist with the rescue work. He also allowed Hartenstein to send a message to Allied vessels that could help guaranteeing their safety. In this way, some 400 people were taken aboard the overcrowded submarines and lifeboats were taken in tow. However, shortly thereafter the rescue operation had to be broken off, when a U.S. Liberator bomber attacked, under the false assumption that the submarines were rescuing exclusively Italian and German prisoners of war.[2] In the end, 1,100 passengers of the Laconia were saved by three French ships; but more than 1,600 lives were lost. In Berlin, Hitler was furious about the rescue operation, because it had endangered the U-boats. This prompted Dönitz to issue the notorious "Laconia order" on September 17, 1942, to all of his submarine commanders:

> No attempt shall be made to rescue members of ships sunk, and this includes picking up persons in the water and putting them in lifeboats, righting capsized lifeboats, and handing over food and water. Rescue runs counter to the most elementary demands of warfare for the destruction of enemy ships and crews. Be harsh. Bear in mind that the enemy takes no regard of women and children in his bombing attacks on German cities. (Davidson, 1966, p. 406)

Submarines had rarely engaged in rescue work, starting with the first casualty of the Battle of the Atlantic,[3] that is, the sinking of the passenger ship Athenia[4] by U-30. At the beginning of the war, U-boats were still conforming to the Hague Convention, which prohibited attacks without warning enemy passenger ships (Salewski, 1970). Thus, the sinking of the Athenia was in direct violation of Hitler's orders and, in fact, the commander of the German submarine was severely reprimanded for his actions. But as time passed and there was no quick end to the war, the restrictions against submarine warfare were relaxed and all merchant ships as well as passenger ships were ordered to be turned back, taken captive, or sunk. With the Laconia order it now became official Kriegsmarine policy not to rescue survivors. It was this order, as well as the sinking of neutral ships, which later constituted the most serious charges against Dönitz at the International Military Tribunal in Nuremberg.

---

[2]The official explanation of the U.S. forces was that the submarines were attacked because they posed a danger to nearby Allied ships.

[3]A misnomer on two counts because rather than a single battle the campaign lasted from 1939 to 1945 and also extended into the Mediterranean and the Arctic.

[4]On September 3, 1939, ten hours after British Prime Minister Chamberlain announced the declaration of war, the Athenia became the first U-boat casualty of the Battle of the Atlantic. Of the 1,400 passengers aboard, many of whom were fleeing the war in Europe, 112 lost their lives, including 28 Americans. A similar incident during 1915, that is, the sinking of the passenger liner Lusitania had killed many Americans and precipitated the entrance of the United States into World War I (Simpson, 1972). Hitler feared that the United States may enter the war as a result of the sinking and therefore claimed that the British had sunk the ship for propaganda purposes.

The Battle of the Atlantic

In January 1943, Hitler became disillusioned with the success of the surface ships and abandoned Germany's shipbuilding program to concentrate on U-boats. As a direct result, Admiral Raeder, who insisted that battleships were not obsolete was forced to retire and Dönitz was promoted to full admiral and commander-in-chief of the German navy (Pope, 1958). He moved to Berlin and issued energetic orders to stop the repair and building of big ships, and to redeploy the crews to the submarine arm that by then had risen to a force of 212 submarines (Bekker, 1974). In March 1943 the Battle of the Atlantic reached its climax when the Allies lost 21 ships against only one U-boat casualty. However, by April more advanced electronic devices for the detection of U-boats (e.g., sonar and radar) were introduced by the Allied forces and were augmented by the success of the ULTRA code breakers, who intercepted reports of submarine positions. In fact, when many of his underwater craft were being ambushed and destroyed before they could even approach the Allied convoys, Dönitz first suspected treason. Between February and May 1943, Dönitz lost 85 submarines (40% of his fleet) and he was forced to withdraw the U-boats from the North Atlantic. His hope of destroying the Allies' Atlantic shipping was shattered. The U-boats did return in September, but in the last 4 months of the year they sank only 67 Allied vessels against a loss of an additional 64 submarines, a ratio that settled the Battle of the Atlantic. This was an important change of fortunes for the Allied forces, because it was during these 12 months of that crucial year that vast stocks of weapons and supplies were ferried across the Atlantic.

Another incident involving Dönitz that the International Military Tribunal had to consider was related to the sinking of the Greek steamer Peleus by U-852 in the Mediterranean on the night of March 13, 1944. The unarmed Peleus (8,833 tons) was struck by two torpedoes and went down in 3 minutes. Of the 35 crew members, 12 managed to get into life rafts only to be attacked with machine guns and hand grenades by *Kapitänsleutnant* Eck's crew. Only 3 of the men survived the massacre, all of whom were wounded by machine gun bullets, and were picked up after 37 days at sea. The Eck case was extremely damaging to Dönitz because Eck claimed that he had acted in accordance with superior orders from the commander-in-chief himself, evidence that Dönitz vigorously contested. Eck's charge was, however, corroborated by other officers who swore that in September 1942 Dönitz had instructed officers in training that not only should they make rescue impossible, but that they should sink rescue ships. Hitler argued that ships were more easily replaceable than the highly qualified personnel required to handle them. Furthermore, he thought it would give Germany a psychological advantage if the crews of ships entering the Atlantic knew beforehand that they would not be rescued if attacked. In this sense, the hate-ridden rhetoric that Dönitz had helped create by 1944 may have contributed to Eck snapping and losing control (C. S. Thomas, 1990). The Eck case, nevertheless, was ambiguous. In the end the actions of U-852 were believed to be caused by Eck himself, who by most accounts was an inexperienced and frightened naval officer. Eck and his officers were sentenced to death by a British court-martial and shot on November 30, 1945.

The U-123, one of Dönitz's U-boats on patrol in the North Atlantic, prepares to engage a merchant vessal with its 37mm flak gun. Bundesarchiv Koblenz.

Dönitz—Chief of State

During the war years, the loyal Dönitz retained the Führer's confidence and in April 1945 Hitler nominated him as the next in succession, much to the surprise of many party leaders all of whom were bypassed. On May 1, 1945, one day after Hitler's suicide, Dönitz assumed the position of chief of state and announced on the Hamburg radio that Hitler had died, as a hero in the capital of the Reich, fighting to the last against Bolshevism and for Germany. Dönitz appointed a nonparty government cabinet of his own choice (including Keitel, Jodl, and Speer), not the one willed on him by Hitler. Then on May 6, 1945, in a move that was calculated to win favor with the Allies, Dönitz sent out letters of dismissal to Himmler and Rosenberg, and ordered Goebbels (of whose death he had not yet heard) and Bormann arrested. Dönitz, who sent an offer of surrender to the British Field

Speer, Dönitz, and Jodl (left to right) are arrested by Allied troops on May 23, 1945, in Flensburg, Germany. Ullstein Bilderdienst.

Marshal Montgomery, knew that it would be difficult to negotiate with the Allies if high-ranking party members were part of his new government. On May 7, Dönitz moved his headquarters to Flensburg near the Danish frontier. For 2 weeks the skeleton of Dönitz's government remained until the Allies instructed him to surrender (Steinert, 1967).

At Nuremberg

It is perhaps a measure of his naiveté that Dönitz was surprised to be included among the major Nazi war criminals to be put on trial at Nuremberg.[5] When confronted with the indictments, he tried to laugh the whole thing off: "None of

---

[5]Dönitz was indicted on Count 1: conspiracy, Count 2: crimes against peace, and Count 3: war crimes, but not on Count 4: crimes against humanity.

these charges concerns me in the least, typical American humor" (Gilbert, 1947, p. 7). At the start of the trial, Dönitz had been fully convinced that the court would never convict him. For some time he had even cherished a faint hope that he might be acquitted so that he could play some part in Germany's revival (Neave, 1978). At Nuremberg, Dönitz was an effective witness in his own case. Moreover, Dönitz was defended by Dr. Flottenrichter Otto Kranzbuehler, a brilliant naval lawyer. From the beginning Kranzbuehler was received at Nuremberg with a courtesy that was extended to none of the other defense lawyers. He demanded and was allowed to appear in court in uniform unlike his client and former commander-in-chief. Allied naval officers on the prosecution staffs treated him as an equal (Neave, 1978).

On May 8, 1946, Dönitz took the stand in his own defense. He declared that as an officer he was not concerned with deciding whether a war was aggressive or not, but rather his concern was to obey orders (Davidson, 1966). The orders for U-boat warfare came from Admiral Raeder. Dönitz further explained that the arming of merchant vessels forced him to issue attack-without-warning orders. Dönitz described Germany as being surrounded by enemies; any attempted revolution in wartime posed a threat to the state and anybody who planned it was, by definition, a traitor. He repeatedly sought to justify his orders to sink ships without notice and to not rescue the survivors as conditions of "military expediency." Dönitz considered the sinking of ships in war zones perfectly proper because they had been warned to keep out. Even Roosevelt, Dönitz argued, recognized that merchant ships that sailed into war zones for the sake of making profit had no right to risk the lives of their crews. For that reason, he forbade ships from going into war zones. He was accused of requisitioning 12,000 concentration camp workers for naval production, a charge he denied. The responsibility for starting the war was a political one, not a military one, he argued. Dönitz added that he was not interested in whether naval arms production was done by foreign slave labor or not, but was only interested in the production itself. Dönitz did not present a likable figure in court, but rather appeared as a fierce U-boat commander fanatically defending himself and his U-boat force.

Dönitz's testimony brought on a discussion among the defendants themselves. Göring for one was pleased with Dönitz, "Ah, now I feel great for the first time in 3 weeks! Now we finally hear a decent German soldier speak for once. That gives me new strength; now I am ready to listen to some more treason again [referring to Schacht and Speer's testimony]" (Gilbert, 1947, p. 327). In contrast, Speer was upset with Dönitz: "Those military men have it much easier. All they have to say is, 'we can only obey orders,' and they don't have to answer any questions about conscience or morality or the welfare of the people" (Gilbert, 1947, p. 329).

Among the 19 defendants standing trial before the International Military Tribunal, it was the Dönitz verdict on which the judges deliberated the longest and were most divided (Smith, 1976; Taylor, 1992). The judges concluded that although Dönitz built and trained the German U-boat arm, the evidence did not show that he was privy to the conspiracy to wage an aggressive war or that he prepared and initiated such a war (i.e., Count 1). The Tribunal further judged that it was not established with certainty that Dönitz deliberately ordered the killing of ship-wrecked survivors. For the Laconia order, he was merely censured. Surprisingly, Dönitz was not held responsible for violating the international laws of U-boat warfare. This was largely based on the fact that the United States and Britain had engaged in similar conduct. But he was found guilty of the overall charges of planning a war of aggression, specifically for setting up war zones (*Sicherheitszonen* or *Speergebiete*) and sinking unarmed neutral ships, as well as the implication of his using forced labor. He was sentenced to 10 years imprison-ment. Dönitz didn't know quite how to respond to the verdict: "Ten years! Well anyway, I cleared U-boat warfare" (Gilbert, 1947, p. 432). After the verdict and in an unusual gesture of sympathy, more than 100 letters from U.S. and British naval officers were received deploring the verdict and suggesting that Dönitz had fought an honorable war.

Although the Dönitz verdict was questioned by many in later years, the Soviets made it clear that they would not release him until he had served his sentence to the very last day. At Spandau prison, Dönitz felt that his appointment as Hitler's successor was a dubious compliment, because he believed that it, not his actions as navy commander, brought him to stand trial at Nuremberg. He complained that it was Speer who suggested to Hitler that he should be the next president, thereby ruining his career (Speer, 1977). In the end, the personality and skill of Kranzbuehler, particularly the permission to interrogate Nimitz on submarine warfare, had more to do with the outcome of the case against Dönitz than the actual evidence against the admiral. A deposition by Admiral Nimitz, who was then commander-in-chief of the U.S. Pacific Fleet, was included in the Nuremberg trial. It stated that it was general and approved practice not to attempt rescue of survivors of submarine attacks (Thompson & Strutz, 1976). Because U.S. submarine prac-tices had paralleled the German's, German naval warfare had been "legal." It was Nimitz's statement that few attempts were made by Allied submarines to rescue German survivors that disproved the more serious charges against Dönitz and that ultimately saved him from execution. He was released in 1956 at the end of the 10-year term.

ANALYSIS

The longest naval battle in history lasted from September 3, 1939, to May 7, 1945 (Hoyt, 1988). A total of 2,882 merchant ships and 149 Allied warships were sunk, including 6 aircraft carriers, 2 battleships, and 34 destroyers. In all, 200,000 men on the Allied side died on the seas or went down in their ships. More than 14 million tons were sent to the bottom of the ocean by German U-boats, approximately 70% of the total losses of the Battle of the Atlantic. Of the 1,170 U-boats that were commissioned during World War II, 863 saw action and 630 never returned. The life expectancy of a German submarine and its crew was less than three missions. Of the 41,000 men who served on U-boats, 25,870 "died gallantly" and 5,100 were taken prisoners (Salewski, 1970). To the majority of the Allies, Dönitz personified the most gruesome form of warfare, the silent and unforgiving slaughter of human life on the high seas.

What kind of person was Dönitz? Did he have a conscience that registered the enormous tolls of war, or was he a career officer engaged in a form of military chess using U-boats as his pawns and the Atlantic as the chessboard? Was he the heroic naval commander that even his enemies admired, or was he a cold-blooded killer who fanatically defended the Nazi doctrine? Historical assessments of Dönitz range from sharply damning to adulatory. For example, his critics point to his role as Hitler's chosen successor or his widely publicized statements of complete loyalty to the Führer and the National Socialistic cause (Bird, 1985). His admirers praise Dönitz's courageous U-boat war and his role in rescuing millions of refugees in the final stages of the war (Thompson & Strutz, 1976).

The Rorschach record may shed some further light on Dönitz's personality and overall level of adjustment. There is very little that we know about this administration of the Inkblot test other than it has never before been published or interpreted.[6] Dönitz himself never mentioned it in his *Memoirs* and Kelley did not address the Rorschach record directly in his comments on Dönitz in *Twenty-Two Cells*. Dönitz's verbatim Rorschach record and interpretative hypothesis can be examined here. For the interested Rorschacher, the scoring of the responses using the Exner Comprehensive System is offered after each response.

Rorschach Record
Subject: Karl Dönitz (1891–1981)
Age: 54
Full-Scale IQ: 138 (Very Superior Range; 99th percentile)
Date of testing: November – December 1945 (specific date unknown)
Examiner: Douglas Kelley, MD

| I. | 1. A beetle. | The entire card seen as living beetle, brisk and very active. |
| | | Wo FMau A 1.0[7] |

| | 2. A bat. | Whole card - alive.   Wo Fo A P 1.0 |

---

[6]Kelley did not give the test with the help of his interpreter Dolibois, although he may have administered it with the assistance of Gilbert. Because Dönitz knew English quite well and improved considerably while at Mondorf and Nuremberg, Kelley could have also administered the test himself without an interpreter (Dolibois, personal communication, July 31, 1994).

[7]The scoring for each Rorschach response is offered for the professional psychologist and Rorschach student. Those not familiar with the Comprehensive System or the scoring of Rorschach responses should understand that a precise interpretation of the Rorschach is only possible with adequate scoring, and for that purpose it is included here (see chap. 5).

3. V^8 A wedding cake.

Whole response. Sort of cake that one puts on the center of the table for a wedding or festival.

Wo F- Fd, Art 1.0 AB

4. A bee.

Wo Fu A 1.0

5. A design for a house.

It looks like a picture of a castle or a house. He would like to build a home like that. It is actually seen as a dimensional drawing with very definite evidence of use of shading for depth.

Wo FVu Art 1.0

6. V A Japanese Pagoda.

This is the same response, only now it is a Japanese pagoda instead of a house.

Wo Fu Sc, Ay 1.0 [9]

7. A coat of arms.

Whole card seen as a family coat of arms.

Wo Fo Art 1.0

II. 1. Two boys at a masquerade, dancing.

He describes this card excellently, mentioning the red hats. States that they are dancing and making steps together. He uses the color only insofar as it appears as part of the masquerade costume.

W+ Ma.FCo (2) H, Cg 4.5 COP

2. South American butterfly.

This is the whole card; the shape and color are both used but the bright colors are what made him think of the South American aspect. The brilliant red and black color is more important than the form. No movement is used here.

Wo CF.C'Fu A 4.5

---

[8]The inverse "carrot" signals to the examiner that the inkblot plate was rotated by the examinee in the direction of the carrot.

[9]Responses 6 and 7 to Card I were not included in the analysis because of the response limit rule of the Comprehensive System.

III. 1. Two gentlemen in formal dress grappling for a bow.

The men are tugging and quarreling about the bow. He describes the men very well and states that you can notice the ends of their coats which are flying about in their struggle, and that their trousers are dropping down because they have no suspenders like the prisoners. He also adds that the center red is their handkerchief and in the struggle their breast pockets, where these handkerchiefs were, have been torn and you can see the ragged edges.

(In testing this card, and asking about the lateral red, he states that when the quarrel started the ladies who were with the gentlemen, left and that the red are their scarves which they left behind. Ladies are always forgetful.)

D+ 1 Ma•ma+ (2) H, Cg, Sc P 4.0 AG, MOR

IV. 1. V Crawfish.

This is the whole card seen as a deep-sea crawfish. He describes the feelers and sees it very clearly. States that it is armored as indicated by the shading. He states that deep-sea crawfish can swim and creep. This one is alive.

Wo FY- A 2.0

2. The skin of a bear.

This is seen as a whole skin, furry as it would be lying before a desk.

Wo FTo Ad 2.0

V. 1. A bat.

This is seen as a real bat with long ears. He feels it is very good and states the ears are important for its flight. It is alive and flying. After looking at the card a little, he states it is such a good bat that is all he can see.

Wo FMao A P 1.0

VI. 1. Skin of an animal, such as you would see on the floor in a lady's room.

He states it is obviously an animal fur but that this was too simple and the lady who owned it altered it by adding feathers. "Only a lady would do this."

W+ FTo Ad P 2.5 DR

VII. 1. This is very nice. Faces of two little girls looking at one another. They have the expression of being curious to learn the secrets of life. They may be dancing together too.

Usual detail—whole card split into two details is used.

W+ Mau (2) H 2.5 COP

2. V A fur muff with appendages; a good lock or a zipper.

This is the entire card with the center detail as a muff; the lateral details as the fur appendages and the center dark line as the zipper.

Wo FTu Cg 2.5 INC

VIII.1. A butterfly camouflaged like a leaf.

The whole card is used with the colors predominant. He feels that it is a butterfly because of general structure.

Wo CF- A 4.5

2. Two chameleons waiting for a choice prey.

These are the two lateral animals seen alive and points for action. He adds their tongues are curled in their mouths and they are ready to push them out.

Do 1 FMpu (2) A

3. V The entrails of a man. Blood. You can see the lungs, backbone, abdomen, bladder and stomach.

This is the whole card and represents a cut-up body; predominantly seen because of the shape and arrangement of parts in their anatomical location. The color itself did not suggest the idea but is used as the blood.

Wo FC- An, Bl 4.5 MOR

IX. 1. A lobster pie with decorations. When you have lobster pie, you make decorations with the lobster and lettuce and tomatoes.

He feels this is an excellent arrangement and the fine color and good appearance of the green lettuce, pink tomatoes and lobster stimulates his appetite. He adds he has a great appetite for lobster anyway.

W+ FCu Fd, Art 5.5

2. V Two animals carrying a load on their shoulders.

Two orange details are seen as animals bearing a load or some sort of construction on their back. Color here is not used.

W+ FMa- (2) A, Fd 5.5 COP

3. A head decoration. Fantastic.

This is the kind of decoration that a vain woman would put on her head.

Wo Fo Cg, Art 5.5

(An umbrella. While giving the inquiry to the previous response, he noticed the center pink detail - V - and stated that it was an umbrella like one that would be over an Indian Maharaja.)

X. 1. Two animals. Crawfish with one sheared.

These are the lateral blue and green details, the green detail being the single claw. They are seen alive.

Ddo 1, 12 Fu (2) A MOR

2. Two mice.

Lateral gray detail; alive.

Do 8 Fu (2) A

3. Flying birds.

Lateral gray detail; alive.

Do FMau (2) A

4. V A cross-section of an experimental bomb - of a mortar type.

This is the whole area seen with the large D section as the motor and the smaller section as a cork or plug which fits into the larger section to block it.

W+ F- Sc 5.5

End of record

INTERPRETATION

The Dönitz Rorschach protocol features 26 responses and, although not in compliance with modern standards of Rorschach administration, appears valid in terms of being able to offer meaningful, interpretative statements.[10] Here, actuarial and objective interpretative hypotheses of the Dönitz record are discussed. The interpretative statements are based on the formal features of the Rorschach protocol, specifically on aspects of the Rorschach structural summary. To this end, computer-generated hypotheses (Exner, Cohen, & McGuire, 1991) are presented that are intended as a guide, from which the interpreter can proceed to study and refine an interpretative strategy. These statements are provided to generate one source of hypotheses concerning the psychological features of Dönitz and are based on actuarial data from empirical studies on over 40,000 responses to the Rorschach test (Exner, 1993). The Dönitz Rorschach record is discussed in terms of different areas of psychological functioning, including the respondent's overall perceptual monitoring and cognitive organizational style, emotional processes, reality testing, stress tolerance, self-esteem, and interpersonal perceptions, and compared to records of adult nonpsychiatric respondents. In each case the most salient and important characteristics of the record are presented first.

Dönitz: Stress Tolerance and Impulse Control.   Dönitz's degree of stress tolerance at the time of the testing was considerably less than that of the majority of nonpsychiatric adult respondents. He was likely, therefore, to display some proclivity for impulsiveness that may predispose a vulnerability to problems with control and a susceptibility to disorganization under stress. This is somewhat surprising because Dönitz had considerable resources available (e.g., intellectual as well as emotional) and is most likely related to the fact that he was under considerable stress while awaiting trial at the Nuremberg jail. Computer-generated statements included:

> The subject has less capacity to deal with stress than might be expected. Some decisions will not be thought through or implemented. People such as this usually function most effectively in familiar environments in which demands and expectations are predictable.

> The limited capacity for control is an unusual finding for this subject because considerable resources are available.

There also was some evidence of situational stress, undoubtedly related to the turmoil in which Dönitz found himself at Nuremberg. His beloved *Vaterland* was

---

[10]At Nuremberg, Dönitz confided to Kelley that he feigned insanity to aid his effort in escaping, "Two companions and I decided it might aid our efforts to escape if we were adjudged insane. We walked about, our heads hunched down, going 'Bzzzz, Bzzzz,' and insisting we were U-boats. The British doctors were too smart for us. We didn't get anywhere. Solitary confinement cured our 'mental state' in no time" (Kelley, 1947, p. 127).

in ruins and occupied by enemy forces, his Führer dead, and he himself faced
serious legal charges.

> The subject is experiencing a significant increase in stimulus demands as a result of
> situationally related stress. As a consequence, some decisions and/or behaviors may
> not be as well organized as is usually the case, and the subject is more vulnerable to
> disorganization as the result of added stresses.

> Some of the stress may relate to some recent emotional loss.

Evidence from the Rorschach suggests that Dönitz was in a chronic overload
state related to the experiences of a prolonged and costly war. During his trial,
however, he was very composed and participated in an organized way on behalf of
his defense. In fact, his defense was so effective that many observers felt that Dönitz
and his lawyer Kranzbühler presented their case better than any of the other
defendants.

Dönitz: Emotional Processes.   Dönitz may be described as ambitensive in
terms of his preferred coping style. This indicates that he has not developed a clear
preference for coping with the environment and tends to vacillate between thinking
through behaviors and trial-and-error behaviors in responding. This ambivalence
in coping style was quite common among the Nazi elite as well as the rank-and-file
(see chap. 6 and 7) and is likely to result in decreased efficiency as well as less
predictability when compared to those who have well-defined styles. It is possible
that Dönitz overcame his vacillation in stressful situations by following and giving
orders "by the book," or by rigidly adhering to Führer and Fatherland. Computerized statements for Dönitz's protocol include the following comments:

> It is likely that the emotions of the subject are inconsistent in terms of their impact on
> thinking, problem solving and decision making behaviors. In other words, in one
> instance thinking may be strongly influenced by feelings, whereas in a second
> instance, even though similar to the first, emotions may play only a peripheral role.

> The subject is prone to deal with feelings on an intellectual level more often than most
> people. Although this process serves to reduce or neutralize the impact of emotions,
> is also represents a naive form of denial that tends to distort the true impact of a
> situation.

From the Rorschach protocol it also appears that Dönitz was monitoring his
environment with an emphasis on detecting threatening or hostile situations. In fact,
Dönitz had repeatedly stated that he felt that Germany was "surrounded by
enemies." There is further evidence that he was, at the time of test administration,
engaging in an introspective process in an attempt to gain self-perspective. This
introspective process was obviously related to the events surrounding his trial at
Nuremberg and was accompanied by affective distress and discomfort.

The subject engages in more self inspecting behaviors that focus on negative features than is common. Excessive introspection such as this often promotes discomfort and frequently becomes a precursor to depression.

Although there is some evidence of distress and perhaps even depression in the Rorschach record, this appears more related to situational stressors than long-term functioning. At Nuremberg, Dönitz was forced to make a transition from German naval leader to war criminal. In addition to having just lost a war he also lost his only two sons.

Dönitz: Self-Esteem and Interpersonal Perception.   At the time of the test administration, Dönitz displayed low self-esteem accompanied by feelings of inadequacy, a negative and damaged self-image, and pessimistic attitudes and thoughts.

This is the type of person who regards him/herself less favorably when compared to others. The self concept or self image includes some very negative, unwanted features that tend to promote a pessimistic view of the self and influence many decisions.

Again, this is thought to be more situational than characterlogical and again related to Dönitz reflecting on his situation at Nuremberg.

This subject engages in more introspection than is customary. This unusual frequency of self inspecting may relate to the negative self-value held by the subject. Some of the self inspecting focuses excessively on perceived negative features of the self image, and as a result, painful feelings that are difficult to contend with often occur. Such a process is expected during the middle period of uncovering psychotherapy but not under other circumstances.

Regarding Dönitz's interpersonal perception and relations, his Rorschach suggests that he displayed relatively little interest in close, emotional relationships with other people. Instead, the Rorschach record reflects that he may have been interested in interpersonal activity. Certainly, Dönitz was almost fanatic about building a fraternity (*Kameradschaft*) among his sailors and was completely loyal to Hitler. This was not a manifestation of interest in other individuals, but rather it gave him a more primitive sense of belonging and structure.

It is likely that this subject tends to be regarded by others as likable and outgoing. Subjects such as this often view interpersonal activity as a very important part of their daily routine and are usually identified by those around them as among the more gregarious in group interactions.

Interpersonally, Dönitz appears needy with strong and unmet needs for emotional sharing and accessibility which may also manifest itself in dependency.

This is the type of person who has stronger needs to be dependent on others than is usually the case. People such as this tend to rely on others for support and often are more "naive" in their expectations about interpersonal relationships.

The subject is experiencing a sense of loneliness or emotional deprivation. This will be quite influential in interpersonal relationships. People such as this are often quite vulnerable to the manipulations of others.

Dönitz: Information Processing.   In examining Dönitz's perceptual monitoring and cognitive organizational style it is quite clear from the Rorschach data that he tends to perceive his environment in an unsophisticated and underincorporative manner. Although capable of obvious and common responses to the Rorschach tests, he makes little effort to organize or integrate the world around him; although he does typically attempt to monitor the entire stimulus field and responds to events in a holistic manner (i.e., with whole blot responses). Much relevant information, however, is not being considered. Such a style of evaluating one's environment is not typical in normal individuals and can be referred to as naive, uncomplicated, or lazy, and may result in maladaptive or inappropriate responses. Computer-generated hypotheses on Dönitz's record include the following statement:

> This is the type of subject who is prone to scan a stimulus field hastily and haphazardly and as a result, may neglect critical bits or cues. This type of less effective scanning is common among children but not for adolescents or adults. It creates a potential for faulty mediation and can contribute to less effective patterns of behavior. This should not be confused with impulsiveness although some decisions and behaviors that result may have that feature.

This finding may come as a surprise, given that Dönitz was one of the highest ranking officers in the Third Reich and was considered to be an efficient military leader. But if one examines his military record closely, he displayed shortcomings as a leader including the neglect of important relevant information. Also, his rigid personality style may have senselessly prolonged the naval struggle. In point of fact, Dönitz's record as a military leader was pathetic. No other unit of the Armed forces, besides the Japanese Kamikaze pilots approached such high rates of attrition as Dönitz's forces. Dönitz's U-boat war was as cruel as any aspect of a war had ever been and his losses heavy. Additionally, many of his subordinates and colleagues felt that Dönitz consistently pursued naval heroics even in the face of impossible odds (C. S. Thomas, 1990). An interesting account of "being out of touch" was given by Speer (1970), who described the charade at Flensburg during the end of the war where Dönitz once more became the professional naval officer, behaving with courtesy and formality, even though the war had been lost. When communication with Field Marshall Montgomery had been established and the capitulation signed, Speer proposed that the Dönitz "Government" should proclaim that it no longer existed. Dönitz, however, considered himself chief-of-state and legitimate successor to Hitler. Even after the unconditional surrender to Montgomery he continued on, making various appointments when there was nothing for the ministers to do but drink whiskey (Speer, 1970). Speer described with disbelief how one of Hitler's large armored Mercedes cars had been brought to Flensburg to drive Dönitz a mere 500 yards to work each day at the new seat of the German Government to preside over "Cabinet" meetings (C. S. Thomas, 1990). The pretense of a working government was particularly strange given that there was general chaos in Germany. Millions of Germans were fleeing from the Soviet forces to the West and in the cities the bombing had practically suffocated life. Within a few days, however, Dönitz was arrested and the final collapse of the Third Reich was complete.

Was it possible that Dönitz may have been in over his head in leading an ever complex naval battle? Was he so far removed from political realities that he thought after the surrender that the Allies might let him continue as head of state? The results from the Rorschach test do suggest that he displayed a propensity for inadequately integrating all features of his environment. Thus, his information-processing style may be described as inefficient, at times irrelevant to sensitive details, and lacking the necessary integration. Particularly when situations became increasingly complex and ambiguous, Dönitz was prone to make errors and rely on a rigid and inflexible problem-solving style. This is further emphasized by the following computer generated statement.

> The ideational sets and values of the subject are well fixed and relatively inflexible. People such as this find it very difficult to alter attitudes or opinions, or to view issues from a perspective different than that which they hold.

Dönitz: Reality Testing.   Dönitz's ability to conform to the realistic features of his environment was less than adequate, even when his environment was structured and the responses to his surroundings were obvious. Thus, the potential for producing responses that were poorly adapted to the realistic features of his environment was considerable. In those situations his behaviors were likely to overlook important reality based concerns and may be perceived by others as unusual, deviant, or eccentric. In this sense Dönitz would "bend" reality to suit his own needs more than a typical normal adult would.

> The likelihood of less conventional responses occurring, even in situations that are simple and/or precisely defined, is significant.

> The subject may display a higher than usual frequency of behaviors that disregard social demands or expectations. This lack of conventionality may be due to the subject's tendency to over-personalize in translating stimuli.

In general, however, there was no evidence of a psychotic adjustment or of a formal thought disorder. Dönitz's thought processes, as manifested in his verbal responses to the Rorschach, did not indicate evidence of cognitive slippage, loose associations, or other forms of autistic logic most often seen in individuals with severe psychopathology such as schizophrenia.

Additional Interpretation.   In examining the sequence of scoring and his verbatim responses for purposes of content analyses, several themes emerge that can be integrated into the previous hypotheses presented about Dönitz's personality. These include his preoccupation with authority and ceremonial processes in his surrounding, by referring in his Rorschach responses to "wedding," "festival," "castle," "coat of arms," "formal dress," and his repeated use of the word "decorations." Also perhaps not surprising, given his life as a career military man, were his sexist references toward women in the protocol, including, "ladies are always forgetful," "only a lady would do this," and "a vain woman." References to war and aggression are obviously expected (e.g., "experimental bomb") as are those responses that were related to naval warfare, specifically with an emphasis on detection and surveillance. Such verbatim examples included "deep sea crawfish," "feelers," "swim and creep," "long ears," "a butterfly camouflaged like a leaf," and perhaps the most telling response of his record "two chameleons waiting for a choice prey." From the content of these responses it is tempting to speculate that Dönitz was somewhat preoccupied with "blending in" with his prevailing environment, in this case the Third Reich and submarine warfare. In general, however, the content of his responses were benign from a psychopathological point of view, and an in-depth content analysis is not attempted here.

SUMMARY

The current Rorschach record revealed some pervasive and interesting personality styles of Dönitz. These are not pathological per se, in the sense that they require psychiatric treatment, but they may result in actions that others would describe on a scale from unusual to maladaptive and are of special interest because of Dönitz's position in the Third Reich. For example, individuals such as Dönitz function most effectively in familiar environments in which demands and expectations are predictable. In this sense his personality is not unusual for a military man. He certainly was not a banal and insipid character. Furthermore, evidence from the Rorschach indicates that Dönitz was rigid in approaching his environment and resistant to rapid changes in attitudes or values. There is evidence that the slaughter of humans on both sides and the loss of his two sons during the war did not change Dönitz's postwar attitudes at all.[11] In 1947, during their imprisonment at Spandau prison,[12] Speer reported the extent to which Dönitz valued military obedience regardless of the cost of life: "After all, this man [Hitler] was the legal head of state in the Reich. His orders were necessarily binding upon me. How else could a government be run?" (Speer, 1977, p. 88). By then, Dönitz may have been the only

---

[11]Dönitz's son, Klaus, was killed in May 1944 on board a torpedo boat in the English channel, and his son Peter perished on a U-boat in May 1943 in the Atlantic (Dönitz, 1968).

[12]Spandau prison, located in former West Berlin served as the exclusive retention site of the seven Nazi prisoners who were given prison sentences by the International Tribunal. Spandau is a historical curiosity because it was built for 600 inmates, but was only used for the seven Nuremberg defendants who received term sentences. The four Allied forces of World War II continued to cooperate during the Cold War watching over the prisoners confinement, each for a month: France in January, Great Britain in February, the Union of Soviet Socialist Republics in March, and the United States in April, with the cycle being repeated thereafter. Early release of the prisoners was only possible if the Allied nations agreed unanimously, which never happened.

person who still believed that Hitler's political testament was "…legally valid and binding" (Weinberg, 1981, p. 41).

The admiral's ability to deny reality came to the forefront when the Allies insisted that the swastika banner be lowered from those garrisons remaining under German control. Dönitz insisted that this be undertaken with all the ceremonies of a bygone era. Similarly when the gruesome details of the concentration camps were brought forward by the Allied media, he assured his men of the navy that this had nothing to do with them (C. S. Thomas, 1990).

Of further interest from the Rorschach data is evidence that suggests that Dönitz was a naive individual who was dependent on others and subject to manipulation by others. For example, by moving the entire German fleet to Western waters before the armistice and declaring that Germany belonged to the Christian West, Dönitz naively hoped that he not only could save himself, but also that he would play a major role in the rebuilding of postwar Germany. Instead, and to his surprise, he was accused of war crimes.

From the vast historical material on Dönitz, it is clear that he was a loyal officer who subordinated himself to Hitler and was faithful to the end. Dönitz felt that Hitler was the only statesman of stature in Europe, often comparing him with Napoleon. He felt that Hitler had extraordinary intelligence and energy and a practically universal knowledge. Part of this unshakable admiration for Hitler is probably attributable to the fact that through Hitler the German navy, Dönitz's true love, was rebuilt, and Germany again became a world power.

The vision of Dönitz as a gentlemanly and heroic naval officer, which his apologists shared with some of the Allied commanders, is decidedly ingenuous. There is no question that he was an intelligent, skillful, and sometimes chivalrous officer who was committed to discipline and order, a man who felt most comfortable in the structured hierarchy of the German navy where he ruled with strict discipline (*mit strengen Regeln*; Boeddeker, 1981). Ideologically, Dönitz was anti-Marxist and anti-Semitic. At Nuremberg he was accused of commending another German officer for the killing of communists in prison camp (Conot, 1983). On other occasions, he spoke of Jews in "tones used by Gauleiters" (Davidson, 1966, p. 393) and told his sailors of the heaven-sent leadership of the Führer whose policies he never questioned. When forced to watch films on the atrocities of the Third Reich at Nuremberg he responded that he could not be accused of knowing of such things. From historical evidence it is also clear that Dönitz was an avid National Socialist and firmly believed in the ideological education of German sailors, suggesting that that the naval officer is the exponent of the state.

Especially revealing is the strong evidence from the Rorschach personality data that suggests that Dönitz was an under-incorporater who may have missed much relevant information when confronted with important decisions. Thus, Dönitz's potential for poor judgments in thinking and behavior may have been considerable and related both to his ambitions in setting unrealistically high goals and to his

---

[13]In fact, Dönitz considered himself as Germany's legal chief of state for years after the war.

inadequate integration of information, particularly in ambiguous situations. Of course, Dönitz had many assistants and much of the plan of operations may have been dictated by political forces outside his control or in response to movement of Allied forces. Nevertheless, at least regarding naval matters of submarine warfare Dönitz "...always made the final decision ..." (Manson, 1990, p. 163). Thus, at the very least, he may have shown poor judgment, as he did with the Laconia order, and at times may have demonstrated gross errors in military decisions. In light of the current Rorschach findings, Dönitz's leadership style and decision making processes are examined in more detail as they relate to the controversial sinking of the *Scharnhorst,* which was sent out by Dönitz "...in what objective observers must call a useless suicide mission for the ship and the 1900 men who went down with her" (Weinberg, 1994, p. 369).

By the time Dönitz became commander-in-chief of the German navy in early 1943, the war at sea had already turned decisively against Germany. Dönitz had been a clever head of the U-boat arm, but he was only an indifferently successful head of the German navy. He may have had better rapport with Hitler than his predecessor Raeder, but he "lacked any long-term strategic vision for the Navy" (Winton, 1983, p. 71). In December 1943 the deteriorating situation on the eastern front, where the German forces were being pushed relentlessly back, encouraged a plan for a naval offensive to attack a convoy from England headed for Russia via the northern route. However, several factors, some of which were related to Dönitz's rigid refusal to incorporate new information and his ambition to execute the operation, set the stage for a naval disaster. The situation was a complex and ambiguous one with the naval leadership divided in its wisdom.

Early developments appeared favorable for success. Dönitz assumed the convoy to be protected by a cruiser escort, no match for a battleship. German reconnaissance, although hampered by long Arctic nights, had not discovered the presence of any heavy enemy formation. Even if such a force was at sea, Dönitz thought that it must have been a long way from the convoy. Thus, Dönitz thought that the *Scharnhorst* seemed to have every chance of delivering a rapid and successful attack.

There was a great deal of reconnaissance information about convoy JW55B regarding its course and speed. The only uncertainty was whether or not there was a British heavy covering force in support of the convoy. The possibility of such a force being at sea had been realized for some days before the *Scharnhorst* sailed. In fact, the "further a staff officer was from the *Scharnhorst,* the more in favor he was of her putting to sea and the more sanguine his view of her chances" (Winton, 1983, pp. 73–74). Dönitz's "wait and see" compromise did not help in this matter. In fact, he rigidly held on to the goals of the operation and demanded much more definitive proof that a British heavy covering force was at sea. In Dönitz's view all evidence was negative; such a force was not at sea. This was in direct opposition to the reports from several sources, both U-boat reconnaissance and staff officers, suggesting that a cover force was closing, that the operation was risky, and that security from the enemy could not be guaranteed. Dönitz, however, felt that the convoy could be taken by surprise. With

Dönitz adamant that the operation proceed orders were given on Christmas Day for the Battle Group to put to sea (Busch, 1990, p. 94):

> Important enemy convoy carrying food and war material to the Russians further imperils our heroic army on the eastern front. We must help. Attack convoy with *Scharnhorst* and destroyers. Exploit tactical situation with skill and daring. Do not end the engagement with a partial success. Go all out and see the job right through. Best chance of success lies in superior firing-power of *Scharnhorst*, therefore try to bring her into action. Deploy destroyers accordingly. Break off according to you own judgment. Break off in any circumstances if faced by heavy units. Inform crews accordingly. I have every confidence in you.

Heil und Sieg, Dönitz

With the weather turning for the worst and no reconnaissance flights available, several high ranking admirals suggested that OSTFRONT should be canceled. The grand admiral, however, insisted that the operation was to go ahead. The final and clearest concerns came from the commander of the *Scharnhorst* himself who signaled that, because of the weather, the use of the destroyers was gravely impaired. In fact, the weather was even worse than expected and with the destroyers steaming at the limits of sea-worthiness and many of the crew of the *Scharnhorst* sea-sick, Dönitz still insisted that OSTFRONT go ahead with *Scharnhorst*—if necessary acting alone, like an armed raider. In the end, the sinking of the *Scharnhorst* by heavy Allied covering forces was among the most tragic in the history of the German navy, taking with her all but 36 of her crew of nearly 2,000 and effectively ending the German surface assaults on the Murmansk run (Bird, 1985). The sinking may have been facilitated by many factors, not the least some unfavorable decisions made by the ship's captain and the up-to-date intelligence ULTRA of the British.

Nevertheless, Dönitz refused to incorporate important reports about the changing weather including newly available reconnaissance information. He failed to understand the hesitation of the force commander and captain of the *Scharnhorst* Vice Admiral Erich Bey about the attack. He furthermore assumed that because it had been very quiet in the north, the British would surely not expect a sortie by the *Scharnhorst*. Ironically, it was precisely because the *Scharnhorst* had been so inactive that the British expected her now (Winton, 1983). Additionally, the pressures resulting from a losing effort at the eastern front, all made Dönitz order the *Scharnhorst* ineffectual. Thus it hardly seemed to matter to Dönitz that Arctic weather grounded the Luftwaffe and drove the *Scharnhorst's* escorts of five destroyers into port, that the location of the enemy covering forces was unknown, or that three admirals had recently advised against the action (C. S. Thomas, 1990).

Dönitz appeared to learn little from the larger events from his years at the head of Service. He remained the arch advocate of offensive action in the face of hopeless odds and of unyielding defense, no matter how exposed the position. From May 1943 to the end of war he remained convinced, even though there was nothing to support his rationale, to fight a defensive war; that is, to continue the struggle even if there was no hope of victory in order to tie down enemy forces. Salewski (1973) observed that such sacrifice of U-boats ultimately did not contribute anything to Germany's defensive war. If his actions often defied rational thought, this is only to suggest that "Dönitz was not thinking" (C. S. Thomas, 1990, p. 125). Padfield (1984) described Dönitz's style of engagement not as that of a rational commander, but that of a National Socialist who was convinced that willpower would overcome numerical inferiority. Salewski (1973) suggested that the losses of the German navy were so great that rather than leading men (*Menschenführung*) the navy leadership was in the business of seducing men (*Menschenverführung*).

Rather than considering troop withdrawal in strategic regions where Allied forces were superior or nonessential to defend more vital areas elsewhere, Dönitz rigidly responded that such consideration was out of the question or not subject to discussion and suggested that the most determined effort even in the face of unfavorable odds can lead to victory (C. S. Thomas, 1990). When the Allied forces in early 1942 prepared for their final assault in North Africa and the Germans still had time to evacuate and save their troops from defeat, Dönitz suggested that an evacuation by sea would only lower morale. A month later the Allies secured their largest haul of Axis prisoners in the war to date—275,000 German and Italian soldiers in 10 days! Only about 800 Axis soldiers managed to escape (Weinberg, 1994).

In another example, Dönitz insisted that the German army hold on to the Courland area of western Latvia to keep the Soviet navy out of the Baltic in order to ensure safe submarine training. Thus, Dönitz's "...immediate operational concern of the German navy in the last months of the war was not...the ongoing activity of submarines in the Atlantic or the hope of reviving effective submarine warfare with new submarines, but the danger threatening its major training area" (Weinberg, 1994, p. 781). The German divisions in Courland, easily evacuated by sea were left stranded fending off a series of Red Army attacks until their final surrender in May 1945. Weinberg (1994) suggested that the surrounded divisions in Courland in essence "...established their own prisoner-of-war camp even as the war was still under way" (p. 721). Certainly, Dönitz was a bright and capable man, but the current findings underscore the notion that he may not have been the leader that many thought he was. Showell (1989) agreed, he suggested that Dönitz was not the master architect of the U-boat arm, that especially non-German writers have made him out to be, "One can definitely say that he contributed virtually nothing to prewar submarine development" (p. 84).

Thus, the current psychological analysis interpreted within the context of the historical data suggests that Dönitz steadfastly held on to his theme to face virtually hopeless odds often sending technologically outmoded boats to fight alone against a host of enemy vessels, whether it was to the Service's escorts in the Mediterranean, the U-boat fleet on the high seas, the surface fleet, or the support units ashore. Bird (1985) further suggested that it is this aspect of Dönitz's involvement in the naval and U-boat war that raises serious questions regarding "...leadership and the German political, technological and military errors and shortcomings...[which]

has been largely neglected by historians" (p. 682). In this respect, a closer examination of Dönitz's handling of military and political affairs is in order.

Taken as a whole, the Rorschach protocol of Dönitz does not suggest evidence of obvious psychopathology. Dönitz was of sound mind. He did not suffer any identifiable mental illness that affected his capacity to know right from wrong or his ability to appreciate the consequences of his actions. The psychological protocol also revealed that Dönitz was experiencing significant stress and anxiety at the time of the administration. This was clearly situational in nature and undoubtedly related to the upcoming trial. The Rorschach record furthermore uncovered a number of personality styles or traits that were potentially maladaptive. In this sense the psychological profile explains Dönitz's problem-solving and operational style. It also provides clues regarding his loyalty to Hitler and his fellow sailors, as well as why he was attracted to the structure of the German navy or a National-Socialistic Germany. In conclusion, Dönitz's psychological protocol suggests that he was relatively well adjusted and that his Rorschach record may compare to those of many military officers of other nationalities.

JULIUS STREICHER (1885–1946): "THE BEAST OF NUREMBERG"

A dirty old man of the sort that gives trouble in parks.
—Rebecca West

The Third Reich's foremost anti-Semite was a short (only 5 feet 2 inches tall), stocky, and muscular man who kept his head shaven bald. His coarse features gave him an intimidating appearance and he became widely known for his corruption, greed, sexual extravagance, and sadism. During his reign as uncrowned ruler of Nuremberg he was seldom seen in public without a whip, and he was fond of boasting about the countless lashings he had meted out. Streicher typified many Nazi stereotypes: the half-crazed sadist, the agitator, and self-proclaimed pornographer. Anyone who dared to challenge the "King of Franconia" risked prison and torture. Yet, despite his unfortunate physique and despite the fact that his constant stream of obscenities did not meet with everyone's approval, he made a remarkable ascent in the Nazi hierarchy. From 1922 to 1939 he rose to become one of the most important men surrounding Hitler[14] (Broszat, 1984).

Volksschullehrer[15] Streicher

Streicher's early life hardly suggested that he would die universally despised. Born in the village of Fleinhausen in southwest Bavaria, on February 12, 1885, he was the ninth child of a Roman Catholic elementary school teacher. After 8 years of formal education he completed preparatory training from 1901 to 1903 to become

---

[14]For a comprehensive historical profile on Streicher, see Bytwerk (1983).

[15]Elementary school teacher.

a school teacher. In 1904 he accepted a position as an assistant teacher and in 1907 he served 1 year as a volunteer in the army. There he behaved so badly that it was suggested he never be given a commission. In 1909 he returned as a teacher to an elementary school in a Nuremberg working-class district where he stayed until 1914. His combat record in a Bavarian unit during World War I was so impressive that he was commissioned with the rank of lieutenant and awarded the Iron Cross, First and Second Class, for bravery in action, despite the earlier entry in his record that he was not officer material.

After the war, Streicher returned to Nuremberg to teach again (1918–1923). Dissatisfied with classroom work he turned to politics as an anti-Communist conservative and a fanatic anti-Semite. In 1919, he joined the German Socialist Party and later joined Hitler's NSDAP after being mesmerized by one of his speeches. At first, Hitler was a bitter rival, but Streicher soon became a loyal follower describing Hitler as a "born leader." By then, Streicher had apparently realized that he himself would not be a leader; he had already failed to dominate two political groups, whereas Hitler clearly controlled the Nazis, and his following was growing (Bytwerk, 1983). During the failed November 1923, Munich Beer-Hall Putsch, Streicher was on Hitler's side and was arrested as one of the conspirators. Hitler showed his gratitude by mentioning Streicher in "Mein Kampf" as one of his early allies involved in his political movement (i.e., *Männer der Bewegung*).

Gauleiter Streicher

Although the Putsch resulted in the temporary disintegration of the Nazi movement, Hitler was set free in 1924 and through hard work soon resurrected his Party. Hitler needed loyal followers to assist him and none was more loyal than Streicher, who declared Hitler's return to politics as a "gift of God." In return for his loyalty, Streicher was appointed Gauleiter of Franconia (viz., northern Bavaria, including Nuremberg) for the Nazi party and was named an honorary SA general. Gauleiters[16] were senior Nazi party administrative figures and Streicher was the most disreputable of all. Although Streicher tried to hold on to his teaching post, he was having increased difficulties. He insisted that his pupils greet him each day with "Heil Hitler!" and the Nazi salute. Finally, in 1928 he was dismissed for conduct unbecoming a teacher. But in 1929 Streicher was elected to the Bavarian Landtag (Legislature) as a Nazi delegate from Franconia. Streicher was never to gain national prominence as a politician, but in and around Nuremberg he had immense power and governed as he saw fit. In 1932 he was given the important post of preparing the annual Nuremberg rallies, also called the *Parteitage* ("Days of the Party"). It was his task to organize the rallies and persuade the world of the prestige of the Nazi movement. Streicher took great pleasure in the foreign visitors and delegations that came each year in growing numbers to examine firsthand Germany's brand of National Socialism.

---

[16]*Gau* is an old Frankish term for a political division within a nation used to describe Nazi party administrative regions, each headed by a Gauleiter. In 1938 there were 32 Nazi party districts.

Julius Streicher, publisher of *Der Stürmer*. Photo by Morris Kiel, courtesy of U.S. Holocaust Memorial Museaum.

But Streicher had many internal quarrels with Party members who accused him of embezzling funds. In addition, his behavior was causing much embarrassment including his friendship with ex-convicts and his sexual exploits. Even fellow Nazis were not amused and most decent Germans denounced Streicher's hate campaign against Jews. Despite the criticism, however, Streicher was re-elected in January 1933. In response to a worldwide boycott of German goods, Hitler appointed Streicher as chairman of the Committee for Counteracting Jewish Atrocity Tales and Boycotts (Ley, Himmler, and Frank were members). Streicher acted swiftly, against what he believed to be a global economic conspiracy against the Third Reich. On April 1, 1933, he ordered SA storm troopers to do sentry duty in every

German town and village, holding placards informing the public that the proprietor of the establishment was a Jew, and challenging citizens and cautioning them not to patronize Jewish stores. Many eager SA and SS complied and additionally smeared shop windows with swastikas and the word *Jude*. But the boycotts also attracted the attention of the international press and was quickly called off.

By this time Streicher acquired a reputation as an eccentric. As a master rabble-rouser, he lost no chance to speak before a crowd wherever he could find one, heaping scorn on his enemies both inside and outside the Party. Time and time again Streicher would be in conflict with social groups and state authorities. He particularly disliked intellectuals and in the course of an address before students and the academic senate of Berlin University he drew a tilted pair of scales on the blackboard. Pointing to the lower scale, he informed his audience that it contained the Führer's brain, while the light one was filled with the composite dirt (*Dreck*) of their professors brains (Grunberger, 1971). On another occasion he told academics assembled at Munich: "I am accustomed to using the whip in order to educate, but here, among you academic men, I suppose the word would have an even stronger effect. You old men with beards and gold-rimmed glasses and scientific faces are really worth next to nothing. Your hearts are not right, and you can't understand the people as we can. We are not separated from them by so-called higher education."

Streicher was a bully and an intimidator of the worst sort. He would admit in public speeches to deriving sexual gratification from horse-whipping political prisoners. On occasion he visited Dachau concentration camp to extract confessions from inmates concerning their sexual fantasies or toured police stations to submit juvenile delinquents to detailed cross-examination about their masturbatory practices. On one occasion Streicher sent this circular to all readers reluctant to renew their subscriptions to his own local daily, the *Fränkische Tageszeitung*:

> Your intention expresses a very peculiar attitude towards our paper, which is an official organ of the National Socialist German Worker's Party, and we hope that you realize this. Our paper certainly deserves the support of every German. We shall continue to forward copies of it to you, and we hope that you will not want to expose yourself to unfortunate consequences in the case of cancellation.

Der Stürmer

Streicher's other and far better known journalistic venture was the notorious and obsessively anti-Semitic weekly, *Der Stürmer*[17] ("To storm forward"). From 1923 to 1945 he served as editor-in-chief of the weekly, which he described as "the best paper in the world." The periodical achieved a phenomenal success, rocketing from an average of 65,000 copies in 1934 to nearly 600,000 in 1935, before diminishing to less than 20,000 during the war years. It became one of the most widely circulated

---

[17]See Showalter (1982) for a comprehensive discussion on *Der Stürmer* and Hahn (1978) for a detailed presentation of letters to the editor.

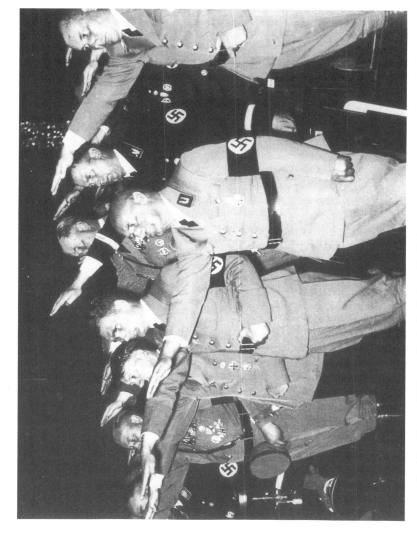

Streicher, Hess, and Hitler at a Nazi rally. Budesarchiv Koblenz.

papers in Germany and brought Streicher national, even international, notoriety. The paper undoubtedly had an even wider audience, since public display boxes on street corners and in school buildings provided cursory reading for millions more. The mendacity of *Der Stürmer* was extraordinary, and it was so nonfactual that the Nazi authorities themselves were occasionally obliged to withdraw it from circulation.[18] However, distorting the truth was only one facet of *Der Stürmer*. Another was open, violent, and sadistic anti-Semitism. Every single issue was devoted to Streicher's favorite theme—sexual intercourse between Jews and non-Jews. In fact, many German citizens banished the paper from their households on grounds of respectability.

Der Stürmer was journalism at its worst. Columns were filled with reports of sex scandals, or cartoons of Jewish faces with grossly exaggerated features. As the years went by, Streicher's propaganda became more feverish as he used the obscene Nuremberg weekly as his outlet for anti-Semitism and pornography. *Der Stürmer* went to grotesque lengths in attacks on Jews, blaming the "Hindenburg" disaster on a Jewish plot, announcing the discovery that Christ was not a Jew but an Aryan or that Pope Pius XI had Jewish blood, entrancing readers of supposed Jewish ritual murders, and reporting of unfortunate German girls being violated by Jewish rapists.

No opportunity was missed to stir up public opinion against what Streicher referred to as the Jewish menace. Anti-Semitism was not new to Germany, but Streicher's brand went far beyond that of his predecessors. The pages of Streicher's paper consisted of one long diatribe against Jews. At first he merely conducted a hate campaign, but gradually his articles and editorials began to call for extermination of "root and branch." Even before the outbreak of World War II he began to call for total annihilation: "Only when world Jewry has been annihilated will it have been solved" (January 1939). In the May 1939, issue, *Der Stürmer* announced that "the Jews in Russia must be killed … utterly exterminated," and in early 1942, Streicher called for the "extermination of that people whose father is the devil."

Der Stürmer was Hitler's favorite reading material. He went through each issue cover to cover, reveling in the dismal tales about Jewish sexual excesses and ritual murders. Streicher spoke and acted aloud what Hitler himself thought and desired. To the outside world Streicher and *Der Stürmer* should have provided ample evidence of the mindset of many who supported the Third Reich. Some issues of *Der Stürmer* were translated into English by U.S. anti-Semitic organizations and it is surprising that non-German governments did not pay closer attention to the Nazi policies of xenophobia. As it was, no one took Streicher's *Stürmer* that seriously.

Dismissal

By 1939, Streicher's behavior was becoming increasingly embarrassing for the Nazi hierarchy. Although Streicher still held Hitler's confidence and was esteemed in some "academic circles" for his "pseudo-scientific" support of anti-Semitism,

---

[18]For example, Issue 32, a particularly violent and untrue account of a sexual murder, was confiscated by deputy police president of Breslau because it was calculated to undermine the public esteem of the police force.

he was loathed for his bizarre and obscene personality. While he did not have any direct influence on policy making, many Party leaders thought it best to remove him from the political limelight. Streicher was charged with corruption and his demise was expedited after he wrote that Göring was impotent and that his daughter, Edda, had been conceived by artificial insemination. Hitler ordered Streicher to resign as Gauleiter without formally stripping him of his title and put him under house arrest on his lavish country estate at Pleikersdorf. But he held no further Party or government post and he was not allowed to set foot in Nuremberg.[19] Hitler, however, was still protective of his loyal supporter, and allowed Streicher to retain the editorship of *Der Stürmer*. In fact, Hitler wanted the paper to continue as Goebbels points out in this entry of his diary (Goebbels, 1983; Reuth, 1990; Schaumburg-Lippe, 1972): "The Führer sent word to me that he does not desire the circulation of the Stürmer to be reduced ... I, too, believe that our propaganda on the Jewish question must continue undiminished."

In this way the former elementary school teacher, after being dismissed from his post, continued to serve as editor of his paper as a private citizen, publishing *Der Stürmer* by telephone, home conference, and personal contributions as author. Hitler ensured that, even during the war, Streicher received all the paper he needed to continue publishing and all the gasoline necessary to maintain a courier between his farm and the *Stürmer's* office. Streicher lived out World War II on his superbly appointed country estate where he lived as somewhat of a folk hero of the Third Reich.

Arrest

His capture by Allied troops was a coincidence. After many of the leading Nazis had capitulated at Flensburg, southern Bavaria became the theater for an intensive Nazi-hunt. On May 23, 1945, U.S. Major Henry Plitt stopped his jeep while on escort to ask for a glass of milk on a farm near Berchtesgaden. Drinking his milk Plitt initiated a conversation with a bearded old man who was sitting on the front porch.

"How do you do? Are you the farmer?"

"No, I only live here. I am an artist, you understand artist ..." the old man responded.

"What do you think of the Nazis?" Plitt asks.

"I don't know about that. I am an artist and have never concerned myself about politics."

"But you look like Julius Streicher?"

The old man looked shocked, "How come you know me?"

---

[19]There is evidence that Streicher during his "exile" made trips to smaller towns and held speeches, although he was "finished" in Nuremberg. The precise reasons for his dismissal were not made public other than that a committee of six Gauleiters, assembled by Rudolf Hess, found him unfit for leadership (*Zur Menschenführung nicht geeignet;* Nadler, 1969).

Something about the old man reminded the major about a Nazi from a wanted poster he had just studied earlier. Plitt intended to say that he looked so much like Streicher, but his faulty German led him to say something to the effect that led Streicher to believe that he had been positively identified (Bytwerk, 1983). Plitt realized immediately what was going on and although Streicher quickly tried to cover by suggesting that his name was Sailer, it was too late. After 25 years of speaking, writing, and preaching hatred of Jews, Streicher—"Jew-Baiter Number One"—was arrested by an U.S. officer who's mother was Jewish (Heydecker & Leeb, 1985). Plitt became an immediate celebrity and was flown back to New York to help sell war bonds.

At Nuremberg

The Allies had wanted Streicher badly, but once they had captured him they had difficulty deciding what to do with him. He simply was not in the same class of defendants like Göring, Ribbentrop, and Speer, men who had held central roles in Hitler's war against the world. Streicher had never belonged to the inner circle of the Nazi elite and had never been personally involved in the execution of Nazi policies (Smith, 1976). It became clear that Streicher was notorious more for his rhetoric than for any specific criminal acts (Bytwerk, 1983). It was the general recollection of Streicher as a Gauleiter of the 1930s that accounted for him being put on trial with the other major defendants at Nuremberg and assigned a seat on "murderer's row" in the dock at the International War Crimes Tribunal. Ironically, Streicher was familiar with the Palace of Justice and its courtroom that in normal times housed the German regional appellate court; he had been tried there and in other courts more than once for slander and corruption. The Tribunal accused him of writing and publishing his "propaganda of death" as part of an indictment of Crimes against Peace (Count 1) and Crimes against Humanity (Count 4).

Throughout his political career Streicher remained consistent on only one point: his virulent anti-Semitism. He did not change at Nuremberg. After the indictment was delivered Streicher responded with agitation that the lawyer's names on Neave's list "looked like those of Jews" and demanded a lawyer who was anti-Semitic—"A Jew could not defend me." He later asked for and got Dr. Hans Marx, a Nuremberg lawyer and former Nazi Party member. To save Streicher from a capital sentence, Marx needed to do two things: persuade the Tribunal that there was insufficient evidence that Streicher had incited the killings of Jews, and prevent the hateful reputation and repulsive appearance of Streicher from crucially influencing the Tribunals' decision. But what did "incitement" mean? Before the war many other Germans "incited the persecution of Jews," but under the charter these acts were not international crimes (Taylor, 1992). Streicher gave Marx a difficult time declaring, immediately after taking his oath, that his "defense counsel has not conducted and was not in a position to conduct my defense in the way I wanted." Streicher's anti-Semitic obsession was so dominant that Marx was unable to get any cooperation for Streicher's defense, and concluded that his client had a "diseased mind" and requested that the Tribunal "consider whether a psychiatric examination of the defendant Streicher would not be proper ... [I] deem it necessary as a precaution in my own interest, since my client does not desire examination of this sort, and is of the opinion that he is mentally completely normal. I myself cannot determine that; it must be decided by a psychiatrist."

The Soviet delegation supported Marx's request because they had noted that Streicher had told them, as he did everyone else, that he was really a Zionist at heart, which prompted the Soviet delegation to have "certain doubts as to the mental stability of the defendant." Assistant Soviet prosecutor Colonel Pokrovsky thought that Streicher was probably shamming: "It is not the first time that persons now standing trial have attempted to delude us about their mental condition." An examination should be conducted immediately, Pokrovsky urged, "to establish definitely whether he is or is not in full possession of his mental capacities." This was not the first time Streicher was considered insane, many Germans themselves thought he was *verückt* (insane), Himmler thought he was *ein Narr* (crazy; Hahn, 1978), and Hitler's onetime adjutant, Fritz Wiedmann suggested that he was "either insane or a very great criminal. I rather think the former is the case" (Conot, 1983, p. 384).

A panel of three psychiatrists consisting of Dr. Krasnushkin of Moscow, Colonel Schroeder of Chicago, and Dr. Delay of Paris took on the task to evaluate Streicher's sanity (Gilbert, 1947). On November 18, 1945, the commission concluded, that whatever shortcomings Streicher may have, they did not amount to insanity or psychosis, but that he suffered from a neurotic obsession (Streicher lectured the psychiatrists on the Jewish problem throughout the examination). The doctors agreed unanimously that Streicher was "sane" and fit (i.e., competent) to "appear before the Tribunal and to present his defense." Gilbert concurred with the psychiatrists and suggested that Streicher had "no true psychiatric diagnosis, but [that Streicher] is of a personality structure which borders on the frankly abnormal and which brought him into difficulties even in the pathological social environment of the Third Reich." Kelley (1947) described Streicher as a "true paranoid reaction ... in other matters he was essentially rational."

The prosecutors knew well that they needed to portray Streicher as one who incited the persecution of Jews, which was best achieved by submitting evidence of what Streicher had publicly written. Streicher's case as presented by Lieutenant Colonel Griffith-Jones drew upon the compilation of the defendant's speeches and publications as proof of their intensity and quantity of Streicher's portrayal of Jews as the major source of evil, and on Streicher's insistence on their extermination. One example will suffice here:

> The male sperm in cohabitation is partially or completely absorbed by the female and thus enters her bloodstream. One single cohabitation of a Jew with an Aryan woman is sufficient to poison her blood forever. Never again will she be able to bear purely Aryan children, even when married to an Aryan. They will all be bastards.

Griffith-Jones continued to quote from issues of *Der Stürmer* to show that Streicher must have been informed of the establishment of ghettos and of the extermination of thousands and millions of Jews in the Eastern Territories. The prosecution concluded:

> In the early days he [Streicher] preached persecution. As persecutions took place he preached extermination and annihilation; and … as millions of Jews were being exterminated and annihilated, he cried out for more and more. This is the crime he has committed. It is the submission of the prosecution that he made these things possible … which could never have happened but for him and others like him.

In his defense, Streicher insisted that it was the Führer's fault and that he was nothing but a cog in a gigantic machine. He vehemently denied any knowledge about mass execution of Jews and defended himself by insisting that he favored the classifications of Jews as aliens. He denied that his actions had incited violence against the Jews or that there was any evidence of such incitement. He declared that the mass killings of Jews first became known to him in 1945 when he was a prisoner at Mondorf. He did acknowledge ordering the destruction of the main Nuremberg synagogue in 1938, but insisted that it was for architectural reasons. Regarding Kristallnacht, he argued that he had been forced, because of the prevailing atmosphere, to speak publicly against Jews the following morning. He furthermore denied that he had preached religious hatred, because Judaism was a race—not a religion. The purpose of his anti-Semitism was not to persecute but to enlighten, he argued (Taylor, 1992). His last words before the Tribunal:

> The prosecution had asserted that mass killings [of Jews] could not have been possible without Streicher and his *Stürmer*. The prosecution neither offered nor submitted any proof of this assertion. …These actions of the leader of the State against Jews can be explained by the attitude toward the Jewish question, which was thoroughly different from mine. Hitler wanted to punish the Jews because he held them responsible for unleashing the war and for the bombing of the German civilian population. …
>
> I repudiate the mass killings … in the same way as they are repudiated by every decent German. Your honors! Neither in my capacity as Gauleiter nor as political author have I committed a crime, and I therefore look forward to your judgment with a good conscience. I have no request to make for myself. I have one for the German people from whom I come. Your Honors, fate has given you the power to pronounce any judgment. Do not pronounce a judgment which would imprint the stamp of dishonor upon the forehead of an entire nation.

Streicher should have confronted the Tribunal with the first and only serious question of criminal guilt among the defendants. His was a unique charge, the other defendants all held important national governmental positions and operated on a national scale. Proof of the charges against them was written in orders, decrees, and memoranda that they wrote, issued, and filed. But Streicher had nothing to do with military decisions and had been a political nonentity since 1940. There was no accusation that Streicher himself had participated in any violence against Jews (Taylor, 1992). He was to stand trial for his incitement of the persecution of the Jews, but he had no connection with Himmler or his subordinates, who were

Streicher at his cell writing desk in the Nuremberg jail. National Archives, courtesy of U.S. Holocaust Memorial Museum.

actually carrying out the Holocaust (Breitman, 1991; Fleming, 1984). Indeed, it would be difficult, for example, to establish a causal relationship between Julius Streicher and the behavior of Rudolf Höss, who was the commander of the Auschwitz death camp (Smith, 1976).

Furthermore, Streicher's membership in the Reichstag was largely ceremonial and his speeches as Gauleiter did not reach a national audience and were stopped by Hitler in 1939. Virtually all of Streicher's Nazism had gone into anti-Semitism, most of it embodied in an evidentiary trail laid out in the issues of *Der Stürmer*, which was his own creation. The periodical was not a governmental agency, but a private newspaper owned and edited by Julius Streicher. Thus, the charges in the indictment were brought against a private newspaper owner and journalist to punish him for publishing statements in which he believed. No question, Streicher was a repulsive personality and he had been an important force in sowing the seeds for anti-Semitic atrocities. But the question before the Tribunal was whether the publication of a German newspaper, no matter how scurrilous, was a crime under international law (Taylor, 1992).

Chief U.S. prosecutor, Justice Jackson, described Streicher as a venomous vulgarian who "manufactured and distributed obscene racial libels which incited the population to accept and assist the progressively savage operations of race purification." He dismissed Streicher's denial that he did not know what was going on: the "Gauleiter of Franconia whose occupation was to pour forth filthy writings about the Jews, but who had no idea that anybody would read them." Marx made little effort to rehabilitate Streicher as a human being worthy of the law's protection. Indeed, at the end of his argument Marx declared that as defense counsel he had "a difficult and thankless task" and left Streicher's guilt or innocence "in the hands of the High Tribunal," thus seemingly washing his own hands of his client (Taylor, 1992).

In *The Anatomy of the Nuremberg Trials,* Taylor (1992), a leading member of the U.S. prosecution staff and chief prosecutor in the 12 follow-up trials, indicated that it would be a difficult legal issue to prove whether "incitement" was a sufficient basis for a conviction. Because there was no charge that Streicher was involved in a conspiracy to bring about aggressive war, Taylor indicated that under Count 1, Streicher's acquittal was a foregone conclusion. On September 10, 1946, as expected, Streicher was found not guilty on Count 1 for lack of evidence implicating Streicher in any conspiracy to wage aggressive war. He was, however, found guilty of Count 4, crimes against humanity, and condemned to death by hanging. Streicher, the four Allied judges proclaimed unanimously, had ordered the boycott of Jewish establishments on April 1, 1933, advocated the Nuremberg Decrees of 1935, and was responsible for the demolition of a synagogue in Nuremberg on August 10, 1938. Most serious was the evidence that proved that Streicher continued to utilize *Der Stürmer* as a vehicle to stir up hatred against Jews and applauded their annihilation. The Tribunal concluded:

> Streicher's incitement to murder and exterminate at the time when Jews in the East were being killed under the most horrible conditions clearly constitutes persecution on political and racial grounds in connection with War Crimes ... as constitutes a Crime against Humanity.

In retrospect, it seems that the Tribunal's hasty treatment of Streicher was difficult to understand from a strictly legal point of view. Taylor (1992) felt that the Tribunal sent Streicher to the gallows in a carefree way "as if they were stamping on a worm." On strict legal terms, Taylor argued that Streicher may have been unjustifiably hanged. After all, Streicher was living on a farm in seclusion from 1940 to the end of the war and his paper's circulation dwindled to about 15,000 copies during most of the war. The Tribunal's opinion had been superficial, perhaps influenced both by his "repulsive appearance and by the likelihood of a negative reaction if Streicher got anything less than the worst" (p. 599). One could argue that Funk's range of crimes was far wider than Streicher's although Funk, the head of the Reichsbank and economics minister of the Third Reich, was given a prison sentence. Many agree that although Streicher's case may have been the most debatable, it was peculiar that his verdict was reached with next to no discussion, in contrast to the detail and length of discussions offered, for example, in the case of Dönitz, whose proof was just as thin. Taylor concluded that it was "hard to condone the Tribunal's unthinking and callous handling of the Streicher case."

The case of Streicher supports once more that in legal trials the most unappetizing members of society will receive the least protection of basic human rights and those from similar socioeconomic classes as the judges will receive the most forgiveness (Smith, 1976). And so it was at Nuremberg. Streicher and Saukel were hanged, Neurath and Speer were given prison sentences, and Schacht and Papen were acquitted. Fifty years later, one need not grieve over the fate of Streicher, but "even an unappetizing, fanatical old Nazi is entitled to careful judgment before being hanged" (Taylor, 1992).

The verdict—death through hanging—was executed on the morning of October 16, 1946 in the prison gymnasium. To the end Streicher was blazingly defiant having to be forced into his court clothing the morning of the execution by struggling guards. At the gallows he angrily shouted, "Heil Hitler!" "The Bolshevik will hang you!" and "Purim festival, 1946."

ANALYSIS

Streicher and his *Stürmer* cannot be interpreted in isolation. Streicher played a very specific but crucial role in the overall success of the Third Reich. He was the embodiment of Hitler' anti-Semitism as well as many a German's subconscious needs. Streicher appealed to the lowest instincts, and he had a following that responded with enthusiasm (Hahn, 1978). Streicher dared to say and write what many Germans were only thinking. In fact, Streicher was closer to Hitler's basic neurosis than anyone. Streicher was one of few men with whom Hitler used the informal *Du* of close friendship, although Speer (1970) indicated that Hitler treated Streicher impersonally. Undoubtedly, Hitler used Streicher for his own purpose of propaganda.

To pass Streicher off as just an obsessed fanatic would not do justice to the fact that his circulation was read by many Germans. Publication meant recognition. Through his weekly paper Streicher brought anti-Semitism to the classroom as well as to the dinning room. *Der Stürmer* also influenced a generation of school children because there were reports that many teachers would routinely read the periodical in class. *Der Stürmer* was among the best known and most profitable of the local Nazi newspapers, and no one could deny Streicher's success in election after election. The paper touched peripherally or extensively, on a broad spectrum of themes and events contributing to the growth of National Socialism (Showalter, 1982). In this way Streicher shaped the perception of Germans significantly and facilitated an atmosphere of hatred and paranoia through street-corner propaganda.

Within this context Streicher's campaign against the Jews prepared the way for the Nuremberg Laws of Citizenship and Race (or Ghetto Laws), by which the status of Jews in Nazi Germany was defined. The result was that German citizenship was withdrawn from all those of "non-German" blood. Jewish physicians were excluded from hospitals, Jewish judges were dismissed, and Jewish students thrown out of universities. It was because of Streicher that the Nuremberg laws were cruelly implemented—for sexual intercourse between Jews and "citizens of Germany or kindred blood" he demanded the death penalty.

Der Stürmer made it permissible to be publicly xenophobic. If viewed from this perspective Streicher was one of the most important men in prewar Germany for the Nazi movement to succeed. To Hitler, Streicher's propaganda was essential in preparing and implementing some of the policies of the Third Reich. Speer (1970), for example, reported that Hitler himself would engage only in a few anti-Semitic statements and it was therefore possible for Hitler to appeal to a much larger and more moderate audience. Streicher represented the most revolting aspects of Nazism and his propaganda aroused deep emotions in the German people. Although many Nazis themselves felt that he stood essentially alone in the world, without him the common man could have never carried out the Final Solution—the Kaltenbrunners and the Himmlers, would have had nobody to carry out their orders. The prosecution had a point when they argued that it was others who had carried out the Holocaust, but that Streicher had prepared the ground.

Today, Streicher is regularly dismissed as a crude, sadistic pornographer, not an entirely unjust description (Bytwerk, 1983). Yet, this unpleasant personality was attractive and persuasive to many. What sort of man was he? Some may argue that it is superfluous to analyze Streicher's personality using standardized psychological testing, since there is enough behavioral evidence, through his writings and his speeches as well as his overall conduct, to describe the man. Although these arguments are noteworthy we do submit, however, that the record presented below is the only personality test that has been collected on Streicher and as such it is of historical significance and may shed additional light on Streicher's personality structure. From Kelley's interpreter we know some of the details of the Rorschach administration:

> The interview was held in Streicher's cell in the war criminal wing of the Nuremberg prison. I remember that I had to 'butter up' Streicher for several days in advance of the test. He was very reluctant to participate. For on thing, he was convinced that Kelley was Jewish—assuring me that all psychiatrists and psychologists were Jewish, and that the test would not be accurate. After getting over those obstacles we undertook the project, with Streicher a somewhat listless and suspicious subject. As I recall, we spent a lot of time on that particular afternoon, and were once interrupted by the officer of the day who had become concerned about the long time we spent with Streicher in his cell (J. E. Dolibois, personal communication, July 31, 1994).

Rorschach Record

Subject: Julius Streicher (1885–1946)
Age: 60
Full-Scale IQ: 106 (Average Range; 66th percentile)
Date of testing: July–December 1945 (specific date unknown)
Examiner: Douglas Kelley, MD

I. 1. A crab or sea animal.   The whole card is used. It is dead.

Wo 1 Fo A 1.0 MOR

  2. A funny airplane.   It is an exaggerated plane such as he has seen in German papers. A drawing for a model of a new type of plane.

Wo 1 Fu Sc, Art 1.0

  3. V Skeleton.   The hip-bones. The whole card is used and it is seen as a simple anatomical specimen.

Wo 1 Fo An 1.0

  4. A dog's head.   This is in the right lateral detail in the shaded area including two small dots on the right side. He sees the eyes and nose and it seems well seen.

Do 2 Fu Ad

He gives at this point a spontaneous additional answer - "Protoplasm." This is the center of the area, bell and figure, and he states that one can see through it.[20]

II. 1. He looks the card over; discusses it, stating that it is pretty. Waves it about his head and finally states that it is two women in the French Revolution times with Jacobean caps.   He states that they have red socks and caps and are dancing. He then gives date of the Revolution as 1789 and is about to go into a discussion on the French Revolutionary in general when he is again attracted by the card.

W+ 1 Ma.FCo (2) H, Cg, Ay 4.5 DR

---

[20]Additional responses occurring during the inquiry are not scored in the Comprehensive System.

2. Red wine glass on a porcelain platter.

Center red and center space detail. He sees glass as red but form is not important. Color is factor for white platter.

In the inquiry, he sees an additional white space, response, "Two Dutch Shoes." Upper white space details.

DS+ 5 FC'.CFu Hh 4.5

III. 1. Two men, counts.

Two waiters.

They are bowing to each other. Seem well dressed of the nobility.
Same response.

D+ 9 Mao (2) H, Cg P 4.0 COP

2. A butterfly or
3. Blood spots.

Do 3 FCo A

He sees the butterfly first in the center and here uses both the form and the color, and at the same time attempts to get the two lateral red details into the same answer and changes over from butterfly to blood spots for all three.

Dv 2 C Bl

4. V A cravat or bow-tie.

This is center red detail form only. At this point he launches into a long discussion on how interesting the card is.

Do 3 Fo Cg

5. V Woman's figures with her hands at her hips.

This is the center space detail as seen in motion.

DdSo 24 Mp- H

6. Negro heads.

In order to see this clearly, he covers up all the other details with his hands.[21]

IV. 1. Fur of an animal, a bear.

He describes the head and feet. Seems very reluctant to give the card back, trying to find some other response. Finally at 60 seconds gives up. The fur is seen with furry side out.

Wo 1 FTu Ad 2.0

[21]In the Comprehensive System, only five responses per card are scored and thus the sixth response is not scored here.

V.   1. A bat.   It is a dead bat; lifeless, and it does not seem to be sleeping or it would be hanging by its feet. It is not flying so it must be dead.

                                            Wo 1 Fo A P 1.0 ALOG, MOR

       2. A flying dog from   This is the same thing in an attempt to improve
           Borneo.   it. It is also lifeless.

                                            Wo 1 F- A 1.0 INC2

       3. A pattern for an airplane.   An airplane model.

                                            Wo 1 Fu Sc, Art 1.0

VI. 1. A fur.   The whole card is used. It is a skin of a unique animal, fur side out. At 20 seconds, he launches into a discussion of the card. Takes off his glasses; looks at the card; puts on his glasses; looks at the card; tells us that it is a card with an ink spot on it and in general attempts to make something out of it.

                                            Wv 1 TFo Ad P

       2. Carved staff.   This is the top center blank detail and he states it is done by a machine. It is very well seen.

                                            Do 6 Fo Hh

VII. 1. The substance taken out   This is one-half of the card and is seen as a
           of an operated knee.   specimen preserved in alcohol of the meniscus which has been removed from the knee joint. He had such an operation and apparently preserved and brought home the material removed from his knee joint which apparently resembles the blot.

                                            Ddv 22 F- An PER, MOR

       2. Two human embryos.   In the inquiry, he states they are not embryos but rather are females dancing. The whole card is split into two details. Usual figures.

                                            Wo 1 Fu (2) (H) 2.5

3. V Skeletons.

These are the same forms which he has been trying to make into something definite. Apparently he realizes the female figures were not good and attempted to make skeletons out of them.

Wo 1 F- (2) An 2.5

4. V A bust.

This is a bust of Napoleon's head-center space detail.

DSo 7 Fu (Hd), Art, Ay

VIII.1. Beautiful colors.

Pastel shades.

Wv 1 C.Y Art

2. Mouse-like animals.

They are like guinea pigs and are alive.

Do 1 Fo 2 A P

3. Oriental pattern.

He becomes very happy about the card; smiles at it. States it has harmonious colors and is an oriental pattern with a combination of figures and colors. This is the whole card; the colors seem to predominate here.

Wv 1 CFo Art

IX. 1. V A plant in bloom. These must be the roots. The green part is eaten up by dogs.

This is a pink plant. Color and form both seem used but the form seems more definite here. When he started, he pointed only to the pink area but had now joined the green part as the leaves. These are the orange details and he has now organized the entire card into a plant with pink blossoms, green leaves and roots. The color does not seem important to the roots but rather the nature-less structure. The card is a whole; is well seen and a good combination of form and color. On careful questioning, it seems most likely that the original response of "Plant in bloom" was suggested more by the color than by the form.

W o 1 mp.CFu Bt, A 5.5 MOR

X.   1. A louse.   Do 1 Fo (2) A

   2. Microscopic animals.   Both these responses are to the lateral blue. Seem to be enlarged which leads to the idea of microscopic sea animals. They seem to be very much alive.

                                                          Do 11 F- (2) An

   3. Skeletons. Human figures.   These two answers started by seeing the top gray area as a skeleton and it was finally played up to the two human figures.

                                                          Do 8 F- (2) H

   4. Tropical flowers.   This is the whole card seen as a collection of flower blossoms and in the inquiry he states they are too pastel to really be tropical. English flowers are brighter like these. These are Nordic flowers.

                                 (He then adds as a spontaneous response:)
                                 This card is not so pretty. In the inquiry at the end, he also notes the center space as a cowboy with a lasso.

                                                          Wv/+ 1 CF.YFo Bt 5.5 DR

                                 End of record

INTERPRETATION

Before interpreting Streicher's record one needs to be concerned with its validity. Specifically, is Streicher's Rorschach data meaningful and interpretively useful? As mentioned Streicher was consistently defiant of any type of examination and may have cooperated only minimally. However, there are several reasons why the Streicher Rorschach record does appear valid. First, it was administered by Kelley and not by Gilbert who evaluated the defendant's intelligence. Gilbert, unlike Kelley, was Jewish, and there was no question that many of the defendants took more friendly to Kelley than to Gilbert, because of this. Second, the Rorschach test was administered quite some time before the stress of the trial as well as before Streicher's "official" psychiatric examination, which he turned into a harangue on anti-Semitism. Perhaps most importantly, the Rorschach record itself appears reliable and valid given that Streicher offered 30 scoreable responses[22] and that many of his responses were rich in detail. Incidentally, the most common strategy of faking or malingering on the Rorschach is to offer very few responses (e.g., less than 14) or to respond with a scarcity of verbalizations typically by reporting that "it just looks like that." Streicher's protocol is not consistent with such an approach and it needs to be remembered that the Rorschach test is one of the most difficult psychological techniques to distort. The testing situation is very ambiguous, offering the examinee very little structure by asking "What might this be?"

Another form of invalidity to be concerned with, particularly in Streicher's case, is that of interpretative bias. Given Streicher's history it is almost impossible to give an objective account of his personality based on the psychological test scores, without responding to the numerous accounts of his repulsive actions as well.[23] An objective interpretation is possible, however, through the use of computer-generated hypothesis. Such computer-assisted statements, which are based on actuarial research, can serve as an objective guide from which one can proceed to study Streicher's personality. As with Dönitz's protocol, Streicher's Rorschach record is discussed in terms of distinctly different areas of psychological functioning in order of importance with the most salient personality described characteristics first.

Streicher: Affective Processes.   The most pertinent aspects of Streicher's Rorschach record lie within the area of emotional functioning. It is within this area of affective control and modulation of emotions that the most noteworthy computer-generated statements are offered:

> The current personality organization is marked by features that give rise to frequent and intense experiences of affective disruption. A basic feature of this personality is a tendency to merge feelings with thinking during problem solving or decision making. People such as this are prone to use and be influenced by emotion.

Streicher is decidedly extratensive, suggesting that his preference is to display emotions routinely to his environment. His problem solving style is markedly rigid and stubborn and not adaptable to different situational demands. This indicates that Streicher does not delay final decisions until he has mentally reviewed alternative and potential results, but typically prefers to test out postulates through trial and error behavior. Thus, Streicher's use of resources regarding coping responses, stress situations, and environmental responsiveness characteristically involves affect in directing behaviors. As a result individuals with this coping style are more willing to display feelings openly and often are less concerned about carefully modulating those displays. This is emphasized by the following actuarial statement:

> Some potentially serious emotional modulation problems exist. People such as this are often overly intense in their emotional displays and frequently convey impressions

---

[22]The average number of responses for normals is 23 in the Comprehensive System.

[23]See Miale and Selzer for examples of interpretative bias (chap. 6).

of impulsiveness. This could be the product of control difficulties; however, it is equally possible that it reflects a less mature psychological organization in which the modulation of affect is not regarded as being very important. This is an unusual finding among adults. People such as this frequently are regarded by others as overly emotional and/or less mature.

This finding does not come as a surprise given that Streicher's behavior could easily be described as impulsive and emotional. Streicher, it appears, finds emotions confusing and may frequently experience both positive and negative feelings about the same stimulus situation. People such as this often experience feelings more intensively than others, have more difficulty in bringing closure to emotional situations, and are more ambivalent concerning the experience and expressions of emotions. The current Rorschach record, however, goes beyond this and suggests that, besides Streicher being immature and very much like a young child in the area of affective control, there is evidence of clinical depression that may serve as a basis for this profound difficulty in modulating his emotions. Usually, patients with these characteristics are diagnosed as having a serious affective disturbance.

Streicher: Stress Tolerance and Impulse Control. It may come as a surprise to find that Streicher's Rorschach record suggests that his capacity for control and tolerance for stress was quite good. Under normal situations Streicher was able to mobilize inner resources that allowed him to function even while experiencing substantial amounts of stress. After all, Streicher had numerous enemies and law suits to contend with, but the current testing indicates that this may not have bothered him too much. Such a high tolerance for stress may have served as a basis for Streicher's vehement anti-Semitism, since such individuals are very resistant to change even in the face of contradictory information or extensive criticism. Computer-generated statements included:

This subject has unusually good capacities for control. Many more resources are readily accessible for use than ordinarily are required. As a result, tolerance for stress is considerable and the subject is readily able to formulate and give direction to behaviors. This feature tends to enhance stabilization of functioning regardless of general or specific adaptability. Thus, nonpatients with this characteristic are often perceived by others as predictably sturdy. Conversely, patients with this characteristic are often more difficult to treat as the stabilization is pervasive and usually will include symptom patterns even though they may be less adaptive or even maladaptive in some situations.

Again there is evidence that situational stressors (e.g., his house arrest of 5 years, the loss of the war, and his indictment) acted on Streicher and may have served to make him more vulnerable to disorganization than in the past. Thus, although there is evidence that this individual had some resources to meet stress demands, there is also evidence that these resources were not as well organized during his imprisonment at Nuremberg.

The subject is currently experiencing distress or discomfort.

The subject is experiencing a sense of loneliness or emotional deprivation. In most instances, this will be situationally related and should be easily identified from the recent history.

The subject is experiencing a significant increase in stimulus demands as a result of situationally related stress. Some of the stress may relate to some emotional loss.

Added psychological complexity is being created by the stress condition.

It needs to be added that this capacity for control would suggest that, most of the time, Streicher was not the "raving lunatic" that he appeared to be, but that under normal situations he was calculating and in control over his behaviors, even though his actions may have been maladaptive. Thus, Streicher was not easily disorganized, in spite of his pathology. The exception would be in instances in which he was emotionally challenged or thrust into overload by intense or prolonged stress. In such situations, he was clearly impulsive, less predictable, and much more likely to act out with little regard to the reality demands around him.

Streicher: Self-Esteem and Interpersonal Perception.   As mentioned earlier there is substantial evidence that Streicher's may have suffered from an affective disturbance, it should not be surprising that he demonstrated a low self-concept and poor self-esteem. On the surface this may not seem consistent with his behavior that indicated a marked emphasis on "racial superiority." It is, however, quite consistent with research and theory in clinical psychology where the need to be perceived as "special" can be related to chronic insecurity. This is particularly true for individuals like Streicher who resisted examining their own feelings and beliefs critically, as the Rorschach record suggests.

The subject is less prone to be introspective than are most adolescents or adults.

Thus, Streicher's insistence on racial discrimination and cultural elitism can be understood as a defense for his own personal shortcoming of being perceived as inferior or weak. Most psychologists believe that this psychological process is not conscious to the person and thereby very resistant to change.

This is the type of person who regards him/herself less favorably when compared to others. The self concept or self image includes some very negative, unwanted features that tend to promote a pessimistic view of the self and influence many decisions.

Some unusual body concern or preoccupation is present. This finding is not uncommon among subjects who have physical problems, but if no health problem exists it signifies the presence of a marked preoccupation body image or functioning.

The area of interpersonal perception suggested that Streicher was generally attracted to people and actually desired to be around others. In fact, he considered himself "A man of the people" (Baird, 1993). One could go as far as to suggest that Streicher was interpersonally needy and thus interested in social stimulation and affection, but he was also vulnerable to the manipulations of others because of this.

> This subject appears to have a marked interest in people. The subject generally perceives positive interactions among people routinely and has a willingness to participate in them. This does not mean that interpersonal relations will be positive or mature.

> The subject is experiencing a sense of loneliness or emotional deprivation. This will be quite influential in interpersonal relationships. People such as this are often quite vulnerable to the manipulations of others.

The suggestion, that Streicher liked being around people does not imply that his interactions with others were necessarily adaptive. To the contrary, he was almost universally loathed. Streicher may have been one of Hitler's oldest companions, but he was always an outsider in the Party because of his sex-obsessed anti-Semitism and his flagrant corruption. For example, before the defendants were brought to Nuremberg, they were in a U.S. prison at Luxembourg. A formal delegation, headed by Dönitz, requested that at least they be treated as gentlemen and not be required to eat at the same table with Streicher (Kelley, 1947). Even during the Nuremberg trial, all the other defendants avoided him (Speer, 1977), and Dönitz announced that neither he nor any of his officers would even touch Streicher's filthy paper (Hahn, 1978).

Streicher: Information Processing.   Streicher is a rigid and significant under incorporator. The current record strongly suggest that he addresses his environment in an extremely simple manner and may often miss important information that other individuals would consider important in coming to decisions and opinions. Thus, Streicher prefers simple solutions to complex problems. This information-processing style is at the heart of Streicher's hate campaign against Jews in which he would take the most complex social phenomenon and reduce them to some simple concept (in this case anti-Semitism). Such an approach almost always neglects important reality-based features as well as social demands which is further emphasized by the following computer-generated statements.

> A basic response style exists that involves a marked tendency to narrow or simplify stimulus fields perceived as complex, or ambiguous. Although this coping style reflects a form of psychological economizing, it also may include problems in the processing of information and as such can create a potential for a higher frequency of behaviors that do not coincide with social demands and/or expectations.

The overall cognitive approach tends to be simple and uncomplicated. In other words, little effort is made to organize and/or integrate fields of information in a more sophisticated way. This is common among children but less so among adolescents and adults. Less sophisticated processing often predisposes less effective translations of inputs and can be a precursor to less effective patterns of adjustment.

Streicher's desire to avoid complexity is easily examined in his capacity as the editor of *Der Stürmer* for which he wrote extensively. His goal was to provide short articles in simple language, often using cartoons, that explained to a popular audience the intricacies of politics and economics. The prose was simple but not of a particularly high quality; it was full of factual, grammatical, and spelling errors (Bytwerk, 1983).

In general, Streicher's psychological functioning can be referred to as naive, overly simplistic, uncomplicated, or lazy, and may often result in maladaptive or inappropriate behaviors. Similar individuals are much more prone for impulsivelike behavior in problem-solving situations and they tend to be negligent in processing information. It needs to be noted that such a style is quite common for individuals with marked intellectual handicaps and much has been made of the fact that Streicher's IQ was the lowest of all the Nuremberg defendants, in spite of his extraordinary influence on Germany. In the IQ test administered by Gilbert's Streicher's score of 106 fell within the average range of intellectual capabilities exceeding approximately 66% of his peers of the same age. Although Streicher may have been less endowed intellectually than Schacht and Frank (both held doctoral degrees) he was not "mentally deficient" or "stupid" as many "experts" have suggested. In contrast, Streicher understood well how to manipulate his surroundings for his own purposes. Streicher was unquestionably a liar and morally corrupt, but he certainly was not of "limited intelligence" (Bytwerk, 1983) or of "low average intelligence" (Kelley, 1947). In fact, some historians have gone so far as to suggest that the lack of Streicher's intelligence formed the basis for his perverted personality and anti-Semitic obsession (e.g., Hahn, 1978).

There is evidence to suggest that Streicher's true intellectual functioning may actually be somewhat higher than that tested by prison psychologist Gilbert. First, Streicher was not well educated and only completed 8 years of formal schooling. Psychometric intelligence is most related to academic achievement and thus his average score reflected to some extend his socioeconomic and educational background. Second, Streicher may not have completely cooperated with the intellectual examination conducted by Gilbert, who was Jewish (see chap. 3). Thus, Streicher the elementary school teacher was by no means a mental degenerate, as many described him to be. His intellectual capabilities were at least average, possibly higher, and Streicher's career showed him to be a man of force and forensic skill, albeit in the environment of the Third Reich. Nevertheless, even the more objective historian has difficulty accepting and more readily believes that because of Streicher's crude presentation and monsterlike behavior he could not have been anything but a mental degenerate.

Scholars, however, must look elsewhere in explaining Streicher's behavior and attitudes. The answers do not lie in the realm of his intellectual abilities.

Streicher: Reality Testing. Streicher's reality-testing capacities are extremely poor even in situations that require an obvious response, where even many psychiatric patients with significant disturbances in reality testing succeed. Not Streicher. His likelihood for less conventional responses is significant, even in situations that are simple and precisely defined.

> The subject is prone to make more unconventional behaviors than do most people. This feature may reflect a strong emphasis on individualism, may result from social alienation, or could be the product of more serious mediational or affective modulation problems. This unconventionality is likely the result of a strong orientation to maintain distance from, and thus cope with an environment that is perceived as threatening, demanding, and ungiving.

> The subject may display a higher than usual frequency of behaviors that disregard social demands or expectations. This lack of conventionality may be due to the subject's tendency to over-personalize in translating stimuli.

> The subject usually merges feelings with thinking during problem solving activity. People such as this tend to be more accepting of logic systems that are not precise or are marked by greater ambiguity.

> Serious problems in thinking are indicated. Instances of ideational discontinuity and/or faulty conceptualization occur too frequently. They tend to interfere with logic and promote faulty judgment and as a result the probability of errors in decision making is increased substantially.

Streicher is manifesting substantial and marked distortions in reality testing in a manner ranging from eccentricity to "bending" reality to suit his own needs to more serious forms of cognitive slippage and perceptual distortions. Although not consistent with a serious thought disorder (e.g., schizophrenia), it does suggest that Streicher violates many important reality based features when responding to his environment. As a result, Streicher would perceive his world quite differently than most individuals do and he would be at high risk for violating important social norms.

Additional Interpretation. In examining Streicher's verbatim responses for purposes of a more qualitative analysis, two findings emerge that can be integrated with previous hypotheses. The first finding, consistent with earlier accounts of depression, includes Streicher's preoccupation with morbid concerns, body functions, and physical well-being. This is emphasized by the content of Streicher's responses to the Rorschach including, "death," "skeletons,"[24] "eaten-up," "anatomical specimen," "hip-bone," "protoplasm," "blood," "lifeless," and "preserved meniscus."

---

[24]Presented three separate times.

Furthermore, Streicher's record indicates numerous responses with anthropological content, "French Revolution," "Negro," "Napoleon," as well as related responses involving art, "drawing," "bust," "shades," and "pattern." Individuals with such response sets typically use intellectualization as a major defensive tactic in situations that are perceived as affectively stressful. Thus, Streicher was prone to deal with feelings on an intellectual level more often than most people. Although this process serves to reduce or neutralize the impact of emotions, it also represents a naive form of denial that tends to distort the true impact of a situation. In effect, it is a "pseudo-intellectual" process that conceals or denies the presence of affect and, as a result, tends to reduce the likelihood that feelings will be dealt with directly or realistically. People such as this tend to become more vulnerable to disorganization during intense emotional experiences because the tactic becomes less effective as the magnitude of affective stimuli increases. This seems important in Streicher's case because he appeared to have used intellectualization excessively to support his preoccupation with anti-Semitism. Almost always he would find some historical half-truth or ambiguous biblical writings from which to rationalize and extrapolate from. For example, he ordered the destruction of the main Nuremberg synagogue, but declared that it was for architectural reasons.

SUMMARY

Streicher's Rorschach record is notable for several reasons. There is clear evidence to suggest that Streicher responds emotionally to his environment, and that his affect tended to be markedly intense and frequently occurred with little or no cognitive controls. The potential for such behaviors to take on impulsive characteristics in a manner that interferes with adaptive responses and social norms is very high. This intensity of his affective experience as well as his inability to modulate his emotional experience appear to be central issues in Streicher's personality and suggests the possibility of a more serious underlying affective disturbance including depressive or manic-depressive disorder.

There is also evidence to suggest that Streicher displayed greater stress tolerance than do a majority of normal respondents on the Rorschach. Thus, he was very resistant to change, predictable in his actions, and comfortable with his behaviors and opinions even in the face of extensive criticism. It was unlikely that under normal situations Streicher would display disorganized behaviors. although there is strong evidence to suggest that when emotionally challenged he became very impulsive and would demonstrate extremely poor reality testing.

Streicher's Rorschach record also indicates a marked low level of self-esteem that may render him particularly vulnerable to ego threatening situations. This finding is frequently accompanied by feelings of inferiority, as well as a negative and damaged self image characterized by pessimistic attitudes and thoughts. It is suggested that Streicher's need to be perceived as "racially superior" and to announce that *Der Stürmer* was "the best paper in the world" is related to this chronic and profound sense of inadequacy.

Streicher's perceptual monitoring style was highly simplistic and unsophisticated. Because of Streicher's unsophisticated style of integrating information, he would come to decisions quickly and without considering all information available. Little effort was expended by Streicher to organize or integrate the world as perceived by others and much relevant information was not considered in coming to decisions. Not surprisingly, Streicher favored simplistic childlike cartoons to convey his political messages in *Der Stürmer*.

Interpersonally, Streicher was attracted to other people to the point where he may be described as interpersonally needy and vulnerable to the manipulation of others (e.g., Hitler). This does not mean that Streicher had adaptive social relationships, in fact, evidence on the Rorschach record suggests the contrary, including substantial distortion in interpersonal relationships and a very unrealistic perception or understanding of others.

Taken together, the features of Streicher's Rorschach record are much more commonly found in children, but not typically seen in adults or even adolescents. Thus, Streicher's personality profile is certainly consistent with immaturity. Moreover, his overly simple information processing style, emotional impulsivity, and poor reality testing do suggest overt psychopathology at a scale that would warrant a psychiatric diagnosis for an affective disorder as well as for a more chronic personality disorder. Thus, the Rorschach record uncovered some basic features of Streicher's personality that explain, to some degree and in psychological terms, his bizarre and unconventional actions. This disturbance in Streicher's personality did not go unnoticed by the German people. Streicher's psychopathology was so profound that he was perceived as unconventional even by the standards of the Third Reich. With the Nazi seizure of power Streicher became expendable and as a result, party officials put him under house arrest in 1939.

These current findings stand in contrast with the panel of three psychiatrists who examined Streicher during the International Military Tribunal. They suggested that there was no evidence of "insanity or psychosis," but that he suffered from a "lesser neurotic obsession." Furthermore, Gilbert suggested that there was "no true diagnosis" and Kelley described Streicher as "rational." The term *insanity* is not a strictly defined psychological diagnosis, but generally means a sense of mental derangement or utter senselessness. The current analyses do suggest that Streicher had the potential to be extremely irrational and may at times have been psychotic; that is, demonstrating an impairment in reality contact, including delusions (false beliefs) and hallucinations (false perceptions). For example, Streicher would talk of supernatural "inner voices" that told him what to do, and he recollected seeing a halo over Hitler's head the first time he heard him speak.

This does not mean that Streicher would have been automatically declared not guilty because of reasons of insanity, although many of his actions were possibly related to an identifiable mental disorder. However, Streicher probably knew right from wrong and there is reason to believe, that although he may have acted many times out of impulse, for the most part he intentionally planned his actions. Furthermore, mental illness per se does not qualify for the insanity defense. His condition during the Nuremberg proceedings does bring up whether he was competent to stand trial and take part in his own defense and his counsel complained that he was unable to get any cooperation. The fact, that Streicher most likely can be considered as having a psychiatric disorder also does not excuse his behavior or trivialize his actions, but it is important to understand that individuals who are emotionally unstable and often irrational, as Streicher was, are capable of assuming a major role in a political movement.

The two Rorschach records presented here clearly suggest that the two subjects varied from normal expectations in a variety of ways with particularly striking evidence in the case of Streicher. Yes, there are some similarities: both Dönitz and Streicher experienced situational stresses related to the upcoming trial, both were attracted to interpersonal situations and sought out social stimulation, both found it very difficult to alter their attitudes or opinions or to view issues from a perspective different than that which they held, and both perceived their environment in an overly simplistic manner. However, while Dönitz did not manifest obvious signs of psychopathology and could be described as a relatively well adjusted individual, Streicher did display clear signs of psychological disturbance. Naturally, one must take into account that Dönitz was acting in a very complex interpersonal field, under a very difficult Führer, and that Streicher was ultimately manipulated by Hitler. Also naturally, one does not need to rely on sophisticated psychological tests to understand that Streicher, as crude a person as there is, and Dönitz, a naval officer, are different, of course they are. Both records differed not only in the degree of adjustment, but also in relationship to the most salient features of their personalities. Although Dönitz and Streicher were both avid National Socialists, their personalities were as different as night and day.

Chapter 9

The Myth of the Nazi Personality

The teacher is faced with the eternal dilemma, whether to present the clear, simple, but inaccurate fact, or the complex, confusing, presumptive truth.

—Karl Menninger

When the preliminary work was begun on this volume, Rudolf Hess had just recently committed suicide in Spandau Prison. At about midpoint in the preparation of this text, the Gulf War "Desert Storm" occurred, with frequent analogies offered between Adolf Hitler's Germany and Sadam Hussein's Iraq, including calls for "Nuremberg-style" war trials against Hussein and high-ranking Iraqi officials. News reports are carrying stories about the rise of neo-Nazism in Germany, particularly as reflected in violence directed toward foreigners. Former East German leader Erich Honecker[1] and five others are being tried in Berlin on charges of manslaughter relating to the deaths of 13 of the more than 200 East Germans killed while trying to flee to the West.[2]

As we conclude our work, civil war rages in what was the nation of Yugoslavia with alarming references to "ethnic cleansing" and concentration camps. In fact, on February 22, 1993, the United Nations Security Council voted unanimously to establish an "International Tribunal to Prosecute Persons Responsible for Human-

---

[1] The charges against Honecker were later dropped because of his severe illness and he was allowed to leave Germany for Chile.

[2] The first verdict, $3\frac{1}{2}$ years in prison for manslaughter, in the trial involving East German border guards accused of shooting to kill at would-be escapees along the Berlin Wall, surpassed the original goal of the prosecution, which had asked for a 2-year suspended sentence. In response to the guards' defense that they were "puppets," following the laws of the German Democratic Republic, Judge Seidel replied that was "simply not justified, the Nazi regime had taught the following generations that those who make the laws can also be in the wrong."

itarian Law Violations in Former Yugoslavia" based on the Nuremberg model (United Nations press release, 1993). Its purpose was to consider all war crimes committed in former Yugoslavia, in accordance with the principles laid down at Nuremberg.

We began this book with an account of the trial of the former SS-Oberscharführer (sergeant) Josef Schwammberger, who stood trial in Stuttgart, Germany, for murders committed between 1941 and 1944 as a commander of forced labor camps in Nazi-occupied Poland. Numerous people have traveled to Stuttgart to testify against the man Simon Wiesenthal called a "beast," including many Holocaust survivors from the United States and Canada. They described murders, beatings, and Schwammberger's penchant for ordering his dog "Prince" to attack prisoners. After a nearly year-long trial, the regional court sentenced the 80-year-old Schwammberger to lifelong imprisonment for committing 25 murders and acting as an accomplice to murder in several 100 cases. Following the sentencing, right-wing extremists gathered outside the courtroom calling for Schwammberger's freedom. Schwammberger said that he "deeply regretted what had happened." This trial brought to an end an era of "big Nazi trials" that included over 19,000 sentences passed in Germany alone.

THE RESURGENCE OF NEO-NAZISM

As we near the close of the 20th century, we reflect that it was 60 years ago that Adolf Hitler was named chancellor and 50 years ago that survivors of Nazi atrocities were liberated by the Allies. Now, 50 years following the fall of the Third Reich, the world appears to face a resurgence of neo-Nazism. In Germany, the process of unification has resulted in the most severe political, economic, and sociological problems since the end of World War II. With the incomplete and, at present, less than successful joining of East and West Germany, this nation may be described ideologically explosive. In particular, East Germany has had the greatest difficulty adapting, with high rates of unemployment and failures in the local business sector. Indeed, the unemployment rate in some areas of East Germany exceeds 20%. Such economic problems can have pervasive effects across generations of Germans. For the elderly, the current economic crises result in everyday commodities suddenly increasing in cost and dramatic decreases in feelings of financial security. The generation of Germans in midlife are confronted with the prospect of unemployment, and adolescents and young adults may feel that they have been cheated out of a meaningful future. It may be particularly the younger generations who have lost a social structure, provided by state organizations (e.g., *Junge Pioniere*), that promoted a sense of social cohesiveness and mutual purpose. As the stress level increases for the younger generation minority right-wing parties have apparently found a fertile soil for their call for a sense of identity based exclusively on nationality.

For the estimated 45,000 to 400,000 neo-Nazis and neo-fascist skinheads, the approximately 6.5 million foreigners living in the total German population of 80 million are the cause of the current painful economic conditions.[3] As a result, there have been an alarming number of violent right-wing attacks, with most incidents occurring within the former area of East Germany where, ironically, only three percent of the foreigners live. In 1992, at least 20 deaths and over 2,285 registered attacks have been attributed to fascist actions, the highest incidence of violent attacks since the conclusion of World War II. Due to these recent events much negative publicity has befallen on the new Germany. Only recently has its government—criticized as being blind in the "right eye"—acted with a clear sense of purpose against the neo-Nazis and moved to ban militant right-wing organizations. Many feel that German law enforcement and legal systems have moved too slowly, particularly when compared to the forceful and rapid actions taken in West Germany against leftist groups in the late 1960s and 1970s. The recent proposed tightening of asylum regulations in Germany—intended primarily to reduce the number of foreigners entering the country to claim asylum—appears to give the impression that the German government is placating right-wing elements, even though the new regulations would be less selective than the immigration standards in most of the European community.[4]

Although xenophobia and right-wing extremism has engendered large scale opposition and demonstrations in most major cities in Germany, there is evidence of substantial sympathy for the neo-Nazi cause by segments of the general public. In confrontations with militant right-wing demonstrators, riot police have occasionally confronted large groups of ordinary citizens who have urged on the radicals. Surveys have indicated that as many as one out of three Germans believe that the Jews were partly to blame for their own persecution during the Nazi era. Sixty percent of the East Germans believe that the presence of foreigners is a significant national problem, whereas 40% of West Germans appear to endorse this view. Current projections indicate that the political right may continue to gain strength if it will be able to clear the five percent political hurdle required in all German states for political representation in the German Parliament. For example, the far-right political party "Republikaner," founded in 1983 and currently headed by former SS leader Franz Schoenhuber, is estimated to have over 20,000 members. In 1992 this party drew 10.9% of the vote and gained 15 seats in the Baden-Württenberg state parliament. Because of its open anti-foreigner programs and the association between this group and violent outbreaks, several recent meetings of the Republikaner have been prohibited by court orders. In the 1994 general elections, however, the "Republikaner," still the largest of the right-wing parties, did poorly. It received less than 2% of the vote, not enough to earn representation in the German Bundestag.

In terms of interpreting contemporary events in Germany, we are often encouraged to understand these phenomena through our understanding of the conflict

---

[3]In 1992, nearly half a million persons applied for asylum, the most ever.

[4]The new regulation was reached through a constitutional amendment. The first time since the founding of the Federal Republic that a basic right was done away with.

which occurred during World War II and the forces that shaped the actions of Nazi Germany. This raises fundamental questions concerning what we believe to be the lessons learned from Nazi Germany and the individuals who participated in that historical drama. It is in this regard that the Rorschach data, which served as the focus of this book, may be of unique value in attempting to understand and evaluate the personality characteristics of those linked to the crimes of the Third Reich. In this chapter, we seek to review both the strengths and weaknesses of these data and to relate the results to other psychological findings from the related field of social psychology and current political events.

THE CONTROVERSY CONTINUES

The painful question of Nazi pathology remains to confront historians of the Third Reich and survivors of the Holocaust. With the 1993 opening of the Holocaust Memorial Museum in Washington, DC, younger generations of Americans are reminded, and sometimes confronted for the first time, with the incomprehensible facts of Nazi Genocide. They ask:

> Were they beasts when they did what they did? Or were they human beings? Can pressures exerted by the environment be so strong as to force us to suspend our moral judgment or act in blatant defiance of it? Is evil done by evil men, or by ordinary people who are responding, not to malevolent drives within themselves, but as creatures of social forces beyond their control; as ordinary men, trapped in an evil situation?

The discussion of the moral basis of Nazi Germany has plagued many historians and social scientists for some time now. Even today the debate is very much alive since our consciences are still troubled. It is related to the idea that the Nazis were perhaps not the pathological demons of a diseased Germany that they were initially made out to be. For many people this issue only has two sides. As one Holocaust survivor stated, "I believe that there are two kinds of people: Those who had the Auschwitz experience, and those who did not. Those who were not in Auschwitz are simply not equipped to understand the value system of those who were there. It is as if each group were speaking a different language on the same subject." This response is entirely understandable, particularly when offered by Holocaust survivors. Most Holocaust survivors today were children during their ordeal. Childhood normally provides moments of great happiness. Unfortunately, during the Holocaust, many children never knew such moments and were forced to endure the unendurable. For those who continue to suffer from it today, it is not mere memories of events that happened in their past. Their pain is still present, many years later, as real as it was on the day it occurred. Such an injury hurts so much, and is so omnipresent, so vast, that it seems impossible to talk about it. One childhood survivor of the Holocaust makes this moving account of her life as "an eternal balance between anger and tears." Another childhood survivor said that "It is in the moment of happiness, that I feel most terrible" (Bettelheim, 1990, p. 216). And now we suggest to those same survivors and their children that many of the Nazis, while engaging in monstrous actions, may not have been monsters. It is, however, important that we re-examine the Third Reich as objectively as possible because by studying the past we may be able to understand the present, and most importantly prepare for the future. We must study the record and learn our lessons.

A very wide range of conclusions has been drawn from the Rorschach data concerning the psychological state of Nazi war criminals. Insofar as a theory of a Nazi personality is concerned, for example, the Eichmann trial may have had more widespread effect on social philosophy than did the Nuremberg trials. Thus, much of this controversy was brought on by the Rorschach record of Adolf Eichmann and Arendt's resulting thesis of banality outlined in *Eichmann in Jerusalem*. It was further fueled by Harrower's article on the Nazi Rorschachs. Selzer (1977), for one, suggested that Arendt "was entirely mistaken" and that Harrower was "entirely erroneous." He further discounted Kelley's contribution as one that was biased because of Kelley's favorable disposition towards the Nazis. "Why is belief in the normality of the Nazis so persistent?" Selzer asked (1977).

Selzer, it can be submitted, missed the point. Suggesting that many of the Nazis may not have been as disturbed clinically as one would expect, given their actions alone, does not suggest that all Nazis were normal. Diagnostic labels are unlikely to account for the complex parameters Hitler used in selecting leaders for his grandiose schemes (McCully, 1980). Furthermore, it does not reduce their responsibility of the actions because it is the madman who may not be able to judge his actions, not the ordinary person. Perhaps the dichotomy of these issues is related to Arendt's definition of "normality" as the absence of any clear psychiatric disturbance. McCully (1980), in fact, disagreed with Arendt's conclusion on Eichmann. He argued that "Eichmann's manner of processing his percepts and certain of his [Rorschach] images themselves, leave in question the validity of his having fit Arendt's proposition, much less having qualified as the prototype who formed the basis for it." Although McCully's interpretations may have been limited in perspective, given that they are based exclusively on interpretations of the content of Rorschach responses, they are relatively robust when compared with Selzer's (1977) interpretation of Eichmann's psychological test drawings. Selzer argued in *The Murderous Mind* that Eichmann's psychological drawings (including the Bender-Gestalt and House, Tree, Person) were "Germanic" belonging to "people who do bad things." Eichmann may not have been the normal "prototype" that Arendt made him out to be, but by most accounts he was far less psychiatrically disturbed and closer to normal than almost everybody would have thought. In this context, the notion of "the banality of evil" does have merit since it stands in contradiction to the prevalent theory of a single Nazi personality—aggressive, militaristic, disciplined, undemocratic, and anti-Semitic in nature.

In contrast to Arendt, Miale and Selzer (1975) found what they believe to be uniform and pervasive evidence of psychopathology among these defendants. These authors concluded that the 16 Nazi protocols presented in their text were "not psychologically normal" and "deemed to constitute, from a psychological standpoint, a highly distinctive group." Selzer (1976, 1977) argued that a small group of fanatic and emotionally disturbed individuals within Germany (a "violently aberrant" group estimated by Selzer to constitute perhaps 10% of the German population) was responsible for the events and atrocities of World War II. Selzer was aware of the arguments that Nazis could be "normal" individuals who behaved as they did because of highly abnormal social structures, but rejected this view as being equivalent to the arguments provided by the defense attorneys of the Nuremberg defendants that these individuals were only "following orders." Similarly, Gilbert (1963) argued, in a quite general and global manner, that a "cultivated personality style" existed among Nazi organizations such as the SS that selected for, and reinforced, personality traits marked by extreme authoritarianism, racially based ideology, and brutal indifference to the suffering of others. Thus, from the perspective of Selzer, Gilbert, and many others, the basic assumption was that the behaviors of the Nuremberg defendants and others in the Nazi leadership represented deviant and aberrant behaviors resulting from marked psychopathology. Such a theory, if in fact accurate, excludes everyday citizens from responsibility, if they did not demonstrate any of those characteristics.

Although the view that the defendants were inherently psychopathological probably resonated with the general view of the Allies in the postwar period, it was also important to many individuals, including the prosecution team at Nuremberg, to demonstrate that the Nuremberg defendants were not "too" insane. For example, there was much concern at the Nuremberg trials that three of the defendants, including Rudolf Hess, might claim insanity as a defense. Thus, particularly in the case of Hess, substantial behavioral and Rorschach evidence of very disturbed and potentially psychotic behavior was discounted because such evidence might serve as an effective defense in the legal proceedings. This point is illustrated by Taylor, a senior member of the prosecution team at Nuremberg and author of the 1992 text *The Anatomy of the Nuremberg Trials*. Taylor (1992) offered the opinion that Hess was "quite unable to defend himself and should not have been tried" (p. 12).

A contrasting perspective developed on the interpretation of the Rorschach materials of the Nuremberg group which did not accept the view of a homogeneous "Nazi personality type" marked by substantial and inevitable psychopathology. For example, Kelley (1946b) argued that the individuals evaluated in Nuremberg were neither insane nor even unique, but could be "duplicated in any country of the world today." Kelley went on to suggest: "We must also realize that such personalities exist in this country, and that there are undoubtedly some individuals who would willingly climb over the corpses of one half of the people of the United States if, by doing so, they could thereby be given control of the other half." Harrower (1976a) essentially concurred with Kelley's conclusion. She noted that "differences in the Nazi Rorschach records greatly outweighed any similarities" and that most of the Rorschach records would not be classified as being produced by emotionally disturbed respondents if blindly reviewed by Rorschach experts. Ritzler, as well as Zillmer and his colleagues, have tended to occupy a more "middle ground" view that emphasizes the broad range of psychopathology exhibited by these defendants, while de-emphasizing any commonalities or homogeneous group characteristics that would apply to all of these individuals.

Indeed, the search for a common personality type has not been restricted to the Nazi leadership, but has also occupied modern psychiatry and psychology in terms of the search for homogeneous personality characteristics that could be related to: Individuals prone to abuse or became addicted to drugs (i.e., the addictive personality), child abusers, serial killers, and even such groups as medical students and homosexuals. All of these pursuits for what were believed to be homogeneous personality traits connected with each of these groups initially appear promising, only to prove to be much more complex and heterogeneous after prolonged research investigation.

THE QUEST FOR THE NAZI PERSONALITY

Nevertheless, our current study did identify a number of personality traits that may have served as predisposing factors for having participated in Third Reich atrocities. These personality characteristics are not universally pathological, in the clinical or psychiatric sense (although they may be maladaptive in certain circumstances), but collectively they may represent a general susceptibility to the influences of the Nazi movement. For example, an overall sense of common personality characteristics were found among the rank-and-file as well as the Nazi elite including an oversimplification in information processing, an inconsistent and therefore ineffective problem-solving style, altered self-esteem, and a diminished regard for the "human" qualities of experience.

Particularly striking among the Nazi protocols studied in this text were the observed deficiencies in cognitive resources that are typically considered necessary for effective stress management. Many of the Nazis (both the elite and rank-and-file collaborators), it can be concluded, were not high-level, creative thinkers and may have had difficulties making their own decisions. As such, they were vulnerable to becoming "stressed out" and for demonstrating a reduced capacity for stress tolerance. Undoubtedly, situational stressors may have contributed to this observed impairment. Nevertheless, when situational variables were taken into consideration, it became relatively clear that the Nazi war criminals' stress reaction was not a function of the acute turmoil of the war crimes trials, but instead a function of their chronically low stress tolerance related to their insufficient personality resources for coping with stress. As a result many of them may have needed an increased amount of structure, guidance, and reassurance in their occupational and social lives, which in turn the Nazi structure may have provided for them. Such individuals, it can be argued, must have been particularly attracted to the rigid and quasi-military structure of the Nazi hierarchy including "following orders."

One of the many myths about the Nazi personality has centered around the Nazis being interpersonally cold and socially aloof. Although many of them showed signs of social skills deficits, we also found, however, that a majority of them were not unresponsive to close, supportive interpersonal relationship. In fact, many of them may have actually felt deprived of close, personal affiliations, which one may speculate was gratified by their membership to a Nazi affiliation. Thus, the "brotherhood" of many of the Nazi sponsored organizations may have served as a substitute for this perceived need for interpersonal intimacy. In this sense, the affiliate needs were gratified by organizational rather than interpersonal involvement.

A further important finding is related to the Nazis' perception of themselves. Current results suggests that the rank-and-file Nazis may have been rather self-effacing and lacking in confidence, while many of the Nazi elite may have felt overconfident (e.g., Göring; Kennedy & Rosenberg, 1993). Thus, a majority of the rank-and-file gave percepts on the Rorschach of being personally damaged or disadvantaged. This is a particularly important observation because it is consistent with their frequently used defense that they were simply "victims of circumstance." In contrast, the Nazi elite very frequently demonstrated increased self-esteem that may have included a sense of entitlement and an overvaluing of self. Such an egocentric style would explain, in part, why many of the Nazi elite viewed themselves as particularly important, to the extreme degree that they considered others as *Untermenschen* (subhumans) not worthy of existing.

In addition, the Nazis as a group (i.e., both the rank-and-file as well as the elite) showed a consistent tendency toward a problem-solving style psychologists describe as "ambitent." The ambitent individual is particularly inefficient in their problem-solving style and is associated with people who have no "mind of their own" or are lacking "an internal compass." Ambitents rely heavily on others as well as on an external structure for guidance in problem solving. Thus, a great majority of the Nazis that were given the psychological records, can be described as ineffectual problem solvers, who were easily influenced by others. These results do, in a general way, support the research findings on conformity reported by Asch and obedience to authority reported by Milgram (reviewed in chap. 1). Very few of the Nazis showed well-established, but reasonably adaptable problem solving styles, that may have been more resistant to Nazi propaganda.

Our results did not confirm the stereotype that the Nazis were psychotic monsters. Although a majority of the Nazi protocols demonstrated unusual thought patterns, only very few Nazi records can be described as psychotic, bizarre, or severely disturbed. Nevertheless, there was evidence in a majority of the records that suggested a propensity for interpreting one's surroundings in a highly simplistic and often unconventional fashion. One could speculate that such a cognitive style draws on inaccurate stereotypes that may take the form of prejudice. This is an important realization because it assumes that the Nazis were not necessarily overwhelmed with sadism and aggression, but rather engaged in an overly simplistic and unconventional cognitive style. Such an approach to one's world can be described as rigid, eccentric, or inefficient, and is consistent with the bigotry of the Nazi propaganda. This finding is also consistent with Arendt's notion of the banality, that is the lack of personal and cognitive depth.

Finally, the present findings also do not confirm the notion of the Nazi sadism. Indeed, there was association between Rorschach indices of sadism and violence associated with an involvement in atrocities, but not to a degree that would explain the violence of the majority of the Nazis. The current results strongly suggest that many ordinary people became involved in violent acts.

One could conclude that the above characteristics may serve as the foundations of a definable "Nazi Personality." This would be too simple of an interpretation, however, for the obvious reason that there was great variability even among those personality constructs that were most prevalent in our Nazi sample and few, if any, Rorschach records contain all the characteristics identified previously. Furthermore, many important other features of personality were not found to be systematically related at all. Differences between the rank-and-file Nazis and the Nazi elite were for the most part not related to personality traits per se, but rather to socioeconomic factors including education, occupation, and social class.

One conclusion that can be firmly drawn from these analysis is related to the myth that the Nazis were highly disturbed and clinically deranged individuals. The current analysis clearly suggests that a majority of the Nazis were not deranged in the clinical sense and that the above described common personality characteristics, while undesirable to many, are not pathological in and of themselves and are actually frequently found in the U.S. population. Thus, as a group, the Nazis were not the hostile sadists many made them out to be. Yet, they were not a collection of random humans either. While the differences among the Nazis studied here far outweigh any similarities, and a Nazi personality cannot be simply defined in strict terms, the above personality traits may nevertheless serve as predisposing characteristics. In this sense the presence of them may make individuals more vulnerable to the influences of a Nazi movement, or for that matter, any political movement. These personality traits are, however, not considered diagnosable. We must therefore conclude that under certain social conditions, just about anyone could have joined the Nazi movement, but that there were individuals who were more likely to join.

THE QUEST FOR THE ALTRUISTIC PERSONALITY

The current search for a homogeneous evil Nazi personality has been, for the most part, an unsuccessful one. Our results suggest that Nazis came in a variety of forms. Would it not prove more meaningful perhaps to examine those individuals who actively resisted the Nazi movement? That is, rather than attempting to understand evilness, it may be appropriate to focus on what makes people behave good. Certainly much has been suggested about the indifference of the general German population to the suffering of others. And yet 50 years later there are individuals beginning to emerge from the terrible history of Nazi Germany who not only saw the horror around them but also risked their lives out of compassion for its victims. Some took great risks by daring to hide Jews in their houses, apartments, or on their farms. Others may have just looked the other way at a check point or slipped some food to those in need. The principle or practice of unselfish concern for or devotion to the welfare of others is known as altruism, as opposed to egotism, a trait we did find in many of the Nazi war criminals.

Why did those who offered help refuse to hide behind the mask of the innocent bystander? A recent analysis of 105 rescuers from 10 different countries (Oliner & Oliner, 1988) suggested that those who demonstrated a "conspiracy of goodness" where relatively ordinary people who demonstrated normal human compassion rather than a special kind of heroism. "We did not think about it, you started off storing a suitcase for a friend, and before you knew it, you were in over your head" said Johtje Vos, age 82, who with her husband saved dozens of Jews in Holland. "We did what any human being would have done," she concluded.

Tec (1986), who studied the Christian rescue of Jews in Nazi-occupied Poland, suggested a series of interrelated characteristics. She noted, for example, that many of the rescuers were individualists who may have been less constrained by the expectations of what society demands at that moment. As such they were more willing to act on their own. In addition, Tec found that many of the rescuers had a history of doing good deeds before the war, including visiting sick individuals in the hospital, caring for the poor, or assisting stray animals. However, a history of helping per se seems not to have protected German physicians. For example, by 1942, 38,000 doctors—one-half of the total in Germany—were members of the Nazi Party and many of those chose to end, rather than preserve, millions of lives. The rescuers are naturally aware that incidents of fellow citizens in Germany, Poland, France, or elsewhere rescuing Jews were the exception rather than the rule. But nevertheless they insist on the "banality of their heroism." To single them out as unusual suggests that there was something abnormal about them, that ordinary people could not engage in this form of helping behavior. This analogy is strikingly similar to the one discussed in this text about the elusive Nazi personality. If one insists that the perpetrators of Nazi atrocities were monsters and that the rescuers were paragons, it would let the rest of humanity off the hook!

In this respect we learn similar lessons from acts of goodness as we do from acts of evilness. Thus, one is confronted with the same difficulty of forcing the rescuers into any specific category, such as altruist. They included the rich and the poor, the educated and the illiterate, believers and atheists. In general, simple terms there were no common personality traits that could explain the behavior of those individuals who became rescuers. One can only conclude that the "gift of goodness" and the "propensity for evilness" is accessible to many individuals. If it were not, it would exclude everyday citizens from their responsibility to perform altruistic behaviors.

If the rescuers were the dormant heroes who often were undistinguishable from those around them, perhaps one may find a different pattern in those who were well known for their resistance against the Third Reich. Indeed, those who resisted the Nazi movement did so with full knowledge of the dangers involved and often did so as part of an organized movement (Kren & Rappoport, 1981). One well-known resistance was the Warsaw Ghetto uprising. This first major resistance mounted on the Nazi-occupied continent took place in the city with Europe's largest Jewish population. Established by the Nazis in 1940 the Ghetto, a walled-in section of several hundred square blocks, held over a quarter million Jews, but the population rose to over a half a million as Jews were brought in from outlying areas. By spring

1943 the size of the Ghetto was reduced to approximately 60,000 mostly related to the shipping of its inhabitants to death camps. On April 19, 1943, German troops in armored vehicles were prepared to enter the Ghetto. Bracing for this final Nazi assault, the resistance fighters, responded with a hail of bullets and grenades. The German SS, ill prepared for guerrilla tactics, initially withdrew, but returned with artillery, airplanes, and flame throwers to level the entire Ghetto block by block. In the end, Hitler's war machine needed a month to subdue a small contingent of under-armed and under-trained Jewish resistance fighters. On May 16, the German troops pronounced that the "Jewish Quarter of Warsaw no longer existed." However, a few dozen resistance fighters made their way to safety to continue their fight. In 1977, the last surviving commander of the Warsaw Ghetto uprising was Marek Edelman, then age 74 and a respected cardiologist and social leader in Lodz, Poland. Edelman helped smuggle weapons to the resistance fighters, spied on German troops, and served as one of five top commanders of the Jewish Fighting Organizations of the Ghetto. In May 1943 he escaped the Ghetto and joined the citywide uprising in 1944 as well as the rescue of Jews in the Nazi-occupied capital (Gutman, 1994). No question, Edelman was prepared to die for his cause, but he refused to be cast in the light of a hero. "Yes, I was ready to die. So what? I wasn't then a hero ... and ... I don't live now as a hero," he shrugged in disgust when questioned about his role in the uprising. Many disagree, like those who anonymously send him bouquets of flowers every year on April 19, the anniversary of the uprising. But like many of the other less visible rescuers, Edelman spurned the hero status explaining simply that "times were different" and that it "was the right thing to do."

The rescuers and resistance fighters informed us that their involvement during the Third Reich grew out of the ways in which they ordinarily related to other people. They reminded us that such courage is not only the province of the independent, intellectually superior thinker or the altruist, but is available to many through the virtues developed in ordinary human interactions (Oliner & Oliner, 1988). In this sense, those who assisted Hitler in atrocities craved power, not morality, and those who could have opposed him were normal men, not heroes (Gordon, 1984).

OTHER PSYCHOLOGICAL PERSPECTIVES

Are there, in fact, lawful relationships between psychopathology and the propensity for violence that form the theoretical basis for the mad Nazi theory? In discussing the relationship between aggressive and violent behavior in psychopathology, Megargee (1984) underscored that violence is not necessarily related to psychopathology and commented: "Although a variety of functional and organic disturbances can lead to aggression and violent behavior, most violence is committed by people suffering from no diagnosable impairment. Even if we exclude legal, socially condoned forms of violence such as warfare, we find criminal violence is often performed by normal people for rational motives" (p. 523).

Megargee's point is that psychopathology is not a necessary precursor for violent behavior, even the type of aggression and violence typically manifested by criminals. Most violent individuals are not mentally ill, and the vast majority of the mentally ill are not prone to violent or aggressive acts. The author notes that if the average individual could not be prevailed upon to engage in violence, nations would be unable to raise effective military forces to provide a viable national defense. Thus, almost all individuals can be placed within a situational context in which they will engage in violent or aggressive behavior. However, virtually all psychology students are eventually taught the basic psychological concept that behavior is a function of the interaction of personality factors or traits and situational stimuli. Put within the context of our discussion, violent or aggressive behavior may be seen as a product of the individual's long-term tendency to engage in violent behavior combined with situational variables likely to increase the probability of a violent response. Although psychopathology can affect or influence the individual's predisposition to engage in violent behaviors, Megargee noted that in many cultures children, especially male children, are generally raised to be aggressive and, in certain situations, violent. The author also noted a variety of situational factors that increase the probability of violence or aggression, including the behavior of the victims, the behavior of other members of the aggressor's peer group, the occurrence of opportunities to engage in violence, and the availability of weapons. As a result, violence is often performed by ordinary, rather than psychiatric disturbed people for very rational, rather than irrational reasons.

This point is reinforced by Browning (1992) in his text entitled, *Ordinary Men: Reserve Police Battalion 101 and the Final Solution in Poland*. Browning convincingly described how 500 seemingly ordinary men became killers, by shooting or deporting nearly 85,000 Jews in wartime Poland. By studying archival documents, including court records, indictments, verbatim quotations, and pretrial interrogations of the decade-long prosecution (1962–1972) of Reserve Police Battalion 101 in West-Germany, the author commented that he had never before "seen the monstrous deeds of the Holocaust so starkly juxtaposed with the human faces of the killers" (p. xvi). Browning questioned whether it required brutal men to perform in the brutalized context of war. These men were not part of the Nazi elite and were not Nazi bureaucrats whose jobs could be performed without confronting the reality of mass murder. No, these rank-and-file men "were quite literally saturated in the blood of victims shot at point-blank range" (p. 162).

Browning concluded that the members of the Police Battalion did not act out of frenzy, bitterness, or frustration, but with calculation. In fact, by age, geographical origin, and social background the men of Reserve Police Battalion 101 were least likely to be considered apt material out of "which to mold future mass killers" (p. 164). They were middle-aged, working-class and did not represent any special selection (e.g., violence prone), but perhaps even negative selection, given their status as reservists of dubious political reliability. Browning pointed out that not anyone in the same situation would have done as the majority of the members of the Police Battalion 101 did (i.e., 80%), and in fact not all men participated in the killing. Nevertheless, Browning concluded, "If the men of Reserve Police Battalion

101 could become killers under such circumstances, what group of men cannot?" (p. 189).

Clinical psychologists, because of their emphasis on the individual's personality traits and characteristics, have typically focused on intrinsic individual character-istics in understanding the origins of antisocial or violent behavior, while paying less attention to the situational factors (including cultural and sociological vari-ables) involved in this phenomenon. Relating to this point, it is interesting to note that the diagnostic label used to describe individuals prone to antisocial behavior has changed several times over the past 50 years, reflecting a confusion and debate concerning the origins of antisocial behavior. The terms *sociopath* and *psychopath* are often used interchangeably in describing the antisocial personality, but each term places a different emphasis on the causes of such behaviors. The term *sociopath* places emphasis on the social and environmental forces hypothesized to shape and maintain antisocial behavior, whereas the term *psychopath* places the primary causation of such behaviors within the personality structure and function-ing of the individual. The fourth version of the *Diagnostic and Statistical Manual–Revised* (*DSM–IV*) of the American Psychiatric Association (1994) has moved away from this etiological conflict by the use of antisocial personality disorder as a more appropriate and descriptive alternative to both the sociopath and psychopath terminology. If the violent, aggressive, and antisocial behaviors displayed by the Nuremberg defendants are not exclusively attributable to gross psychopathology, psychopathy, or homogeneous personality characteristics, then to what other influ-ences or factors can such behaviors be attributed?

CONCLUSION

Before we place too much emphasis on the Nazi Rorschach data, it is necessary to mention a number of limitations and weaknesses that limit the use of these data. It should be noted, for example, that the Nuremberg Rorschachs (and to a lesser extent those reported by Ritzler on Danish collaborators and German Military Occupa-tional Personnel) were not consistent with modern standards of administration. At Nuremberg, Rorschach protocols were collected by Kelley and by Gilbert (some prisoners produced protocols for both), and each of these examiners had substantial administration problems. Kelley, by far the more accomplished Rorschach expert, did not speak German fluently and required the services of an interpreter in order to accomplish the administrations. In contrast, Gilbert was fluent in German, but it appears that his understanding of the Rorschach was substantially limited in contrast to Kelley's mastery of it. By modern standards, the inquiry used in these Rorschach records was often restricted or even occasionally nonexistent and did not permit complete and adequate scoring of all of the Rorschach protocols.

Because of these inadequacies, as well as changes in scoring criteria over the years, there are reliability problems in scoring of these protocols as manifested in some disagreement among Rorschach experts who have reviewed the protocols. This latter issue is illustrated, for example, by the scoring interpretation differences found for the same Rorschach protocols as seen in the review by Zillmer and his colleagues in 1989 in contrast to the work published in 1991 by Resnick and Nunno (Ritzler, Zillmer, & Belevich, 1993). It is important to note that even when protocols are scored reliably, these protocols would still be "underscored" because of the limitations of the inquiry procedure used in the original administrations. Perhaps a reasonable way of thinking about these protocols is that they represent very valuable materials through which to gain a unique insight into the personality characteristics of both high ranking Nazi officials and those of the rank-and-file, but their use requires much labor in order to piece together the potential pool of information represented in these records.

Another limitation in the interpretation of these data concerns the tendency to overgeneralize findings from the Nuremberg defendants to the psychological functioning of other groups. Borofsky and Brand (1980) specifically noted this issue in their discussion of methodology problems related to the interpretation of the Rorschach findings from the Nuremberg group. These authors stated:

> It must be kept in mind that the Nuremberg war trial criminals are probably not a representative sample of Nazis. As a group the Nuremberg war trial criminals represent individuals who were successful, high-level administrators and leaders. One can raise serious questions as to whether conclusions drawn from the Rorschach records of the Nuremberg war trial criminals are generalizable to the psychological functioning of Nazis as a population. For this reason we would very much like to encourage research that uses the Rorschach records of Nazis in addition to the Nuremberg war trial criminals. (p. 400)

Ritzler's data is so important in this latter regard, because it provides information on nearly 200 Nazi collaborators, a much larger and potentially more representative group than the very select group of Nuremberg defendants.

Not only were the Nuremberg war trial criminals a very small and heterogeneous group, but the Rorschach protocols were administered to individuals under uniquely stressful conditions. The Nuremberg defendants had watched their country disintegrate, with all the major social institutions of Germany in collapse, and many of the defendants were awaiting a grim and foreseeable outcome: Death sentences from the tribunal. Despite all of these issues, many authors have generalized findings from the Nuremberg war trial group to "Nazis in general" and, occasionally, even to a German national character. On the level of scientific inquiry, confusion concerning the generalization of data from these individuals is also exhibited by researchers in decisions concerning whether the data are treated individually or on a group basis. Expressed most directly, should the researcher average findings to generate group means and standard deviations, or should each individual Rorschach record be treated as a "separate group?" If this group consisted of unique individuals, group level data (such as mean values) would be misleading and may not accurately represent any single member of the group.

A further restriction of the current data is related to the potential difficulty in attempting to sort out transient or "state" personality characteristics from long-term, enduring trait personality characteristics and features as manifested in the

Rorschach protocols of the Nuremberg defendants. To illustrate this point, almost all individuals will experience a state of anxiety if placed under intense and prolonged stress, but individuals who maintain a high level of trait anxiety are particularly vulnerable to this emotion when placed under even relatively low levels of stress, and the term *anxious* may be accurately applied as a descriptor for these latter individuals. As previously noted, all of the Nuremberg group were imprisoned, all tried on serious offenses, and most being tried on capital offenses with a reasonable expectation of eventual execution. Yet, the personality characteristics shown by the Nuremberg group, despite the very unique context of these Rorschach administrations, has often been linked to these individuals' antisocial behaviors occurring from several years to several decades prior to the Rorschach administration. Without a longitudinal series of Rorschach administrations, the question of whether such features as depression, antisocial personality characteristics, or unusual/schizoid thinking represents an acute response to the circumstances surrounding the trial, or to more longstanding features predating these circumstances, cannot be answered with certainty for many of this group. It does seem possible, however, to offer reasonable speculations in selected individual cases, when biographical data is sufficiently rich and descriptive, concerning the individual's life experiences over an extended period of time.

Perhaps the most striking problem in evaluating these data is the degree of bias which has often been present in the interpretation of these protocols, compounded by the lack of clearly stated hypotheses. It is likely that all researchers have some preconceived notions about what these Rorschach protocols should reveal and an "unbiased" review of these protocols is not possible. The use of clearly stated research hypotheses would, however, have made explicit the hidden assumptions and preconceptions of a researcher's agenda. Research perspectives on these data have ranged widely: From Harrower's view that these protocols represent an average group of U.S. citizens, to the viewpoint of Gilbert and others that these protocols display very marked psychopathology and antisocial characteristics. Indeed, Gilbert's (1948a, 1963) titles for many of his publications (e.g., *The Mentality of SS Murderous Robots* or *Göring, Amiable Psychopath*) leaves little doubt concerning his overall perception of these individuals and the fact that he disliked most of them, especially Göring (Taylor, 1992). Unquestionably, the actions of the Nuremberg war trial criminals would stir emotions which were likely to tempt even the most objective individual to revert to subjective interpretations when dealing with this sample. As noted by Borofsky and Brand (1980), however, "if one starts off with an a priori assumption that the Nuremberg war trial criminals were psychologically disturbed, then any clustering of responses ... will be interpreted as indicating that these individuals were psychologically disturbed, independent of the validity of such a statement" (p. 381). The tendency to readily identify evidence of psychopathology in Rorschach responses is particularly seductive to psychologists and other mental health clinicians who are typically better trained at focusing on psychopathology than on normality.

This point is unfortunately well illustrated in the nationally publicized investigation of the tragedy related to the battleship USS Iowa. On April 19, 1989, an explosion occurred in gun turret No. 2 of the USS Iowa. This explosion killed 47 U.S. Navy sailors entrapped within the gun-turret when five 94-pound bags of powder ignited while being loaded into the open breech of a 16-inch gun. The Navy sought to identify the causes of the explosion in an extensive investigation following the accident. After initially ruling out the possibility of accidental or unintentional causes for the explosion, the Navy's investigation of the USS Iowa incident centered on the possibility of an intentional act of sabotage. Extensive interviews and investigations were conducted by the Naval Investigative Service (NIS), and these data were, in turn, provided to FBI specialists at the National Center for the Analysis of Violent Crime. In this investigation FBI behavioral scientists testified before Congressional House and Senate Subcommittees that their analysis of the background and investigative information available on one of the sailors killed in this explosion led them to the unequivocal conclusion (with complete certainty) that this disaster was the result of a homicidal/suicidal action on the part of this Iowa crewman.

   This interpretation was widely criticized from a variety of sources, and the U.S. House of Representatives Armed Services Committee invited the American Psychological Association to appoint a special panel of experts (which included Archer) to review the NIS evidence and decision of the FBI behavioral scientists. The 12 panelists were selected based on their credentials and expertise in areas including suicidology, forensic psychology, personality assessment, and the assessment of factors related to the occurrence of violence. In addition to the panelists selected by the American Psychological Association, two psychiatrists were appointed by the House Armed Services Committee, to ultimately form a panel of 14 members. The Committee asked the panelists to comment on the validity of the Navy's conclusions, the adequacy of the database used by the Navy, any conclusions that could be drawn concerning the personality characteristics of the accused, and an estimate of the validity of the approach taken by the Navy and FBI in determining the posthumous determination of suicidal tendencies of the accused Navy sailor. Each of the 14 panelists worked independently, and submitted a written report to the House Armed Services Committee. Six of these panelists (five psychologists including Archer and one psychiatrist) were requested to testify before the Investigations Subcommittee of the Armed Services Committee on December 21, 1989. A clear majority of the panelists (11) were critical both of the Navy's investigation of the incident and the conclusions drawn by the Navy and FBI based on this evidence. Following these committee hearings, the investigation into the USS Iowa incident was reopened. The murder/suicide hypothesis was largely discounted following the subsequent discovery that such an explosion could be accounted for by an accident scenario in simulation tests conducted by independent experts at Sandia National Laboratories.

   The Navy and FBI initial investigation provides strong evidence for the pervasive effects of bias in the interpretation of psychological data. Just as Miale, Selzer, and Gilbert began with the assumption that the Nuremberg group must have been psychologically disturbed, and then found ample evidence to support this conclusion in the records of all the defendants, the FBI behavioral scientists began with the assumption that the USS Iowa gun turret explosion could only be accounted for by the sabotage of a homicidal/suicidal and allegedly homosexual sailor. Unsurprisingly, they found ample evidence of such suicidal and homicidal impulses based on the interpretations of what were, in many cases, relatively normal developmentally related life events. In a recent review of the lessons to be learned from the USS Iowa incident, Poythress, Otto, Darkes, and Starr (1993) offered conclusions that might also be relevant to those reviewing the Nuremberg Rorschach protocols. These authors stated:

> Although psychologists and other mental health professionals clearly have expertise in many aspects of human behavior, this expertise has limits. We are obliged to define our expertise carefully and to note our limitations. This is particularly necessary when the stakes are so high and the effects of errors so great as in the case of EDA (Equivocal Death Analysis), psychological autopsies, and psychological profiling. The repercussions of the USS Iowa explosion and investigation demonstrate this very clearly. We should tread slowly and carefully when entering such relatively uncharted waters: To do any less would be a disservice to the public and to our profession. (p. 14)

Another type of limitation related to the Rorschach protocols discussed in this book is the issue of the complexities involved in cross-cultural assessment. This issue has been recently discussed by Potash, Crespo, Patel, and Ceralvolo (1990) in the following quote:

> Responses to projective techniques can be viewed as reflecting the underlying personality dynamics of the subjects as well as their family psychodynamics. It is also possible to see individuals' test responses as reflecting their particular culture or society, because the individual's view of the world is largely shaped by the overall culture. Consequently, individuals raised in different cultures are likely to have different perceptions of the world; those differences should be revealed in varying response patterns to projective techniques. (p. 657)

The degree to which the definitions and meanings of psychopathology are dependent upon cultural or societal standards has been subject to substantial debate. As noted by Butcher and Bemis (1984), there have been at least three major approaches to this complex issue. The relativistic view of psychopathology, originally stemming from the work of anthropologists in the 1930s and 1940s postulates that "psychopathology" is always related to social acts conducted within the bounds of cultural values and beliefs. In the relativistic view abnormal behavior may be said to be whatever a particular group defines as beyond the bounds of acceptable or normal behavior. Thus, the meaning of abnormal behavior varies from culture to culture with little cross-cultural consistency. The same behaviors that would result in a label of schizophrenia in a western culture, for example, may result in the perception of a religious prophet in a non-western culture. Among the Nuremberg defendants, Dönitz appears to refer to this relativistic perspective in his final presentation at the Nuremberg trial which was as follows: "If I have incurred guilt in any way, then this was chiefly in the sense that in spite of my purely military position I should perhaps have not only been a soldier, but up to a certain point a politician, which, however, was in contradiction to my entire career and the tradition of the German Armed Forces" (Taylor, 1992, p. 541).

The relativistic position was also part of the defense offered by Hoess, the commandant of Auschwitz,[5] in an interview with Gilbert described in a recent text on the Holocaust by Porpora (1990). Hoess was asked by Gilbert if he considered not obeying orders and he responded:

> No, from our entire training the thought of refusing an order just didn't enter ones head, regardless of what kind of an order it was. ... Guess you cannot understand our world. I naturally had to obey orders and I must now stand to take the consequences. ... At that time there were no consequences to consider. It didn't even occur to me at all that I could be held responsible. You see, in Germany, it was understood that if something went wrong, then the man who gave the orders was responsible. So I didn't think that I would have to answer for it myself. (p. 17)

In contrast, a second approach to the definition of abnormal behavior postulates that there is a single, cross-cultural set of diagnostic criteria that can be applied across diverse societies and cultures. From this perspective, for example, it is noted that the occurrence of hallucinations, delusions, and disorientation characterized abnormal behavior in almost all cultures and societies. Although the specific symptoms related to a disorder may vary somewhat across cultures, most of the salient behaviors associated with a particular form of abnormal behavior can be consistently found cross-culturally.

A third approach to defining abnormal behavior is described by Butcher and Bemis (1984) as beginning to supplant both the relativistic and absolutist perspectives. This third view maintains that it is possible to distinguish between individual psychopathology and culturally bound or determined deviance. The former is capable of evaluation on a cross-cultural basis with reference to standard indices of psychological functioning, whereas the latter form of deviance must be assessed in reference to the specific culture within which it occurs. For example, the violent and aggressive actions of the Nuremberg war trial criminals could be reflective of individual psychopathology that may have provoked such behaviors regardless of the cultural or societal norms these individuals found themselves within. Or such behaviors may have resulted from unique cultural and societal definitions, values, attitudes, and contingencies that promoted such behaviors. To complicate the issue further, it is also possible that the behaviors of the Nuremberg war trial criminals and others of the Nazi leadership may have represented combinations of both individual psychopathology and societal conditions which perpetrated behaviors and attitudes viewed as deviant by other cultures. The central importance of the Rorschach protocols discussed in this text relate to the issue of the possibility of making a distinction between individual psychopathology versus cultural deviancy in the etiology of the actions of the Nuremberg group.

---

[5] Also see *Kommandant in Auschwitz* (Broszat, 1963).

It should also be noted that the Rorschach protocols not only involve cross-cultural issues, but also cross-sectional sampling issues because these protocols were collected nearly 50 years ago. A unique cultural and historical context surround these data. Despite these observations, several studies of these Rorschach protocols have employed control groups or normative groups based upon contemporary samples of data collected in the United States. Ritzler (1978), however, made a concerted effort to deal with these issues by using several subject groups including subjects over 35 years of age (to be reasonably comparable to the Nuremberg war trial group that had a mean age of 54 years) and collected in the 1940s, as well as the use of Rorschach markers or techniques derived from Rorschach research in Germany during the 1930s. Despite the best efforts in this area, however, it is impossible to adequately control for historical and cultural factors that may have shaped or influenced the subtleties of the Rorschach responses of the Nuremberg group.

Finally, scientific progress in the analysis of the Rorschach protocols discussed in this book has been hampered by the use of very different Rorschach scoring systems, research perspectives, and research methodologies. This issue deals with an inevitable problem given the very substantial changes and improvements in our understanding of Rorschach data over the past decades. Miale and Selzer (1975) utilized a content approach to Rorschach interpretation, Harrower (1976a) used the Klopfer scoring system, Ritzler (1978) used the Rappaport and Beck systems of Rorschach interpretation and Zillmer et al. (1989) and Resnick and Nunno (1991) used the now popular Comprehensive System of Rorschach interpretation developed over the past 20 years by Exner and his colleagues. Combined with these differences in scoring and interpretive systems, no two groups of researchers used the Rorschach data in an identical manner. Ritzler (1978) emphasized the use of a between-group research design, whereas Harrower emphasized discrimination of the individual Rorschach protocols from the Nuremberg group with individual control group protocols based on the judgments of experts in the Rorschach field. Zillmer and his colleagues emphasized the use of an objective computerized interpretation system as applied to individual Rorschach records as a means of attempting to control for the subjective biases that enter in the interpretation of Rorschach records from this unique group of individuals. Ritzler's contributions to this area in his evaluation of the Rorschach records of Danish collaborators has centered on his use of group analysis techniques to find meaningful patterns in group data. As a result of these varying approaches to these data research results have not tended to build as systematically in this area as one might desire, and studies are often not directly comparable with one another. On the other hand, it should be noted that all of these researchers did employ the research methodologies of their day to control for biases present in preceding studies, and most of these researchers did pay close attention to the work of their colleagues in attempting to understand their own Rorschach findings. Unfortunately, no clear consensus has as yet spontaneously emerged concerning the most effective means of evaluating and analyzing these data, and each approach represents a compromise with distinct advantages and disadvantages.

Despite the many limitations presented here, the Rorschach protocols presented in this text represent one of the few scientific records available through which to understand the salient personality characteristics of those individuals involved in the events surrounding the Third Reich. These data include two perspectives: the highly select group of Nazi leadership represented at the Nuremberg trials and a large group of Danish collaborators presented through the work of Ritzler. These data do not provide, however, for an "easy" understanding of the dynamics of these individuals. To illustrate this point, in 1947 Harrower, acting as a representative of the First International Congress of the World Federation of Mental Health, invited 10 Rorschach experts of that period to review the 16 Rorschach protocols produced by the Nuremberg defendants. Not one of the 10 invited experts responded to the invitation to publicly present their findings after receiving and reviewing the Rorschach records. Although these experts probably had many reasons for their lack of response to this invitation, it seems reasonable to infer (as did Borofsky & Brand, 1980) that at least some of these Rorschach experts were concerned about the potential political implications that could become attached to any conclusions based on these data. The view of the personalities of Nazi leadership in the immediate postwar period was heavily colored and influenced by the effects of extensive wartime propaganda efforts by the Allies. These beliefs stemmed from intensely held political and religious frameworks, and the deep human emotions felt in response to the atrocities committed by Nazi Germany. As a result, these Rorschach data are particularly important within this context as one of the most "objective" source of information available through which to try to understand the personalities and psychopathology of Nazi war criminals.

In 1945–1946, historical events came together to result in the administration of Rorschachs to the Nuremberg defendants and Danish Nazi collaborators. As a consequence, modern psychologists have available to them a fascinating record, a historical window, through which to shed light on the personality organization and psychopathological characteristics of this unique group of individuals. The Rorschach records were never introduced as evidence during the war crimes trials, and they remained largely unavailable to researchers and scholars for several decades.

Indeed, the research undertaken for the purposes of this book produced several new Rorschach protocols from the Nuremberg group that have been previously lost to the community of scholars. Based on our review of these protocols, it is concluded that the Nuremberg group shared few common traits or characteristics with the exception of above average intellectual functioning. Thus, there appears to be no central psychological or personality characteristic found commonly for this group. On the other hand, it can also be observed that many of the Nuremberg group produced Rorschach protocol that provided evidence of significant psychopathology, representing a wide range of psychopathology related to personality disorders (e.g., antisocial personality disorder), affective disorders (e.g., depression), and disorders of thought (e.g., schizophrenia).

Despite this latter observation, however, it would be appropriate to conclude that the Rorschach protocols which served as the central focus of this text are not sufficient, in themselves, to explain the inhumane and violent actions taken by the

Nazi elite as well as by those in the rank-and-file. In reaching a similar conclusion, Borofsky and Brand (1980) offered the following observation:

> At the present time we as psychologists have been unable to satisfactorily explain the motivations and personality organizations that prompted ... war trial criminals to such grotesque and inhumane actions. Given our ignorance on such an emotionally charged issue, it is not surprising that some individuals might attempt to attack the efficacy of the Rorschach as a tool for measuring psychological functioning and personality organization. If such individuals could convince themselves that the Rorschach was not a sensitive psychological test, they might be able to maintain intact their *Weltanschauung* that only emotionally disturbed psychopaths could have functioned in the manner of [Nazi] war trial criminals. Fortunately, or unfortunately, as the case may be, there is ample evidence to demonstrate the diagnostic and heuristic value of the Rorschach test. (p. 399)

If the Rorschach data does not indicate a salient or core set of personality characteristics or traits that can account for abhorrent Nazi behavior, then is it possible that we could search for the unique characteristics of German society to explain the Nazi atrocities? This type of search, however, is also likely to prove fruitless and seeks false reassurance concerning the "unique" circumstances surrounding barbaric behavior and the likelihood that it "couldn't happen again" or "couldn't happen here." However, as we noted in the beginning of the chapter, actions similar to those found in Nazi Germany have happened before and are continuing to occur even as we prepare this monograph.

Annas and Grodin (1992) authored text e.:titled *Nazi Doctors in the Nuremberg Code: Human Rights in Human Experimentation*. This outstanding text documents the "doctors' trial" conducted at Nuremberg in 1946 and 1947 to try 23 defendants on charges related to human experimentation carried out by Nazi physicians. In reference to this historical context, the authors noted the following:

> On December 21, 1990, the U.S. Food and Drug Administration published a new regulation permitting the commissioner to determine that the requirement for obtaining informed consent from all human subjects prior to the use of an experimental drug or vaccine could be waived for Desert Shield participants when it was not feasible in certain battlefield or combat-related situations. (p. 5)

Annas and Grodin argued that the U.S. Defense Department's use of experimental drugs and vaccines on U.S. military personnel without their consent was a direct violation of the Nuremberg Code. They further noted the irony that the action was justified on the basis of military expediency.

The work of Stanley Milgram in the 1970s, cited in the introductory chapter to this text, provides a chilling reminder that obedience to authority, even when such obedience results in the inflicting of pain or death on innocent others, is not uniquely related to Nazi Germany but can be found among typical U.S. citizens, politicians and corporate managers included. In Milgram's experiment, over half of his subjects complied with the request to apply shock up to the 450-volt level that was clearly designated on the equipment as "Danger: Severe Shock." Perhaps most importantly, the rationale offered by Milgram subjects in follow-up group discussions for their actions were very similar to that offered by many of the Nazi defendants at Nuremberg and Copenhagen: They were following the orders or instructions they had been given or saw themselves as victims of circumstance.

Borofsky and Brand (1980) stated:

> It seems that much of the acrimony surrounding the debate as to whether or not the Nuremberg criminals were emotionally disturbed has to do with the anxiety and conflict generated by threats to our individual world views and our inability to adequately comprehend the behavior of the Nuremberg war trial criminals. In such an affect-laden situation we are extremely vulnerable to invoke dogmatism in order to temporarily quiet our anxieties. (p. 399)

Although anxiety is inevitably associated with examining issues related to aggression and violence, these issues are clearly far too important to be determined solely by the operation of primitive defense mechanisms such as denial or projection. Thus, a purely clinical explanation, let alone psychological characteristics of Germans who either supported or resisted the Third Reich, is not possible. The current data do not support a prototype of "good guys" or "bad guys." Gordon (1984) summarized this position in *Hitler, Germans, and the Jewish Question* as follows: "The psychological interpretations of 'bad guys' that emerge from studies of such phenomena as the 'authoritarian personality' have been subjected to serious, thoughtful, and probably justified attacks" (p. 309).

The Rorschach data discussed in this text deserve an evaluation free of dogmatism and prejudice. If interpreted within this context one can only reach one conclusion. Namely, that many individuals, including high-ranking Nazi war criminals, as well as those of the rank-and-file, participated in atrocities without having diagnosable impairments that would account for their actions. In this sense, the origins of Nazi Germany should be sought for primarily in the context of social, cultural, political and personality, rather than clinical psychological factors.

Appendix

Complete verbatim records of the Rorschach data from Nazi war criminals are presented, including Gilbert's administrations of 16 Rorschachs, Kelley's 6 protocols, an example of a Danish Nazi collaborator administered during the 1946 war crimes trials in Copenhagen by Nancy Bratt-Oestergaard, and the Eichmann record collected by Kulcsar before the 1962 trial in Jerusalem. It is important to note that several features of the Nazi records listed here do not entirely conform to modern Rorschach administration (see Exner, 1993), which may subsequently influence the scoring and interpretation of the Nazi material. For the purpose of this summary, the responses and inquiry (if available) were exactly transposed with the exception of reaction time that was not included here. No attempt has been made to change the records to make them conform with the Comprehensive System (Exner, 1993) regarding the accuracy of the number of responses, issues of testing the limits, or the presence of additional responses during inquiry. Thus, when scoring these protocols, the Rorschacher must use their own judgment in evaluating the validity of these protocols and whether they comply with the Comprehensive System. The irregularities of the Nazi Rorschach administrations were discussed in detail in chapter 5 and the interested reader should review this section carefully.

In essence, the protocols collected by Kelley, Gilbert, and Bratt-Oestergaard are simply reproduced here as they were recorded. The Eichmann record was transposed from McCully (1980) and Miale and Selzer (1975).[1] The 23 Nazi Rorschach records presented here summarize, for the first time, the protocols of all major Nazi Rorschach records available, including seven previously unpublished protocols.

---

[1] Both sources were used because they did not correspond entirely. Many of the Rorschach verbalizations in Miale and Selzer's *The Nuremberg Mind* did not match with the Gilbert recordings. In this appendix, all records are presented from the notes of Gilbert and Kelley, to remain as close as possible to the original source.

Protocol administered by Nancy Bratt-Oestergaard, PhD:
- Danish rank-and-file Nazi collaborator #1303

Protocols administered by Douglas Kelley, MD:
- Karl Dönitz
- Hans Frank
- Hermann Göring
- Robert Ley
- Alfred Rosenberg
- Julius Streicher

Protocols administered by Gustave Gilbert, PhD:
- Hans Frank
- Hans Fritzsche
- Walther Funk
- Hermann Göring
- Rudolf Hess
- Ernst Kaltenbrunner
- Wilhelm Keitel
- Constantin von Neurath
- Franz von Papen
- Joachim von Ribbentrop
- Alfred Rosenberg
- Fritz Sauckel
- Hjalmar Schacht
- Baldur von Schirach
- Arthur Seyss-Inquart
- Albert Speer

Protocol administered by I. M. Kulcsar, MD:
- Adolf Eichmann

Rorschach Record
Subject: Sample protocol of a Danish rank-and-file Nazi collaborator (#1303)
Age: 44 years
Date of testing: 1946 (specific date unknown)
Examiner: Nancy Bratt-Oestergaard
Notes: No inquiry

I.	1.	Beetle with claws. (W^2)
	2.	Bird with wings, flapping its wing. (2 "wing" = 7)
II.	1.	Two headless men, sitting at a bar drinking. (1)
	2.	A heart in the middle, no, it's not a heart, it doesn't look like that. (5)
III.	1.	Two men that stand arguing. (W)
	2.	Bow-tie in the middle. (3)
	3.	Blood-stains. (2)

---

[2]Refers to the location of the response according to the Beck system (Beck et al., 1961).

IV.	1.	A fancy animal with two eyes. (W)
		It is the eyes and antennae, if anything. (28)
	2.	A masked person having two eyes—at a fancy-dress ball, a helmet on his head. (3)
V.	1.	Bat. (W)
VI.	1.	Skin of cat hung out to dry. (W)
	2.	Two little claws. (21)
VII.	1.	Butterfly. (4)
	2.	Monkey. (3)
	3.	A pair of clouds. (W)
VIII.	1.	Chameleon. (1)
	2.	Lung-tissue. (2)
	3.	Skeleton in the middle. (3)
		Is this made public too, in the papers? That is why one is so afraid to say anything.
IX.	1.	Shrimp or the like. (3)
	2.	Fountain. (6)
	3.	Head of an animal. (2)
X.	1.	Colored stains.
	2.	One has knocked off a pen. (W)
	3.	Sweet pea flower. (15)
	4.	A face—two men looking at each other. (26)
	5.	Butterfly pupa. (13)

End of record

Rorschach Record
Subject: Karl Dönitz (1891–1981)
Age: 54
Estimated IQ: 138 (Very Superior Range; 99th percentile)
Date of testing: November 1945–February 1946 (specific date unknown)
Examiner: Douglas Kelley

I.	1.	A beetle.
		The entire card seen as a living beetle, brisk and very active.
	2.	A bat.
		Whole card—alive.
V[3]	3.	A wedding cake.
		Whole response. Sort of cake that one puts on the center of the table for a wedding or festival.
	4.	A bee. A design for a house.
		It looks like a picture of a castle or a house. He would like to build a home like that. It is actually seen as a

---

[3]The inverse "carrot" signals to the examiner that the inkblot plate was rotated by the examinee in the direction of the carrot.

			dimensional drawing with very definite evidence of use of shading for depth.
V		5.	A Japanese pagoda.
			This is the same response, only now it is a Japanese pagoda instead of a house.
		6.	A coat of arms.
			Whole card seen as a family coat of arms.
II.		1.	Two boys at a masquerade, dancing.
			He describes this card excellently, mentioning the red hats. States that they are dancing and making steps together. He uses the color only insofar as it appears as part of the masquerade costume.
		2.	South American butterfly.
			This is the whole card; the shape and color are both used but the bright colors are what made him think of the South American aspect. The brilliant red and black color is more important than the form. No movement is used here.
III.		1.	Two gentlemen in formal dress grappling for a bow.
			The men are tugging and quarreling about the bow. He describes the men very well and states that you can notice the ends of their coats which are flying about in their struggle, and that their trousers are dropping down because they have no suspenders like the prisoners. He also adds that the center red is their handkerchief and in the struggle their breast pockets, where these handkerchiefs were, have been torn and you can see the ragged edges.
			(In testing this card, and asking about the lateral red, he states that when the quarrel started the ladies, who were with the gentlemen, left and that the red are their scarves which they left behind. Ladies are always forgetful.)
IV.	V	1.	Crawfish.
			This is the whole card seen as a deep-sea crawfish. He describes the feelers and sees it very clearly. States that it is armored as indicated by the shading. He states that deep-sea crawfish can swim and creep. This one is alive.
		2.	The skin of a bear.
			This is seen as a whole skin, furry as it would be lying before a desk.
V.		1.	A bat.
			This is seen as a real bat with long ears. He feels it is very good and states the ears are important for its flight.

		It is alive and flying. After looking at the card a little, he states it is such a good bat that that is all he can see.
VI.	1.	Skin of an animal, such as you would see on the floor in a lady's room.
		He states it is obviously an animal fur but that this was too simple and the lady who owned it altered it by adding feathers. "Only a lady would do this."
VII.	1.	This is very nice. Faces of two little girls looking at one another. They have expressions of being curious to learn the secrets of life. They may be dancing together too.
		Usual detail—whole card split into two details is used.
V	2.	A fur muff with appendages; a good lock or a zipper.
		This is the entire card with the center detail as a muff; the two lateral details as the fur appendages and the center dark line as the zipper.
VIII.	1.	A butterfly camouflaged like a leaf.
		The whole card is used with the colors predominant. He feels that it is a butterfly because of general structure.
	2.	Two chameleons waiting for a choice prey.
		These are the two lateral animals seen alive and points for action. He adds their tongues are curled in their mouths and they are ready to push them out.
V	3.	The entrails of a man. Blood. You can see the lungs, backbone, abdomen, bladder, and stomach.
		This is the whole card and represents a cut-up body; predominantly seen because of the shape and arrangement of parts in their anatomical location. The color itself did not suggest the idea but is used as the blood.
IX.	1.	A lobster pie with decorations. When you have lobster pie, you make the decorations with the lobster and lettuce and tomatoes.
		He feels this is an excellent arrangement and the fine color and good appearance of the green lettuce, pink tomatoes and lobster stimulates his appetite. He adds he has a great appetite for lobster anyway.
V	2.	Two animals carrying a load on their shoulders.
		Two orange details are seen as animals bearing a load or some sort of construction on their back. Color here is not used.
	3.	A head decoration. Fantastic.
		This is the kind of decoration that a vain woman would put on her head.
		(An umbrella. While giving the inquiry to the previous response, he noticed the center pink detail—V—and

		stated that it was an umbrella like one that would be over an Indian Maharaja.)
X.	1.	Two animals. Crawfish with one sheared.
		These are the lateral blue and green details, the green detail being the single claw. They are seen alive.
	2.	Two mice.
		Lateral gray detail; alive.
	3.	Flying birds.
		Lateral gray detail; alive.
V	4.	A cross-section of an experimental bomb—of a mortar type.
		This is the whole area seen with the large D section as the motor and the smaller section as a cork or plug which fits into the larger section to block it.

End of record

Rorschach Record
Subject: Hans Frank (1900–1946)
Age: 46
Estimated IQ: 130 (Very Superior Range; 98th percentile)
Date of testing: before December 8, 1945 (specific date unknown)
Examiner: Douglas Kelley

I.	1.	Skeleton.
		Whole response. He describes it as part of the hip-bone with some of the upper part and chest. He feels from its small shape and contours it is feminine.
	2.	The upper part of an emblem.
		This is excellently seen as a flag emblem of the old Roman type. He describes two eagles laterally around a single standard.
	3.	An antique insignia.
		This is seen from above looking down on it with some perspective. He describes it as having a staff and wings such as was used by a messenger of the gods.
II.	1.	Two little bears holding a bottle.
		These are the two black areas, with the central detail as the bottle. They are grizzly bears and their front leg is lifted.
	2.	Two furs hanging on a wall.
		These are the black details; seem to be hanging and which at the same time in addition to being furry are wrinkled and as yet untanned.
	3.	A top spinning in the dark.

		This is the center white detail with the black detail as the darkness. He adds here spontaneously that the red are lamps or red flames which light up part of the scene.
III.	1.	Two men in top hats … clowns making faces.
		He starts off immediately describing the card and discusses little details such as the men's faces, coats, legs, slippers, etc.
	2.	Masqueraders.
		These are the same figures seen in the same fashion.
	3.	The red is like a butterfly.
		This is the center area and the color is most important. It is alive and its wings are moving. It is the shape of a butterfly but if it were a different color it would probably be something else.
	4.	The whole picture is an advertisement of a masquerade.
		This is an attempt to use the entire card and he feels it is a grotesque sign in which the two central figures indicate the action and the red are special attention getters or bits of large red print.
IV.	1.	A man dressed in a fur coat. His feet are seen from the close front.
		This figure is seen first as dead, lying in state, but then he adds that if he was laid out dead, he would not have a fur coat on and he feels that the man must have just lain down and is alive.
	2.	Double railroad tracks running between two lakes as seen from above; lighted up by the moon after a flood.
		The entire card is used as a scene with the white space as lakes, central line as railroad tracks and the black area as woods in the moonlight which accounts for the great predominance of shade.
V.	1.	A bat.
		This is seen as lifeless, stuffed and hanging from a wall.
	2.	Animal with legs and horns.
		This is the center detail and he feels it is perhaps an antelope.
VI.	1.	A fur … silver fox hanging on a standard made of black lacquer with feathers on the edge, with a large fur in the background.
		It is a complicated response and is seen as a dimensional set-up with the large outline of the fur as the background and then the standard on which are supported the two lighter furs, which are the two light areas in the lateral details. It is well seen and the whisker details are added as nails driven into the wall to hold up the fur.
VII.	1.	Two grotesque women with rococo hairdos.

He feels these are two Negro women with white wings. They are alive but it seems to be a drawing of them rather than the real things. A sort of a drawing you find in ladies' magazines. Negroes because of shading on faces.

2.   A powder box, with white puffs.
This is the white space seen as the powder box with the lower detail as the puffs. The top of the box is the white space between the upper details.

VIII.   1.   Very pretty. Two old Bourbon flags. Beautiful blue.
These are the center blue details seen as 18th century flags standing in the corner of a museum; the upper gray detail being used as a corner of the wall. They are in the place of honor and are fastened to the wall. The rest of the card is merely decoration around the corner.

IX.   1.   A symbol of belief. A sword set in flames. The green represents the world; the pink, fire; and the golden color, the rest of the scene becomes lost in the golden light above. The center is the sword.
This is the entire card and is a combination response utilizing all details. He states it is a symbol of belief but is unable to state what belief.

X.   1.   The Eiffel Tower seen from a distance.
This is the top gray detail.

2.   An advertisement in Paris
This is a development from the first response. Here the whole card is used, the gray being the Eiffel Tower; the white being the Seine River and the other colors indicating the important centers in Paris.

3.   A poster against venereal disease.
Here the lateral blue are seen as bugs carrying disease, lateral green, to the skeletons, central gray. The entire card is used around this theme as advertising matter focused on this bringing of disease to the body.

End of record

Rorschach Record
Subject: Hermann Göring (1893–1946)
Age: 52
Estimated IQ: 138 (Very Superior Range; 99th percentile)
Date of testing: before December 9th, 1945 (specific date unknown)
Examiner: Douglas Kelley

I.   1.   A bat.
The entire card is a flying animal, but it looks more like a bat.

| | | 2. | A June bug because of the feelers. |

2.
A June bug because of the feelers.
The entire card. You can see the claws. It is alive and spread out.

II.   1.   Two dancing men. A fantastic dance.
Two men, here are their heads, their hands together, like whirling dervishes. Here are their bodies, their feet.

(These figures are seen extremely well; colors are not used except that they can be part of the costume of men.)

III.   1.   Two men.
Usual men. Are seen in very close detail with eyes, forehead, legs, beard, etc. During inquiry he mentions the red center which means nothing to him. On testing states it might indicate the hearts of the two men.

    2.   Skeletons.
This is the center gray detail and is seen as the chest cavity. Form used, not shading.

IV.   V   1.   Fantastic fish.
Card was turned several times before answer was given. Fish is seen as a flat fish, prehistoric type such as is found in deep ocean bed. The eyes, feelers, fins are pointed out. The fish is alive.

V.   1.   Bat.
Card is turned for some twenty seconds and he then adds, "A night bat." He states bat is fantastic, not entirely true to detail; but the main parts, head, wings, legs are there. He calls it a night bat for no particular reason. Color not used. It is seen as the whole card and is alive.

VI.   1.   Comments: "Interesting." A flying or crawling night animal.
Card was turned many times and the animal is seen as a whole. He calls attention to the head and the feelers, and states that it is "one of the things that come out of the night." It is seen alive.

    1.   Fur or skin.
This is the blot without the top detail. It is seen with the fur side out.

VII.   1.   Fantastic figures.
He sees the usual two figures and indicates the faces and jaws sticking out. They seem to be in movement and are covered with capes.

    2.   Hands.
These are the top two details which look like hands waving.

VIII.   1.   Two animals climbing up a plant.
The plant is of a fantastic form but the animals are good. The entire center area is the plant. The plant is seen primarily for its form with some effect because of its color. The rats are not fantastic. He has seen big rats like this before.

IX.   1.   Before giving this response, the card is turned repeatedly, moved backward and forward and he holds his two fists over his eyes and peers through them muttering "fantastic." Finally he says "Plant and dwarfs."
Plants are the pink and green areas; dwarfs the top details. Plants are described as being colored with the form of bushes and dwarfs are seen as spooks with fat stomachs and are alive.

X.   1.   This is the prettiest card. "Witches Sabbath."
Whole card is used with sense of motion and he builds this response into his second response.

                   2.   Two figures.
These are fantastic figures, half man and half animal and are the upper gray details. They are seen alive and are what made him think of witches using the rest of the blot as figures in motion.

                   3.   Two more figures.
Top part of pink detail. Usual faces. He points out nose, etc. These two figures are also alive.

                   4.   Scorpions.
Lateral blue seen as scorpions crawling.

                   5.   Two caterpillars.
Center green details. Caterpillars are seen alive and crawling.

End of record

Rorschach Record
Subject: Robert Ley (1890–1945)
Age: 55
Date of testing: before October 25, 1945 (specific date unknown)
Examiner: Douglas Kelley

I.   1.   A dragon. (It looks like a medieval dragon attacking with its claws out).
This is the whole picture and Ley has never seen a dragon. It is what he has always imagined an angry attacking dragon would look like.

                   2.   A bat. (Two wings moving and flapping).
This is poorly seen; the body being mostly the loose wings with a center indistinct.

3.   Mountains and valleys.

These are on the wings of the bat, seen as a relief map—lateral details.

4.   Dots.

These are high points in the mountains like on a map. This is purely descriptive addition to the previous answer.

5.   Shadows and lights.

This is a poor descriptive response to the entire card.

6.   A line down the center here is a spot at the top. This is very confusing. It must be an airplane.

Small spot is seen just below the center top detail; it is confusing because it appears to be in motion and he finally decides it is a small airplane. A four-motored airplane flying over a valley seen from above.

7.   Feelers and mouth.

These are the top center two tiny details.

V   8.   It depends on how you look at it. Here is a head.

This is the top center detail reversed and is seen merely as an eagle head.

II.   1.   A butterfly. There are colors here. That's funny. It is a funny butterfly.

The whole picture is used and he states that it is a form of a butterfly but the colors are important. The colors actually struck him first.

(An additional response, spontaneous at this point is lamp. This is the center white space form only.)

2.   Black and red and white.

He repeats this several times and then moving the card near and far, states the colors look different when you consider the distance. At this point, he brought the card close to him and went over the description of the butterfly again.

3.   A stork, or goose would be better.

It looks like it was tipped over with its legs pulled in. It seems unique. This top is red. Form is vague—no movement except perhaps tension. It is alive.

4.   Jaws of the butterfly.

These are the top red details which he described previously as the mouth of the butterfly.

III.   1.   Two men at a table greeting each other. (They actually seem to be fighting. They are excited men.) They seem to be tearing a bouquet apart or throwing it at each other. Perhaps they had corsages on their chests.

2.   They could be men with horses' feet. They seem broken in two at the middle. They have goats' beards.

This response is simply a description of the men and he continues by describing their foreheads and faces. At 40 seconds he again starts over and describes their horses' feet, which seems to fascinate him. He then points to their chests and shows how the corsages have been torn off as indicated by the ragged lines.

IV.   1.   A funny bear fur spread out.

You can see the head and tail. Terrific legs. It has shadows and peculiar arms. It is alive and represents Bolshevism over-running Europe.

He starts out with a discussion of Bolshevism and how the bear symbolizes Bolshevism to him. He describes the eyes of the bear and then returns to his Bolshevistic theme.

V.   1.   It is more like a bat.

All of these are funny types of bats. Horns and legs, back and wings. It is flying.

2.   It could also be a butterfly.

Identical figure as above.

VI.   1.   What is this?

Subject seems extremely puzzled. Turns the card all over; looks at the back; seems very confused and finally gives a response. A bee torn apart. It was a large bumblebee. You can see the small head and legs with a line on the back. It is dead. Answer is very poorly seen.

VII.   1.   Cloud formations. Thunder clouds.

He repeats this response several times to himself.

2.   Like an animal. A mouth. There seems to be a backbone. It also has a mouth. You can see it in relief.

He again repeats this answer several times. This response is to the tiny black center detail, the upper end being the mouth.

3.   Spongy, foamy clouds.

These are thunder clouds gathering as seen from a plane. He does not seem to realize that he has given this answer previously.

VIII.   1.   Two bears with big heads on a flower getting honey.

The bears are honey bears. The flower is seen only in general details, color playing a more important role than the form. The bears are alive and are actually eating on the flower.

2.   The colors are very beautiful like a dress. Pastel shades.

3.   Pretty little pictures of peacocks fighting.

These are central tiny white details.

		4.	The white part looks like animals. Each time there is that line.
			These are the same peacocks previously seen. Subject turns card continuously during this period.
IX.		1.	Large flowers. The cup type.
			He points out the stem of the upper part of the pink detail. The form and color are both used but the form here is predominant. He used the pink as the stem. The flowers are the orange details.
		2.	A chalice.
			This is the entire card seen as a chalice or cup and the form and color are also used.
		3.	Green. This is an ugly color. It is spotty. The beige though is very pretty.
X.	V	1.	Spiders right and left.
			They seem to be alive or killing some animal and sucking its blood, with lateral green detail as the animal being killed.
	V	2.	One bowl in another.
			This is the green detail fitting into the red detail. Form alone is used.
		3.	Blue, yellow, red, gray. The colors are very unique.
		4.	The card is turned numerous times finally right side up. Buffaloes fighting. They are unique.
			Top gray details.
	V	5.	Little flower cups. A pattern of flowers.
			He uses the whole card and points to different color details and finally adds: "See, here are the seeds." Center yellow detail.

End of record

Rorschach Record
Subject: Alfred Rosenberg (1893–1946)
Age: 52
Estimated IQ: 127 (Superior Range; 96th percentile)
Date of testing: before December 9, 1945 (specific date unknown)
Examiner: Douglas Kelley

I.		1.	A beetle.
			The whole card is used and the beetle is seen flattened out or squashed. He notes the feelers and other little details quite well.
II.		1.	Two hooded figures dancing.
			Usual figures are seen and he states they are hooded, describing the red hoods and black capes, saying they look bearlike.

III.	1.	Two figures around in a basin.
		Usual figures with a center detail at the base. The red is not used but on later questioning, he states that the red spots are lamps giving off red light. He states the men are grotesque and describes them well.
IV.	1.	Fur.
		He spontaneously adds very fine fur and obviously used the texture quite well.
V.	1.	A bat.
		He states that it is hard to tell whether it is alive or dead. It appears flattened out and does not seem plastic enough to be alive. Finally decides it is dead.
VI.	1.	A fur.
		Describes shape but emphasizes again it is a soft furry pelt.
VII.	1.	Two children's heads.
		These are the upper detail only and he states that the children are laughing at each other.
VIII.	1.	Two pink mice, climbing up a tree.
		He states he called them pink mice because they just happen to be pink. He does not feel that mice are pink, but is willing to accept these as pink because the color just happens to be there. He describes the plant as a nondescript one, stating that he thought of a tree because of the center and upper detail which look like a tree and feels that the tree is dead because of its gray color. He states that it is not a very good tree and it is, in general, poorly seen except for its top.
IX.	1.	Nothing. Absolutely nothing.
		(In rechecking card, he states it is almost like a crab, but it does not fit together. You can see the crab-like claws, but the rest of it does not go with the claws.)
X.	1.	Two spiders.
		Usual blue detail seen as extremely active spiders.
	2.	Two little gray animals.
		These are the center gray details seen as seahorses and are very much alive. The color is not used but again is simply mentioned because they happen to be gray.
	3.	Coral reefs.
		These are the center pink details and here the color is more important then the shape.

End of record

Rorschach Record
Subject: Julius Streicher (1885–1946)
Age: 60
Estimated IQ: 106 (Average Range; 66th percentile)
Date of testing: July–October 1945 (specific date unknown)
Examiner: Douglas Kelley

I.		1.	A crab or sea animal.
			The whole card is used. It is dead.
		2.	A funny airplane.
			It is an exaggerated plane such as he has seen in German papers. A drawing for a model of a new type of plane.
	V	3.	Skeleton.
			The hip-bones. The whole card is used and it is seen as a simple anatomical specimen.
		4.	A dog's head.
			This is in the right lateral detail in the shaded area including two small dots on the right side. He sees the eyes and nose and it seems well seen.
			He gives at this point a spontaneous additional answer. Protoplasm. This is the center of the area, bell and figure, and he states that one can see through it.
II.		1.	He looks the card over; discusses it, stating that it is pretty. Waves it about his head and finally states that it is two women in the French Revolutionary times with Jacobean caps.
			He states that they have red socks and caps and are dancing. He then gives date of Revolution as 1789 and is about to go into a discussion on the French Revolution in general when he is again attracted by the card.
	V	2.	Red wine glass on a porcelain platter.
			Center red and center space detail. In the inquiry he sees an additional white space response, "Two Dutch Shoes." Upper white space details. He sees glass as red but form is not important. Color is factor for white platter.
III.		1.	Two men, counts.
			They are bowing to each other. Seem well dressed of the nobility.
		2.	Two waiters.
			Same response.
		3.	A butterfly. Or blood spots.
			He sees the butterfly first in the center and here uses both the form and the color, and at the same time attempts to get the two lateral red details into the same

			answer and changes over from butterfly to blood spots for all three.
	V	4.	A cravat or bow-tie.
			This is center red detail form only. At this point he launches into a long discussion on how interesting the card is.
	V	5.	Woman's figure with her hands at her hips.
			This is the center space detail as seen in motion.
		6.	Negro heads.
			In order to see this clearly, he covers up all the other details with his hands.
IV.		1.	Fur of an animal. (A bear).
			He describes the head and feet. Seems very reluctant to give the card back, trying to find some other response. Finally at 60 seconds gives up. The fur is seen with furry side out.
V.		1.	A bat.
			It is a dead bat; lifeless, and it does not seem to be sleeping or it would be hanging by its feet. It is not flying so it must be dead.
		2.	A flying dog from Borneo.
			This is the same thing in an attempt to improve it. It is also lifeless.
		3.	A pattern for an airplane.
			An airplane model.
VI.		1.	A fur.
			The whole card is used. It is a skin of a unique animal, fur side out. At 20 seconds, he launches into a discussion of the card. Takes off his glasses; looks at the card; puts on his glasses; looks at the card; tells us that it is a card with an ink spot on it and in general attempts to make something out of it.
		2.	Carved staff.
			This is the top center blank detail and he states it is done by a machine. It is very well seen.
VII.	V	1.	The substance taken out of an operated knee.
			This is one-half of the card and is seen as a specimen preserved in alcohol of the meniscus which has been removed from the knee joint. He had such an operation and apparently preserved and brought home the material removed from his knee joint which apparently resembles the blot.
		2.	Two human embryos
			In the inquiry he states they are not embryos but rather are females dancing. The whole card is split into two details. Usual figures.

		3.	Skeletons.

3. Skeletons.
    These are the same forms which he has been trying to make into something definite. Apparently he realizes the female figures were not good and attempted to make skeletons out of them.

V   4. A bust.
    This is a bust of Napoleon's head—center space detail.

VIII.   1. Beautiful colors. Pastel shades.

2. Mouselike animals.
    They are like guinea pigs and are alive.

3. Oriental pattern.
    He becomes very happy about the card; smiles at it. States it has harmonious colors and is an oriental pattern with a combination of figures and colors. This is the whole card; the colors seem to predominate here.

IX.   V   1. A plant in bloom.
    This is a pink plant. Color and form both seem used, but the form seems more definite here.

V   2. The green part is eaten up by dogs.
    When he started, he pointed only to the pink area but has now joined the green part as the leaves.

V   3. These must be the roots.
    These are the orange details and he has now organized the entire card into a plant with pink blossoms, green leaves and roots. The color does not seem important to the roots but rather the natureless structure. The card is a whole; is well seen and a good combination of form and color. On careful questioning, it seems most likely that the original response of "Plant in bloom" was suggested more by the color than by the form.

X.   1. A louse.

2. Microscopic animals.
    Both these responses are to the lateral blue. Seem to be enlarged which leads to the idea of microscopic sea animals. They seem to be very much alive.

3. Skeletons.

4. Human figures.
    These two answers started by seeing the top gray area as a skeleton and it was finally played up to the two human figures.

5. Tropical flowers.
    This is the whole card seen as a collection of flower blossoms and in the inquiry he states they are too pastel to really be tropical. English flowers are brighter like these. These are Nordic flowers.

(He then adds as a spontaneous response: This card is not so pretty.)

In the inquiry at the end, he also notes the center space as a cowboy with a lasso.

End of record

Rorschach Record
Subject: Hans Frank (1900–1946)
Age: 46
Estimated IQ: 130 (Very Superior Range; 98th percentile)
Date of testing: December 8, 1945
Examiner: Gustave Gilbert

I.	1.	I know just exactly what I said before—the top of a Roman staff, looking at it diagonally from above ... *senatus populusque Romanus* (SPQR).
		It's the top (of the staff) with the legion eagle ... strong symbolism. ... Hmm ... also a world power ... how they come and go ... (W)
	2.	Photo of a pelvic girdle and back-bone—a cross section. Has bone and marrow texture. (W)
	3.	Bell hanging from a cross-bar. Just the shape. (D)
	4.	Grotesque profiles looking out. Outline of outer edges. (D)
	5.	Two little birds. Little birds or cuckoos sitting on mountain top. (top peaks) (D)
	6.	Two breasts—women's breasts. Outline. (de)
	7.	Little angle's heads, lips protruded as if blowing—cherubs. Outline. (de)
	8.	Horn stumps of a deer - first and second stages. (Dr)
	9.	Caduceus without staff ... Just the shape. (W)
	10.	Two little bears—a grizzly bear looking up. Grizzly fur—very clear fur coloring. (top peaks) (Dr)
II.	1.	Those are my darling bears (laughs). They're holding a bottle—just the top part of the bears and the furry texture. (D)
	2.	Beautiful prima ballerina dancing in white dress with red light shining from below. (Afterthought) Black cloak spread out, about to wrap it around her.

        She is stepping toward you on the stage, red light coming from the footlights. (S + D)

3.   If you glance at it quickly, it is a top spinning.

        It is balanced by spinning—just the shape. (S)

4.   White luminescent glass lamp.

        It is so bright (glaring) because it is in the darkness. (S)

5.   The red spots could be part of a red butterfly.

        Two red wings. (top red) (D)

6.   ... or a flower.

        Red leaves. (top red) (D)

7.   A lake (S) with a canal and a distant tower, moonlight gleaming on the water, a little bridge up here.

        Perspective as from an airplane at night, with moonlight reflected in the water. (WS)

III.   1.   Ah, yes, the two Negroes bowing to each other with tailcoats and top hats, a piece of white vest showing, flower in lapel.

        Usual figures. (cutoff W)

2.   Flying fish.

        Jumping. (lower side) (Dd)

3.   A crab.

        Shape. (lower center) (D)

IV.   1.   A big fur for a North pole traveler—a hunter. It lies spread out; upper appendages are not arms but straps to tie it with; the fur stands out clearly and plastically.

        It's the outside hairy fur side of the animal hide ... very clear. (W)

2.   A railroad track through a dark forest and water (S) left and right, dammed up to make way for the railroad embarkment (DS).

        The coloring is like dark woods; trees and grass indicated by the shading. The center line is a straight track through it. (S + DS)

3.   Snakes or eels (appendages).

        Just the shape. (D)

V.   1.   A bat - wings, head, legs; it is mounted; could never be like that in real life. Just the shape; it is furry, but the color isn't clear—it is opened and mounted. (W)

2.   Two ugly heads ... one-eyed Cyclops ... one eye in a criminal head and a beard ... scheusslich! ... the nose is illuminated ... like a mask.

        Profile ... it has an alcoholic nose ... ugly... (D)

        (Comment: *"Scheusslich! Widerlich!* ... like Stalin. Did you know that I knew Lenin as a kid in Munich?)

VI.   1.   Two silver fox furs hanging elegantly on a turned coat hanger pole … soft fur.

                    It has the texture of soft fur—the pole is a masterpiece; shiny black wood. (D)

         2.   The outside is spread out fur, cat's fur; top a feathery thing … whole thing makes a fur display as in a show window.

                    Outside fur is a different texture. (D) (1 & 2 make combined W)

         3.   Could be a grave … cross on top, wreaths still on grave and four stakes marking it off. … a symbol of sorrow … flaming metal golden rays from Christ's body on top.

                    Symbol of death; pieta…wreaths hanging from cross over grave; two weeks after burial, therefore Christ's figure not finished on cross … that's just how it looks . (well seen) (W)

         4.   Grotesque heads.

                    Shape of side profiles. (D)

         5.   Two big fish … shimmering silver bodies.

                    Middle shiny areas. (D)

VII.   1.   Two Negresses dressed up with eighteenth century head-dresses or wigs; kinky hair visible under wigs.

                    They are making mocking gesture to each other. (upper 2/3) (D)

         2.   Bottom part is clouds.

                    Brightly illuminated like clouds. (D)

         3.   (Excited) Just look! … a powder box … very elegant … wonderfully shaped, even the screw-thread in the neck.

                    Outline. (S)

         4.   Melted snow running down the drain, dirty.

                    Shading of melted snow, running down the drain dark and dirty. (lower D)

         5.   Two Mongolian heads … Sultans with head-dress.

                    (middle D)

VIII.   1.   Wonderful symbols … blue silk banners of 18th century hanging across corner of trophy room.

                    Bottom part might be paper flowers, red and orange, banner in middle is typical eighteenth century blue silk; a victory display. (D)

         2.   (Surprised) And here are two animals … they could be chameleons.

                    Just the shape, climbing. (D)

IX.   1.   (Enthusiastic) A wonderful sword going up into the light … it comes from the fire inside the earth, through the green earth into the sunlight … Herrlich! (Magnificent) … You could write above *pax eterno en suelo* (dramatic gesture).

                    (Gasps on seeing the card again) "Red flames … golden handle of sword, lost in heavenly light above

... it is a cosmic symbol of life; we rise from the earth through life, into the heaven above ... you see, they just wanted to make an inkblot, but a symbol of life resulted!" (W)

2.   There's the coast of Norway.

Upper inner right outline. (D)

3.   Reindeer horns. (That sword symbol is wonderful! ... inspiring!)

Just shape. (D)

("That sword symbol is wonderful! Inspiring!)

X.   1.   Eiffel Tower up here, that's clear ... and the Seine River ... and the Ile de France ... It's a poster, "Travel to Paris."

Eiffel Tower shape of upper gray, Seine River (center S), Ile de France (two long red strips) ... "just the shape—not so good." (built up WS)

2.   Terrible looking crablike animals.

Microscopic crab shape, blue as in water or crystal. (D)

3.   Poster against venereal disease, because it shows backbone and pelvic area.

Just a colored chart. (DW)

4.   Antelope head mounted on a board like a trophy.

Shape. (lower green) (D)

5.   Sun with yellow light around it.

(D)

6.   Engine governor.

Usual wish bone figure. (D)

7.   Flower with roots and earth clinging to roots.

Shape. (upper gray) (D)

8.   Two ducks; wild ducks flying together carrying something in their beaks together.

Not exactly blue, but you can see the coloring. (D)

9.   Two heads.

Profile shape. (edge of red D)

(Comment: "It's uncanny ... they're just inkblots, but it shows that beauty and a deeper meaning can be concealed in the most unassuming forms. ... You know, it is terrifying ... a man wants to make an inkblot ... and the ink itself makes a symbol of life! It just shows that the spiritual world is greater than any man's will. You psychologists are ingenious in using such methods.")

End of record

Rorschach Record
Subject: Hans Fritzsche (1900–1953)
Age: 45
Estimated IQ: 130 (Very Superior Range; 98th percentile)
Date of testing: November 5, 1945
Examiner: Gustave Gilbert

I.   1.   Butterfly.
                   Just the shape ... mounted, not alive, somewhat torn.
                   (W)

          2.   Dancing girl with hands in the air.
                   Outline of dancer in the middle with half-transparent
                   veil around her and other veils flying, all in motion.
                   (W)

          3.   Parachute jumper.
                   Fleeting impression as he jumps; body in middle, head
                   bent under,
                   parachute just opening. (W)

          4.   A priest standing before an alter, hands raised in prayer,
                   head bowed.
                   Priest is praying; stained glass window behind is only
                   partly represented, with varying shades of light coming
                   through. (W)

          5.   I also saw a bird without a head, but that's same as
                   butterfly.

II.   1.   Two dancing bears—very clear; or gnomes or dwarfs.
                   Makes a revolting impression—not at all friendly.
                   The bloody color made me uncomfortable ... it doesn't
                   fit the picture at all. The black shape and shading of fur
                   gives the impression of dancing bears. (cutoff W)

                   Additional. [When told to include red]. Yes, I can
                   finally include the red—two clowns with red caps and
                   red painted faces or masks, dancing. (W)

III.   1.   Two waiters fighting over a wine-cooler. ... the red just
                   doesn't belong.
                   Just the shape of the black part. (cutoff W)

          2.   The red just doesn't belong.
                   Additional. [When asked about the red]. Well, they
                   could be fighting over a torn heart.

IV.   1.   Two animal furs, one lying on top of the other.
                   A long fox fur in the middle on top of a broad bear fur;
                   both hairy and distinguishable by their shape. (W)

V.   1.   A bat, just taking off, because his legs are still down.
                   Just the shape. (W)

VI.   1.   Animal fur ... so clear that it eclipses anything else.

Somewhat similar to cat's fur texture, aside from the obvious cat's whiskers above. (W)

2. Also makes a musical impression; there's a certain harmony.

Not only the violin shape of the central portion, but the harmoniously matched texture of the wood in the lower back part; symbolic of music, not realistic. (W)

Testing the limits: Recognizes sex symbols.

VII. 1. A torn map.

Just the rough outline ... nothing definite. (W)

Additional: Could also be white silhouette of head and shoulders of soldier in steel helmet. (S)

Testing the limits: Recognizes dancing figures.

VIII. 1. Combination of two chameleons and delicately colored blossoms.

Chameleons are red at the moment, very lively; blossoms are red and brown. (D)

2. Withered leaves above.

Tries to combine it with 1, but decides they are separate. Color and texture; outline isn't very good. (gray and blue D)

3. Could be the breastbone of a chicken.

Shape of ribs and white spaces. (DS)

Additional: Could also be colored top. (cutoff W)

IX. 1. Oil or gasoline lamp blowing out bright light under pressure.

Curved glass lamp shade, center glowing flame gives light above red base of lamp. (WS)

V 2. Burning oil well or volcano with fiery smoke, lava, and ashes.

Eruption of Vesuvius—brown lava running down mountain, dark ashes and smoke (green), red burning gas or reflection of fire on cloud above. (W)

X. V^ 1. Torn flower—stem and calyx are there and colored pieces are scattered around.

^V ... Just a little botanical study

Color and form give impression of botanical charts with enlargement of cross-section of a flower and various flower parts scattered around. (W)

Testing the limits: Sees rabbit's head.

Additional: I saw two sea horses (V) at first but paid no attention because I was looking for an organized picture of the whole thing. (large green D)

End of record

Rorschach Record
Subject: Walther Funk (1890–1960)
Age: 55
Estimated IQ: 124 (Superior Range; 95th percentile)
Date of testing: October 31, 1945
Examiner: Gustave Gilbert

I.	1.	(Laughs) Two men are grabbing a woman and she's protesting with hands in the air ... or maybe they're dancing. They're probably dancing around her. (W)
II.	1.	Could be two men dancing an ecstatic dance, but I don't know why the head and feet are red ... maybe from exertion; they're sweating.
		They are harlequins clapping hands together; the little specks around their heads show they're sweating; head and feet are flushed (red) from exertion. (W)
III.	1.	Two apes greeting each other and taking their hats off ... half monkey, half man.
		Just the shape of the black part. (cutoff W)
	2.	Monkeys hanging by their tails.
		Just the shape ... there are no red monkeys ... although there was a famous whorehouse in Leipzig called "The Blue Monkey." (red D)
	3.	Hip-bone, I suppose.
		Just the shape. (center D)
IV.	1.	Dancing bear, but the head doesn't belong.
		Shape and movement of a dancing bear and the hairy hide. (W)
	2.	Head of a grotesque animal.
		Shape of jackal's head. (lower D)
V.	1.	A bat, very clear.
		Shape of a flying bat and the dark night color. (W)
VI.	1.	(Comment: "Oy-oy-oy, they're getting crazier.")
		A sword that's been thrust in somewhere.
		Dark shape of sword above, thrust into this center line. (D)
	2.	Animal hide stretched out.
		Valuable dachs fur has black–gray texture like this. (W)
VII.	1.	Two children or cherubs dancing on a cloud.

Shape of children's chubby cheeks and texture of clouds. (W)

2. Monument with two figures.
    Outline. (lower gray inside black) (dr)

VIII. 1. Two bears.
    Just the shape of climbing bears. (D)

2. Fruit blossom, stalk, and leaves.
    Red and brown blossoms below, center stalk, green leaves. (D)

IX. 1. Two deer.
    Shape of their faces and horns. (di)

2. Woods with tree in middle.
    Green woods with tree in middle. (D)

3. Man holding grotesque animal by his hand and foot, a pole projecting out of his stomach ... maybe giving birth to these animals—oxen, dragons, deer.
    Shape of a man (pink D) and oxen (green D), deer (di inside green) dragons (orange D) but the colors don't apply. (built-up W)

X. 1. Again the hip-bone or pelvic girdle.
    Shape. (center blue D)

2. Two gremlins busy with human vertebrae.
    Animal figures gnawing at the base of the spine. (upper gray D)

3. A lot of gremlins and witch animals have torn a man's body apart; the red is the two halves of a man's body and there are pelvic bones top and middle. A representation of the witches' kitchen in Faust, the Walpurgisnacht.
    The red is flesh color, but the colors don't apply to the other figures ... it's all confused. (W)

Explanation: That last picture might be in a concentration camp. "I can't stand reading about those things - I get sick to my stomach. I've been occupied with art and beautiful things all my life ..."

End of record

Rorschach Record
Subject: Hermann Göring (1893–1946)
Age: 52
Estimated IQ: 138 (Very Superior Range; 99th percentile)
Date of Testing: December 9, 1945
Examiner: Gustave Gilbert

I. 1. Funny beetle.
    Just the shape. (W)

2.   A bat.

It is the shape of a bat, but really not so good; the gray-black color gives an involuntary impression of a night animal. (W)

II.   1.   (laughs) Those are the two dancing figures, very clear, shoulder here and face here, clapping hands (cuts off bottom part with hand, including red).

Top red is head and hat; face is partly white. (WS)

III.   1.   Two caricature figures, with high collar like Schacht ... but the red spots...I can't figure that out...can't figure out (gets impatient, snaps forefinger at three red spots as though to brush them off) what these things are...damned if I know....

They are debating over something...maybe two doctors arguing over the inner organs of a man (laughs). (W)

                2   ...You might also say that it is an opened figure of one man— opened up, with two identical halves and the insides in the middle (points to lower D and center red— offers the idea as though not to be taken seriously).

Yes, of course, the opened man...(brushes it off—turns card down, ready for next one). (W)

(Always puts card down when he is satisfied he has said enough; indicates he is ready for the next one.)

IV.   V^V   1.   Funny animal, sea animal, the kind you make smoked fish out of, has eyes.

Just the structure. (W)

V.   V   1.   Night animal—a flying animal, not exactly a bat—
        V^   It is very symmetrical; if you fold it together it's the same.

It is more like a bat... the dark color is important. (W)

VI.   V   1.   Hide of an animal—here are the legs and the backbone line— a bedroom rug...this way (turns it), I don't know— this thing here (top) I can't figure out. (puts card away)

It is the shading and the shape of the thing without the top piece.—I can see it lying on the floor right before me—very clear—short- haired fur. (W)

VII.   1.   A face—grotesque—half-man, half-animal.
Upper 2/3 heads and shoulders. Does not indicate M. (D)

Testing the limits: Can see usual female figures ^ & V when suggested.

VIII.   V   1.   Only two things clear here—two animals climbing up, very clear.

It is very clear no matter how you hold it. (usual animals) (D)

		2.	Fantastic sea plants in the middle.

2.   Fantastic sea plants in the middle.

Of course, it's the color—could also be exotic flowers.

IX.   V   1.   Very fantastic plant.

Chiefly the color; also form. (D)

2.   There are the trolls from Peer Gynt.

The grotesque shape. (usual orange details, D)

X.   1.   Two crablike animals.

Just the shape its alive. (blue D)

2.   Two troll figures, or parrots.

Just the shape; alive. (side gray D)

3.   Little dogs.

They are sitting on their haunches; it is independent of color. (yellow D)

4.   Fantastic profiles—I don't know what that blue stuff is that they are blowing out.

Grotesque caricature—not really alive. (inner edge of large red D)

End of record

Rorschach Record

Subject: Rudolf Hess (1894–1987)
Age: 51
Estimated IQ: 120 (Superior Range; 91st percentile)
Date of testing: January 6, 1946
Examiner: Gustave Gilbert

I.   1.   Microscopic pictures of something; cross-section of a stem.

Outline of a stem cross-section, with spaces for the sap, like a fern; enlarged from microscopic picture. (WS)

2.   An insect.

Just the shape of the head and horns, body, and wings. (W)

II.   1.   Also microscopic cross-section; parts of an insect with blood spots.

The shape of the cross-section of the leg of a fly with red blood spots; space in the middle is the marrow, although I don't know if the leg of an insect has marrow. (WS)

2.   A mask.

Mask of an island savage, like Fiji Islanders, though I don't know them; the opening is for the mouth; it is devilish, that is why the eyes and beard are red. (W)

Testing the limits: Can see female figures.

III.   1.   Two gentlemen greeting each other.

			They are holding hats in their hands, it is very ornamental because it is symmetrical; you might say the whole thing represents an expressionistic illustration for a crime novel, with the blood spots; the red tie plays some part, I suppose. (built-up W).
		2.	A red bow-tie between them.
		3.	Two blood spots.
IV.		1.	An animal fur—stretched and hung on the wall. The head is down here; the whole thing gives the impression of long-haired fur. (W)
V.		1.	Skin of a bat. The shape of a stretched-out skin, from the head and tail—night-gray like a bat; hooked ends for grasping prey. (W)
VI.			(When asked if he remembers seeing these before, he says Yes.)
		1.	A stretched fur. Also long haired, but more the shape; would still look like it if coloring was different. (W)

Testing the limits: Can barely see sex symbols.

VII.		1.	Old-fashioned cravat, kind of moth-eaten—the sort of cravat men used to wear. It should be silk, but this doesn't look like silk; just the shape of a cravat they used to drape around their necks. (W)
VIII.		1.	A decoration with two animals at the edge…that is all. Design on Indian tapestry; the color just supports the design; the animals just look like animals, but they are not alive; the colors are immaterial … could be other colors just as well. (W)
IX.		1.	A technical representation of the cross-section of either a carburetor or a fountain. The idea comes mainly from the vaporized stream of gas or water in the middle and a receptacle underneath; the color has nothing to do with it, unless it represents different metals in a mechanical drawing. (DW)
X.	V	1.	Decoration with sea animals … crabs, et cetera. Just the general shapes, like the crabs; the color doesn't have anything to do with it. (W)
	V	2.	Seeds here. Yellow and shaped like acorn seeds that float in the air. (D)

Additional: Could also be the cross-section of an orchid with red leaves; there the color plays a greater part. (D)

> Additional: There are also sea horses here, by the shape of it. (usual D)

End of record

Rorschach Record

Subject: Ernst Kaltenbrunner (1903–1946)
Age: 42
Estimated IQ: 113 (Bright Normal Range; 81st percentile)
Date of testing: October 29, 1945
Examiner: Gustave Gilbert

I.
(Approaches problem very cagily: "Of course, the first impression is a folded inkblot...")

1. Upper half is mothlike figure or bat—but all thoughts are disturbed by the symmetry of the symmetrical inkblot. After a while the possibility of an animal is excluded by this.

> Upper center part has feelers and claws...just the shape. (D)

More comments on symmetry.

II.
(Comment: "Here too there is symmetry, but no middle line")

1. The red spots are big crabs.

> It has the appendages and head of a crab (center red), but the claws make it impossible because they are out of place. (confabulated D)

2. Bottom red spots are crab's claws.

> (Responses very slow, unsure and painful—"I can't make a final decision about this." Studies card very carefully.)

3. Two people holding hands—but it requires a lot of imagination.

> They are carnival figures with red caps—I don't think it is, but a child might think so. The red socks are blotted out at the bottom. It's all fantastic. (cutoff W)

III.
1. Caricature of two waiters taking something away from a table. (Comments on symmetry)

> Has the shape of waiters wearing tailcoats. (cutoff W)

2. Perhaps two hats there which they are holding.
> (DW)

3. Red spots blotted when paper was folded together.
Red bow-tie in the middle.

> The shape, but it's red and pink. (D)

IV.
1. Dried skin of an unknown marine animal—mounted specimen.

		It has the head and eyes of an animal and the shading looks like fur. I must emphasize that it is only fantasy— there is no furry underwater animal.

It has the head and eyes of an animal and the shading
looks like fur. I must emphasize that it is only fantasy—
there is no furry underwater animal.
(more comment on symmetry)

V.   1.   (Inspects carefully, comments on symmetrical folded ink-blot)
                   Could be a bat, but such a fantastic one I have never seen.
                   Two big wings, big head and ears—just the shape. (W)

VI.   1.   Opened flounder.
                   The tail is above—the shape. But understand, I don't
                   really believe it's a flounder. (W)

VII.   Rejected. "Same process—inkblot—can't imagine what. . ."
                   Testing the limits: When old women are suggested he
                   barely sees two cherub heads. (Do)

VIII.   (Keeps commenting on folded blot with every card)
               1.   Two chameleons.
                   Just the shape. [Usual side animal] (D)
               2.   Impossible for leaves, because they're four cornered.
                   The color is for leaves, but not the shape—I thought of
                   that because chameleons live on trees. (blue D)
               3.   Prepared specimen of a marine animal with two eyes and
                   two feelers. (All answers very slow, unsure, and cautious.)
                   Crablike shape. (upper D)
                   All answers very slow, unsure, and cautious.

IX.   1.   General impression is of a cuttlefish. [Holds hand down
                   center line: "it was certainly not the purpose of the folded
                   blot to make a cuttlefish, but that's what came out. Of
                   course it's not a cuttlefish at all."]
                   It's an awful-looking animal that can pour out ink-like
                   fluid to hide itself. The colors are not right—it's the
                   contours and general impression. (W)

X.   1.   Rejected. "The most colorful of all the representations. It
                   tells me nothing besides the colored impression."
                   Nothing there. If you ignore the color, you might see a
                   Chinese garden with bridges, islands, and ponds,
                   etc.—but the colors spoil everything.

End of record

Rorschach Record
Subject: Wilhelm Keitel (1988–1946)
Age: 57
Estimate IQ: 129 (Very Superior Range; 97th percentile)
Date of testing: October 30, 1945
Examiner: Gustave Gilbert

I.   1.   Clearly a butterfly with wings and feelers.

Just the shape of the whole thing. The body is transparent like X-ray picture here. (W)

II.   1.   (Comment: "Hmmm ... remarkable—rather similar to the one before. The red repulses me—it irritates me.") Could be two dogs' heads with eyes, nose, and neck. But the red doesn't belong—and the white space, I don't know.

Could be bears' heads putting their snouts together, playing, not the whole animal; it's just the shape and normal color. (cutoff W)

Testing the limits: Cannot recognize clowns.

III.   (Studies it, tilting head from side to side, comments, stalling.)

1.   Could be sort of bird's head, kind of torn below, like bird's head and breast.

Just the shape and feathery breast. (upper black D)

2.   Spider legs below.

Exactly the shape of spiders' legs. (D)

Testing the limits: Rejects suggestion of waiters, but accepts apes bending over. "But the red really doesn't belong at all. You see, I'm an outdoor man, not a barfly."

IV.   1.   (Mutters under breath; turns card over) Also a kind of birdlike insect; feelers and eyes above, torn wings, backbone—same class as bats and butterflies.

More a marine animal with big eyes and feelers; might be a picture taken through the water because of shading; looks dark in water. (W)

V.   1.   Well, there's the head and wings, feelers, and legs—but I've never seen a butterfly like that.

It's looking down at a flying animal from my balcony; maybe a bat. (W)

VI.   1.   The hide of a beast of prey—the middle line here—and spread out on the ground.

Just like a stretched out tiger hide; arms, tail below, kind of leopard texture; head missing. (W)

VII.   1.   [Holds it near and far, turns, comments, stalls] Maybe a cat's fur—very poorly done, pieces hanging together—rabbit fur.

Just the color and shading of cat's fur; rabbit's fur texture; a miserable job of skinning; I'm a hunter and nature lover. (W)

VIII.   1.   Dandelion bud prepared on a slide and enlarged.

Just the colored drawing of a microscopic slide projection with natural colors in a botany book. (W)

2.   If fantasy goes to work, one can see two animals with head, nose, legs.

		Just the shape. They're in motion. (usual D)

IX.

[Looks it over and throws arm up helplessly. *"Das ist ein tolles Ding!* (That's an amazing thing!)—The plant world ends here."]

1. Eruption of a volcano with clouds of smoke rising out of the depths and becoming brighter clouds above.

    The red is fire; green is dark clouds coming out of the crater and the sun is shining through the clouds on top, making them brighter. (W)

2. An animal with snout and eyes and beard; looks like an elk on one side, crocodile on the other.

    Just the features. (inside detail in both greens) (di)

X.

[Almost rejected. Comments on colors, turns, studies, stalls. "It is entirely without relationship.]

1. Some kind of flower in the orchid family, but nothing definite; gray stem, red leaves—the other things are inorganic.

    The red belongs; there are such flowers, and it has the calyx shape; but the other things don't belong. (attempt at W) (D)

End of record

Rorschach Record
Subject: Constantine von Neurath (1873–1956)
Age: 67
Estimated IQ: 125 (Superior Range; 95th percentile)
Date of testing: November 1, 1945
Examiner: Gustave Gilbert

I.   1.   Angel figure without a head, seen from behind.
                 Shape of angel with wings, standing. (cutoff W)

II. 1.   Two women or Chinese greeting each other.
                 Women or Chinese with red turbans, hands together. (W).

III. 1.   Two men greeting each other, hat in hand—don't know what that middle thing is.
                 The black part just looks like that. (cutoff W)

         2.   Could be a bow-tie.
                 Just the shape (Center D).

                 Testing the limits: Gives red devils for corner red.

IV. 1.   Bear skin.
                 Shape and appearance of fur—yes, long-haired fur.

V.   1.   A bat.
                 The shape. (W)

	2.	A loaded donkey from behind.
		He is going away; poorly loaded. (cutoff W)
VI.	1.	Clothes rack.
		Shape of pole with hooks (upper projections), and fur hanging on it—short haired, woolly, like llama. (W)
VII.	1.	Door hinges down here.
		The shape. (bottom center dr)
		Testing the limits: Yes, with a lot of fantasy it could be two dancing girls.
VIII.	1.	Two chameleons climbing up on a plant.
		Just the shape—the bottom part might be the color of a flower, but otherwise color doesn't apply. (W)
IX.	1.	Two deer.
		Shape of top part. (D)
		Additional: Green part might be green bush.
X.		Rejected. "Don't know what that could be."

Testing the limits: Recognizes rabbit head, but laughs, "That requires a lot of fantasy." Recognizes lions (top center) but tends to reject suggestions like red blood smear, brown leaves; recognizes shape of dogs (yellow) alive but independent of color.

End of record

Rorschach Record
Subject: Franz von Papen (1879–1969)
Age: 66
Estimated IQ: 134 (Very Superior Range; 99th percentile)
Date of testing: October 30, 1945
Examiner: Gustave Gilbert

I.	1.	A butterfly.
		Head and feelers and torn wings; it's dead and mounted; just the form. (W)
II.		[Laughs—stalls for time]
	1.	Footprint of a shot animal; but there's really no resemblance.
		Just the footprint with blood from the wound; doesn't resemble any part of an animal. (W)
		Testing the limits: Can barely see dancing figures.
III.	1.	Caricature of two men quarreling over a pot.
		Heads, feet, arms—like Secessionist art of 1900. (excluding red) (cutoff W)
IV.	1.	Hide of an animal.

		Shading gives impression of fur; could be long-haired because it's dark. (W)
	2.	Crawling animal or insect. Dead specimen of insect or crawling animal; by the shape. (W)
V.	1.	Same thing—butterfly, or something like that (not satisfied). Mounted specimen, dead; just the shape. (W)
VI.		[More stalling for time]
	1.	Some kind of insect with head and feelers. Either a specimen or X-ray photo of the insect; upper part with wings. (D)
VII.	1.	Torn clouds - but clouds don't look like that; not so black. General effect of the lighting—but that black center strip doesn't belong. (W)
	2.	Two fauns looking at each other. Just the faces and headdress and arms—they're laughing. (upper 2/3 D)
VIII.	1.	Two animals crawling up a tree. Just looks plantlike from shape and color, but there are no red animals—that's just the shape. (W)
IX.		Rejected
X.	1.	An anatomical picture, perhaps. Well, I'm not well versed in anatomy. [doesn't explain] (W)

End of record

Rorschach Record
Subject: Joachim von Ribbentrop (1893–1946)
Age: 52
Estimated IQ: 129 (Very Superior Range; 97th percentile)
Date of testing: October 1945 to February 1946 (specific date unknown)
Examiner: Gustave Gilbert

I.	1.	As I've already said, that is something like a crab. Shape of body, small claws (omits outer projection). (W) Additional: Could also be a night-bird from Dante's Inferno —fantastic figure—dark gray-black, like bat.
II.	1.	Harlequins doing a wild dance. They are clapping hands. [Examiner: "Happy?"] No, grotesque; a mummer's dance. Top part is heads, independent of color. (W)
III.	1.	Two waiters.

The shape. [Examiner: "Lively?"] Well, yes, a little crazy. (W)

2. A butterfly in the middle.
    Just the shape. (D)

IV. 1. Fur hide, hanging on the wall—from Africa.
    Long-haired fur. (W)

V. 1. Here I said a butterfly or bat—a night animal.
    Night animal, because it's dark and the form is grotesque. (W)

VI. 1. Again a hide.
    Short-haired; a little fantastic, but looks like a hide. (W)

VII. [Rejected] "I don't know what that is - it doesn't convey anything to me."
    Testing the limits: Yes, could be two women with a lot of imagination; (V) yes, two dancers without heads; top part are capes, grotesque dance.)

VIII. 1. Right and left are skunks; otherwise, I don't know.
    They're climbing up a tree; independent of color. (D)

    Additional: Could be a butterfly below, but only the shape of one. Flags in the middle; only the form.

IX. [Rejected] "Doesn't convey anything—you must have an awful fantasy for this."

X. [Rejected] "Doesn't convey anything. What would you want? How it looks? I can't say—it has nice colors."

End of record

Rorschach Record
Subject: Alfred Rosenberg (1893–1946)
Age: 52
Estimated IQ: 127 (Superior Range; 96th percentile)
Date of testing: December 9, 1945
Examiner: Gustave Gilbert

I. 1. Same as last time … beetle with spread out wings.
    It is the feelers and torn wings and the body shape of the beetle … more dead or mounted. (W)

II. 1. Two clowns with red caps clapping hands, one foot up, elbows out.
    Black costume with red dunce caps and red socks … just caught in the middle of a movement. (W)

III. 1. Two withered old men, standing by a pot, holding on, pulling apart.
    Two men in tuxedos. (usual cutoff W)

2. Two red torches.

			Just flickering red light—not really red lamps—torches. (D)
IV.		1.	Long haired, soft fur rug before a hearth.
			The shape and shading of a fur rug. (W)
V.		1.	A bat, just about to fly away.
			Has the pointed head and massive wings of a bat.
			(Excluding color?) Yes, it is dark, as in nature. (W)
VI.		1.	Two little boys talking to each other.
			They are porcelain figures, not really alive. (W)
			(Testing the limits on dancing female figures: "No, there are vertebrae, though")
VII.		1.	A rug, soft fur.
			Shape of stretched fur ... shading shows soft fur. (W)
VIII.	V	1.	Two field mice, climbing down a tree ... if you ignore the color.
			Red leaves on top, but animals are independent of color—the rest is branches and trunk. (W)
IX.	V		(Comment: "This is one on which I couldn't see anything...")
	V	1.	At best, two crabs crawling out of a mixture of red and blue plants.
			The crabs should really be darker but otherwise it's more the impression from color than form. (W)
X.		1.	Animal pictures on a coral reef, with sea horses and crabs and green snakes.
			Long red strips of coral, form and color of gray sea horses, shape of crabs but not color. (W)

End of record

Rorschach Record
Subject: Fritz Sauckel (1894–1946)
Age: 51
Estimated IQ: 118 (Bright Normal; 88th percentile)
Date of testing: October 31, 1945
Examiner: Gustave Gilbert

I.	V	1.	Skeleton and bones.
			Mammoth skeleton by the shape. (middle DS)
		2.	Kind of bug.
			Middle part has shape of bug. (D)
II.		1.	Fantastic butterfly.
			Black butterfly with red tips. (W)
		2.	Lamp shade.
			Shape of white space. (S)
		3.	Dance pose.

			Black Spanish mantilla, white dancer dress, spinning toe-dance. (DS)
III.		1.	Two fops in tailcoats, greeting each other, hat in hand.
			Just the shape of the black part; red doesn't belong. (cutoff W)
IV.		1.	Could be hide of a bear.
			Symmetrical hide, hairy edges. (W)
V.		1.	A bat.
			Shape of head, wings, et cetera. (W)
VI.		1.	X-rayed body.
			May be lung X-ray with windpipe in middle. (W)
		2.	Turned leg of a stool.
			Shape of upper black part. (D)
VII.			Rejected
VIII.	>V>	1.	Futuristic attempt at a tree with two wolves at sides; bottom doesn't belong.
			Shape of wolves at side; top looks like tree-top; don't know about the rest; not real … no perspective. (D)
IX.		1.	Two gnomes in a fairy tapestry; stage designer's fancy.
			Shape of gnomes on top, but a scene painter probably just threw green and red paint on below. (W)
X.			(Comment: "This is crazy…all imaginable colors.")
		1.	I'm not an anatomist…it's a fantastic conglomeration of colors.
			Maybe something anatomical…I don't know. (W)
	V	2.	Fantastic blossom, but too many colors; maybe a big flower here.
			Green calyx and red blossom. (D)

End of record

Rorschach Record

Subject: Hjalmar Schacht (1877–1970)
Age: 63
Estimated IQ: 143 (Very Superior Range; 99.8th percentile)
Date of testing: November 1, 1945
Examiner: Gustave Gilbert

I.		1.	A bat.
			The shape. (W)
		2.	Tanned hide; an animal skin without the holes.
			The shape of an opened hide. (W)
		3.	(Covers sides) The center could be two men with one arm around each other and one hand held up taking an oath.
			They're swearing brotherly love and eternal allegiance to the Versailles Treaty. (D)
		4.	Egyptian mummy inside.

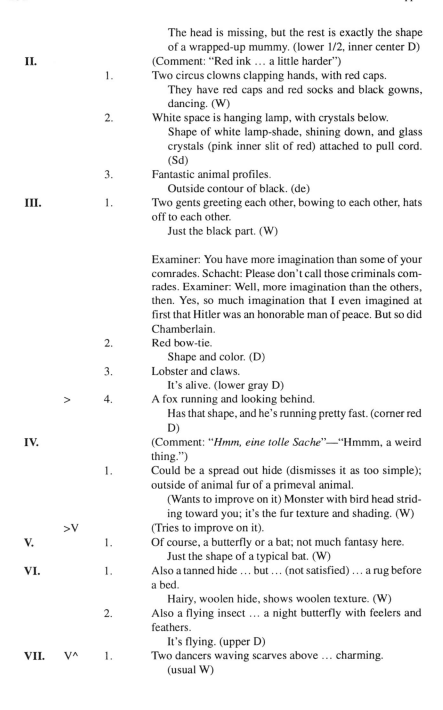

			The head is missing, but the rest is exactly the shape of a wrapped-up mummy. (lower 1/2, inner center D)
II.			(Comment: "Red ink … a little harder")
		1.	Two circus clowns clapping hands, with red caps. They have red caps and red socks and black gowns, dancing. (W)
		2.	White space is hanging lamp, with crystals below. Shape of white lamp-shade, shining down, and glass crystals (pink inner slit of red) attached to pull cord. (Sd)
		3.	Fantastic animal profiles. Outside contour of black. (de)
III.		1.	Two gents greeting each other, bowing to each other, hats off to each other. Just the black part. (W)

Examiner: You have more imagination than some of your comrades. Schacht: Please don't call those criminals comrades. Examiner: Well, more imagination than the others, then. Yes, so much imagination that I even imagined at first that Hitler was an honorable man of peace. But so did Chamberlain.

		2.	Red bow-tie. Shape and color. (D)
		3.	Lobster and claws. It's alive. (lower gray D)
	>	4.	A fox running and looking behind. Has that shape, and he's running pretty fast. (corner red D)
IV.			(Comment: "*Hmm, eine tolle Sache*"—"Hmmm, a weird thing.")
		1.	Could be a spread out hide (dismisses it as too simple); outside of animal fur of a primeval animal. (Wants to improve on it) Monster with bird head striding toward you; it's the fur texture and shading. (W)
	>V		(Tries to improve on it).
V.		1.	Of course, a butterfly or a bat; not much fantasy here. Just the shape of a typical bat. (W)
VI.		1.	Also a tanned hide … but … (not satisfied) … a rug before a bed. Hairy, woolen hide, shows woolen texture. (W)
		2.	Also a flying insect … a night butterfly with feelers and feathers. It's flying. (upper D)
VII.	V^	1.	Two dancers waving scarves above … charming. (usual W)

2. Snow on branches ... settled in the angle formed by branches.

> The shading and texture of snow piled on branches. (W)

3. Horns of reindeer ... not too good.

> Just roughly the shape. (W)

4. Girls' heads about to kiss each other, with hair-do and feather here.

> Shape of top part. (D)

VIII. (Comment: "That's tough")

1. A blossom.

> Red and brown orchid. (lower part of blot) (D)

2. Two chameleons crawling up on flower; could be mice, but lack tails; if seen alone they might be bears, but that's too big in relation to the flower.

> Just the figure. (shape) (D)

3. Christ on the cross, with loin cloth; arm, head to side.

> (Faint outline inside right blue patch, apparently well seen.) (di)

4. Small xylophone.

> Shape. (Dr)

> 5. Reclining dog looking back.

> (Left appendage of orange.) (Dr)

IX. V^V 1. Floor lamp and red lamp-shade.

> The base is rising, but the center line and red lamp-shade are there. (D)

> 2. A shot rabbit's head.

> (Inside detail in green) (di)

^ 3. Wizard with pointed hat, stretching out hand.

> Outline of upper right piece. (orange detail, D)

V 4. Caterpillar eating green leaf.

> Shape and color. (edge orange and green) (Dr)

5. Two Dutch girls with blue caps and green aprons, holding hands.

> (part of green just below pink, well seen original response) (Dr)

6. White speck is South America.

> (S)

7. Gargoyle.

> (edge of green facing lower left corner of card) (de)

X. 1. Fantastic devils dancing, two on each side.

> Shape of dancing figures, one is waving torch. (outer blue D)

2. Young animals.

> Alive, looking at each other. (D)

3.   Pelvic girdle of human skeleton.
            The shape. (middle blue) (D)
4.   Rabbits heads.
            The shape. (usual green) (D)
5.   Venetian lions.
            Statues, just the shape. (yellow) (D)
6.   Bird's nest.
            Shape. (side gray) (D)
7.   Mussels.
            Brownish mussels. (D)

            ("Can't make much of the red ... let's try this way (V)
            Too much confusion")

            End of record

Rorschach Record
Subject: Baldur von Schirach (1907–1974)
Age: 38
Estimated IQ: 130 (Very Superior Range; 98th percentile)
Date of testing: October 27, 1945
Examiner: Gustave Gilbert

I.   (Approaches problem cautiously; doesn't answer until
                        he's sure.)
        1.   A bat.
                        Additional: Now I can see two Santa Clauses with
                        Christmas trees under their arms.

                        It's the painful gray tones, but it's mostly the shape and
                        it's alive. If it was colored I would have thought of a
                        dancer. The outside specks are only the mess from the
                        airbrush; the white spaces just don't belong. (W)

                        Additional: Now I can see two men with helmets
                        raising gloved hands.
II.   1.   Two grotesque dancing men clapping hands with red
                        turbans and red boots, red waistband shimmering through
                        ... happy motif.
                        Clearly just the shape, but the color gives the impres-
                        sion of gaiety. I forgot to mention that they had white
                        beards; yes, I saw that originally. No, blood would
                        never have occurred to me. On further observation,
                        they're holding a glass together. (W)
III.   1.   Caricature of two men in coat-tail dress holding a pot;
                        waiters, maybe. Behind them on the wall are red orna-
                        ments and in the middle something like a butterfly orna-

ment. Corner ornaments are like something falling down. Whole thing is like an illustration for an E. Th. A. Hoffmann story [author of fantasies]. It's fantastic because they don't have any human heads.

Main figures are alive but the background figures are not. The pot is shiny, metallic, but they're putting a cloth over it, perhaps because it's hot; the waiters have white aprons with white strings around their waists and white ties and high collars. (WS)

IV.	1.	Fantastic animal god with powerful legs and slit eyes and a kind of widow's peak on his forehead. Gives impression of fur. Belongs to Rococo period-dance pantomime in a Rococo festival.

Form is strong, but texture is also clear; it is soft, deep fur with an animal skin on soles; probably a dancer carrying animal skin over him for festival dance. (W)

V.   1.   First impression, like a bat.

It's alive; the shape and darkness give impression of a bat, but the goat's feet don't correspond. (W)

2.   Figure in Midsummer Night's Dream or Merry Wives of Windsor ...

Shakespeare in any case. (Shows he has Shakespeare book with him in cell.) The figures that dance around Falstaff in the last act of Merry Wives of Windsor.

Horns and fat central figure suggest Falstaff; rest are light wavy figures hidden behind his cloak ... just vague forms. (W)

VI.   1.   A wall decoration - a large animal fur.

Furry texture, probably tiger skin because of shading on legs. (W)

2.   Wooden rod or table leg.

Polished black wood. (upper center D)

3.   Something feathery behind.

Gray tone. (D)

4.   Part of a brick wall with gate or fountain in the middle; yes, a fountain in the distance with water gushing up—a definite scene in depth.

Definite vista; fieldstone wall because of mottled tones, like Maxfield Parrish; angle of perspective at bottom. (lower ½ of card) (D)

VII.   1.   Two women with coquettish hats looking back at each other. (upper 2/3) (D)

2.   Impression of snow or sugar—texture of something baked with fancy icing.

From shading and texture; icing or snow has fallen on it. (W)

VIII. 1. Two animals standing on a mountain grasping the gray and blue parts, perhaps bears; gives strong impression of heraldry ... animals on a coat-of-arms ... pleasantly shaded colors, but no real construction.
They're balancing on one foot, holding onto coat of arms, climbing up. (W)

IX. 1. Orchids.
Shape and color equally; orange flower, green leaves, pink blossoms. (W)

2. Something oriental ... Chinese dragonlike figures above and green jade—a Chinese vase for burning incense with smoke rising in the middle.
The brown is bronzelike and the green is jadelike, but there is no surface texture; just the color. (upper 2/3) (D)

3. Mysterious animal with round head and slit eyes and green protectors before the face, blowing out red smoke—very artistic.
Brown suggests horns; center bulge face with eye space; pink clouds on bottom are smoke. (W)

X. 1. Whole thing is a page out of a fairy-tale book.
Fairy-tale because of color; all are figures in a story. (W)

2. Two mountains with two little animals on top with big eyes and open mouths.
Just the shape. (pink strips with gray figures on top) (D)

3. Two blue devils running and laughing toward the mountain, waving leaf.
Color is cheerful even though they are devils. (outer blue and green) (D)

4. Mole on each side.
Alive, but sleeping. (center gray) (D)

5. Green dancers bending their backs, holding ornament with horns.
Mostly the movement. (lower green) (D)

6. Two yellow lions or dogs sitting, looking up.
Form is very pronounced. (D)

7. King's cape and crown.
Wouldn't have thought of a king's cape if it wasn't blue. (center) (D)

8. Tree-trunk behind the birdlike figures.
(top center) (D)

9. Brown spots below are only decorative.
Perhaps they belong to the mountain. (D)

End of record

Rorschach Record
Subject: Arthur Seyss-Inquart (1892–1946)
Age: 53
Estimated IQ: 141 (Very Superior Range; 99th percentile)
Date of Testing: November 4, 1945
Examiner: Gustave Gilbert

I.		1.	Vertebrae.
			Three vertebrae—shape of center part. (D)
II.		1.	Grotesque dance.
			Two figures with red caps and socks and black gowns and they're clapping hands. (cutoff W)
III.		1.	Similar to the one before, but salon style—in tailcoats.
			Two men bowing, paying compliments to each other, hat in hand; just the shape of the black part. (cutoff W)
		2.	This belongs to the vertebrae in the first figure.
			Shape like a vertebra and belongs to the first card. (lower D)
		3.	Red bow tie.
			Grotesque shape, but bright red bow tie. (D3)
IV.	^V^	1.	Hide of a beast of prey—furry texture; head with glass eyes, whiskers.
			Hairy hide and the shape of the head is very clear, even if you turn it > (tries reflection picture); could be dark reflection in water too. (W)
V.	V	1.	Butterfly with feelers.
			Mounted, as in a collection. (W)
		2.	Bat.
			Stylized, not alive. (W)
VI.	^V^V>^	1.	If you take off this projection (covers it), its a fur hide.
			Has the shape and texture of fur. (D)
	>	2.	This way it's interesting; a scene reflected in water with trees, house, field, and woods, all reflected in water.
			The dark shading inhibits the fantasy, because its tragic; but it has the shape of a reflected scene; trees (feathery projections), house (small indentations), field (grayish expanse), woods (dark areas). (W)
VII.	V>^	1.	Symmetry suggests dancing; two people dancing.
			Children's dance with feather cap and skirts in motion. (W)
	V	2.	Two people running away from something, grabbing hat with hand and jumping or dancing away.
			Impressive dance of flight, better than the other. (lower 2/3) (D)
	V	3.	White space stands out, but I don't know what it is—stone monument, maybe.
			Outline of some kind of monument. (S)

VIII.	^V>	1.	A reflection again; an animal climbing from one object to another and reflected in the water. [offers same thing in different positions]
			Shape of climbing animal is very distinct; colors don't have much to do with this. (W)
	V	2.	If you cover the animals [does so], it is a flower with leaves here and blossoms here—maybe an orchid.
			The colors play an important part in this conception. (cutoff W)
IX.	^V^V>		(Comment: Can't get a reflection picture out of this)
		1	... could be seahorses.
			Approximate shape. (D3+D3)
		2.	Fantastic plant picture; has flower, leaves, roots, but exaggerated.
			Red blossom and green leaves, but roots are not so good. (W)
X.		1.	Profile with pug noses—can't organize all the details.
			Shape of the edge here. (center red edge) (de)
	V	2.	A bridge between two cliffs—an ice bridge in a mountain crevice.
			The blue is icy, but the red does not belong—it is very grotesque, not very good. (center red and blue D)

End of record

Rorschach Record
Subject: Albert Speer (1905–1981)
Age: 40
Estimated IQ: 128 (Very Superior Range; 97th percentile)
Date of testing: October 30, 1945
Examiner: Gustave Gilbert

I.		1.	Like a bug; but I don't know any bug that looks like that.
			Center part looks like a shelled bug because of the shape; not alive. (Center D)
II.	V	1.	A butterfly.
			Just the shape, with red tips. (W)
			Testing the limits: Cannot see dancing figures.
III.		1.	Could be a drawing by Kubin, can hardly say what. (stalling)
			(1 is tentative, stalling, until he decides on 2.)
		2.	Could be two people daubed on the card. (very uncertain)
			Well it's expressionistic, but very vague. They have arms, legs, high collars. No, I paid no attention to the red spots. (W)
IV.			(Comment: This is damned hard.)

		1.	Cross between a bug and a butterfly.
			Now I would say more like a butterfly; shape of appendages on top; shape of the whole thing. (W)
V.	V	1.	A butterfly—a bit clearer.
			(Comment: I understand architecture better.)
			The shape drawn in black and white. (W)
VI.			Promptly rejected.

Testing the limits: Rejects suggestion of sex.

VII.   Rejected.

Testing the limits: Cannot see suggested women.

VIII.   (Blinks in surprise)

   >^ 1. Coat-of-arms, two animals on the side, butterfly on bottom and parts on top belong to design.

           They're shaped like that, but in heraldry the color is independent of the objects it represents. (W)

IX.   Rejected. (Studies it. Gives up after 2 1/2 minutes)

X.   (Comment: Too torn apart, can't make out a thing.)

         1. Could call this a sea horse.

           Just the shape. (green D)

Additional: Bottom figure (gray) could be cross-section of a flower.

Comment: "My fantasies run into musical channels. I can entertain myself here in the cell for hours by running over classical musical compositions in my mind. But I can't visualize very well."

End of record

Rorschach Record

Subject: Adolf Eichmann (1906–1962)
Age: Approximately 55
Date of Testing: 1960–1961 (specific date unknown)
Examiner: I. M. Kulcsar

I.	1.	Bat, from a collector or a museum, with spread-out wings. (W)
II.	1.	Two brown bears pressing against a glass, hats on their heads which are blown away as in dueling. Even the snout is drawn on the left one, and the ear on the right one. Very clear bear ears. Quickly drawn with sketching ink. (W)
III.		("This is also a humorous sketch.")

	1.	Two very polite dandies tipping their hats to each other, greeting each other very formally; there are even patent leather shoes there.
	2.	Two clowns who want to do their best, masked; white collars at the neck. (W)
	3.	The red could be an eye-catching stage decoration in the background. (D)
IV.	1.	A stretched-out cowhide, stretched for drying, or already treated. It is also trimmed—the forepaws and the rear. The head is very badly drawn; the backbone well drawn; it also goes well toward the side. (W)
V.	1.	Bat, much better than the first one. (W)
VI.	1.	Also a skin, but the head part doesn't fit - also a skin of a wild animal. (W)
	2.	The head part like the head decoration of the Aztecs. (upper D)
VII.	1.	Outlines of continents, if I cover the lower part. (D)
V	2.	South America down to Tierra del Fuego; Caribbean Sea with Brazil,Argentina, Chile. (D)
	3.	Again a humorous drawing: two dancing elephants, trunks raised, eyes slightly indicated, standing on one foot. (D)
VIII.	1.	A leaf chewed up by insects, pressed for (display in) herbarium; the color shading would look different in a fall leaf, but there is a leaf in Argentina whose color is similar. (W)
IX.	1.	A coat of arms (covers half); above is the helmet, heraldry in the middle, drawing below, but one side must be covered. It's more the color. (D)
X.	1.	A colored drawing from botany, a flower with pistil and stamens. (W)
>	2.	A detailed drawing of stamens, drawn for a better view for school use. (W)

End of record

References

Abel, T. (1938). *Why Hitler came to power: An answer based on the original life stories of six hundred of his followers*. Englewood Cliffs, NJ: Prentice Hall.

Abel, T. (1945). Is a psychiatric interpretation of the German enigma necessary? *American Sociological Review, 10*, 457–464.

Abel, T. (1965). *The Nazi movement*. New York: Atherton.

Adorno, T. W., Frankel-Brunswick, E., Levinson, D. J., & Sanford, R. N. (1950). *The authoritarian personality*. New York: Harper.

Allen, B. P. (1984). Inattention to history yields faulty conceptions of Nazi leaders. *Journal of Personality Assessment, 48*(3), 257–258.

Allport, G. W. (1961). *Pattern and growth in personality*. New York: Holt, Rinehart & Winston.

American Psychiatric Association. (1994). *Diagnostic and statistical manual of mental disorders* (4th ed., rev). Washington, DC: Author.

Andrus, B. C. (1969). *I was the Nuremberg jailer*. New York: Coward-McCann.

Annas, G. J., & Grodin, M. A. (1992). *The Nazi doctors and the Nuremberg Code: Human rights in human experimentation*. New York: Oxford Press.

Archer, R. P., Marush, M., Inhof, E. A., & Piotrowski, C. (1991). Psychological test usage with adolescent clients: 1990 survey findings. *Professional Psychology: Research & Practice, 22*, 247–252.

Arendt, H. (1958). *The origins of totalitarianism*. New York: Meridian Books.

Arendt, H. (1963). *Eichman in Jerusalem: A report on the banality of evil*. New York: Viking Press.

Asch, S. E. (1952). *Social psychology*. Englewood Cliffs, NJ: Prentice Hall.

Bailey, G. (1991). *Germans: The biography of an obsession*. New York: Free Press.

Baird, J. W. (1993). Julius Streicher: Der Berufsantisemit [Julius Streicher: Antisemit by profession]. In R. Smelser, E. Syring, & R. Zitelman (Eds.), *Die braune Elite II: 21 weitere biographische shizzen* (pp. 231–242). Darmstadt, Germany: Wissenschaftliche Buchzesellschaft.

Beck, S. J. (1943). Review of "The Rorschach Technique." *Psychoanalytic Quarterly, II*, 583–587.

Beck, S. J., Beck, A., Levitt, E., & Molish, H. (1961). *Rorschach's test: I. Basic processes*. New York: Grune & Stratton.

Bekker, C. (1974). *Hitler's naval war*. Garden City, NY: Doubleday.

Bettelheim, B. (1990). *Freud's Vienna and other essays*. New York: Knopf.

Bird, K. W. (1977). *Weimar: The German naval officers corps and the rise of national socialism*. Amsterdam: Grüner.

Bird, K. W. (1985). *German naval history*. New York: Garland.

Birn, R. B. (1986). *Die höheren SS- und Polizeiführer: Himmlers Vertreter im Reich und den besetzten Gebieten.* [High ranking SS and police leaders: Himmler's representatives in the Reich and the occupied territories]. Düsseldorf, Germany: Droste.

Boeddeker, G. (1981). *Die Boote im Netz: Karl Dönitz und das Schicksal der Deutschen U-boot-Waffe.* [Boats in the net: Karl Dönitz and the fate of German submarine warfare]. Bergisch Gladbach, Germany: Bastei-Lübbe.

Borofsky, G. L., & Brand, D. J. (1980). Personality organization and psychological functioning of the Nuremberg war criminal: The Rorschach data. In J. E. Dimsdale (Ed.), *Survivors, victims, and perpetrators: Essays on the Nazi Holocaust* (pp. 359–403). Washington, DC: Hemisphere.

Bosch, W. J. (1970). *Judgment on Nuremberg: American attitudes toward the major German war-crime trials.* Chapel Hill, NC: University of North Carolina Press.

Bracher, K.D. (1976). *Die Krise Europas 1917-1975.* [Crisis in Europe 1917–1975]. Propyläen Verlag.

Brackman, A. C. (1987). *The other Nuremberg: The untold story of the Tokyo war crimes trials.* New York: Quill/William Morrow.

Bratt-Oestergaard, N. (1950). Rorschachtests von Dänischen Landesverrätern [Rorschach tests of Danish traitors]. *Beiheft der Schweizer Zeitschrift der Psychologischen Anwendungen, 19,* 93–101.

Breitman, R. (1991). *The architect of genocide: Himmler and the final solution.* New York: Knopf.

Brickner, R. M. (1943). *Is Germany incurable?* Philadelphia: J. B. Lippincott.

Browning, C. R. (1992). *Ordinary men: Reserve Police Battalion 101 and the final solution in Poland.* New York: HarperCollins.

Broszat, M. (1963). *Kommandant in Auschwitz: Autobiographische Aufzeichnungeng des Rudolf Höss* [Commander of Auschwitz: Autobiographical sketches of Rudolph Höss]. München, Germany: Deutscher Taschenbuch Verlag.

Broszat, M. (1984). *Die Machtergreifung: Der Aufstieg der NSDAP und die Zerstörung der Weimarer Republik* [The seizure of power: The ascend of the NSDAP and the downfall of the Weimat Republic]. München, Germany: Deutscher Taschenbuch Verlag.

Busch, F. O. (1990). *Holocaust at sea: The drama of the Scharnhorst.* New York: Rinehart.

Butcher, J. N., & Bemis, K. M. (1984). Abnormal behavior in cultural context. In H. E. Adams & P. B. Sutker (Eds.), *Comprehensive handbook of psychopathology* (p. 111–140). New York: Plenum.

Bytwerk, R. L. (1983). *Julius Streicher.* New York: Stein & Day.

Christiansen, K. O. (1950). *Male collaborators with the Germans in Denmark during the occupation* (Danish with English Summary). Copenhagen: University of Copenhagen Press.

Cocks, G. (1985). *Psychotherapy in the Third Reich: The Göring Institute.* New York: Oxford University Press.

Conot, R. E. (1983). *Justice at Nuremberg.* New York: Harper & Row.

Davidson, E. (1966). *Trial of the Germans.* New York: MacMillan.

Diamond, R., Barth, J. T., & Zillmer, E. A. (1988). An investigation of the psychological component of mild head injury: The role of the MMPI. *International Journal of Clinical Neuropsychology, 10,* 35–40.

Dicks, H. V. (1950). Personality traits and National Socialist ideology. *Human Relations, 3,* 111–154.

Dicks, H. V. (1972). *Licensed mass murder: A socio-psychological study of some SS killers.* New York: Basic Books.

Dolibois, J. E. (1989). *Patterns of circles: An ambassador's story.* Kent, OH: Kent State University Press.

Dönitz, K. (1959). *Memoirs.* Westport, CT: Greenwood.

Dönitz, K. (1968). *Mein wechselvolles leben* [My life in transition]. Göttingen, Germany: Musterschmidt-Verlag.

Dr. Robert Ley's brain (1946). *Medical Record, 159,* 188.

Durkheim, E. (1982). *The rules of sociological method.* New York: The Free Press.

Exner, J. E. (1974). *The Rorschach: A comprehensive system, Vol. 1, basic foundations.* New York: Wiley.

Exner, J. E. (1978a). *The Rorschach: A comprehensive system, Vol. 2, current research and advanced interpretation.* New York: Wiley.

Exner, J. E. (1978b). *A Rorschach workbook for the comprehensive system.* New York: Rorschach Workshops.

Exner, J. E. (1985). *A Rorschach workbook for the comprehensive system* (2nd ed.). New York: Rorschach Workshops.

Exner, J. E. (1986) *The Rorschach: A comprehensive system, Vol. 1, basic foundations* (2nd ed.). New York: Wiley.

Exner, J. E. (1989). Searching for projection in the Rorschach. *Journal of Personality Assessment, 53,* 520–536.

Exner, J. E. (1990). *A Rorschach workbook for the comprehensive system* (3rd ed.). Asheville, NC: Rorschach Workshops.

Exner, J. E. (1993). *The Rorschach: A comprehensive system, Vol. 1, basic foundations* (3rd ed.). New York: Wiley.

Exner, J. E., Cohen, J. B., & Mcguire, H. (1991). *Rorschach interpretation assistance program - version 2* [computer program]. Asheville, NC: Rorschach Workshops.

Exner, J. E., & Murillo, L. (1975). Early prediction of post hospitalization relapse. *Journal of Personality Assessment, 12,* 231–237.

Fest, J. C. (1970). *The face of the Third Reich.* London: Widenfeld & Nicolson.

Fleming, G. (1984). *Hitler and the final solution.* Berkeley: University of California.

Freiwald, A., & Mendelsohn, M. (1994). *The last Nazi: Josef Schwammberger and the Nazi past.* New York: Norton.

Friedman, P. (1957). *Their brothers' keepers.* New York: Crown.

Fritzsche, H. (1953). *The sword in the scales.* London: Alan Wingate.

Gilbert, G. M. (1947). *Nuremberg diary.* New York: Signet.

Gilbert, G. M. (1948a). Hermann Göring, amiable psychopath. *Journal of Abnormal and Social Psychology, 43,* 211.

Gilbert, G. M. (1948b, August). *Nazi authoritarianism and aggression.* Paper presented at the first annual meeting of the International Conference on Mental Hygiene, London, England.

Gilbert, G. M. (1948c, August). *The problem of German authoritarianism and aggression.* Paper presented at the first annual meeting of the International Conference on Mental Hygiene, London, England.

Gilbert, G. M. (1950). *The psychology of dictatorship.* New York: Ronald Press.

Gilbert, G. M. (1963). The mentality of SS murderous robots. *Yad Vashem Studies, 5,* 35–41.

Goebbels, J. (1983). *The Goebbels diaries.* New York: Putnam.

Golden, C. J., Zillmer, E. A., & Spiers, M. (1992). *Neuropsychological assessment and intervention.* Springfield, IL: Charles C. Thomas.

Gordon, S. (1984). *Hitler, Germans, and the "Jewish question."* Princeton, NJ: Princeton University Press.

Greenstein, F. (1969). *Personality and politics, problems of evidence, inference, and conceptualization.* Chicago: Markham.

Grunberger, R. (1971). *The 12-year Reich, a social history of Nazi Germany, 1933-1945.* New York: Holt, Rinehart & Winston.

Guilford, J. P. (1959). *Personality.* New York: McGraw-Hill.

Gutman, I. (1994). *Resistance The Warsaw ghetto uprising.* Boston: Houghton Mifflin.

Hahn, F. (1978). *Lieber Stürmer: Leserbriefe an das NS-Kampfblatt 1924 bis 1945* [Dear Stürmer: Letters to the editor 1924 to 1945]. Stuttgart: Seewald Verlag.

Harris, R. (1986). *Selling Hitler.* New York: Pantheon.

Harrower, M. (1943). Personality testing in penal institutions. *Probation, 23,* 1–6.

Harrower, M. (1955a). A new pattern for mental health services in a children's court. *Journal of Orthopsychiatry, 25,* 1–50.

Harrower, M. (1955b). A psychological testing program for entering students at the University of Texas School of Medicine, Galveston—A preliminary report. *Texas Reports on Biology and Medicine, 13,* 406–419.

Harrower, M. (1957). The relevant use of psychological tests in medical education. *British Journal of Medical Psychology, 30,* 19–26.

Harrower, M. (1961). Desirable and undesirable aspects of large scale projective evaluation. *Acta Psychologica, 19,* 1–4.

Harrower, M. (1965). *Psychodiagnostic testing: An empirical approach.* Springfield, IL: Charles C. Thomas.

Harrower, M. (1970). Projective classification. In A. R. Hahrer (Ed.), *New approaches to personality classification* (pp. 139–164). New York: Columbia University Press.

Harrower, M. (1976a). Rorschach records of the Nazi war criminals: An experimental study after 30 years. *Journal of Personality Assessment, 40*, 341–351

Harrower, M. (1976b, July). Were Hitler's henchmen mad? *Psychology Today*, pp. 76–80.

Harrower, M., & Bowers, D. (1987). *The inside story: Self-evaluations reflecting basic Rorschach types.* Hillsdale, NJ: Lawrence Erlbaum Associates.

Herzstein, R. E. (1988). *Waldheim: The missing years.* New York: Arbor House/William Morrow.

Heydecker, J., & Leeb, J. (1985). *Der Nürnberger Prozess: Neue Dokumente, Erkentnisse und Analysen.* [The Nuremberg trials: New documents, insights and analysis]. Köln: Kiepenheuer & Witsch.

Hilberg, R. (1971). *Documents of destruction: Germany and Jewry 1933-1945.* Chicago: Quadrangle.

Hilberg, R. (1992). *Perpetrators, victims, bystanders: The Jewish catastrophe 1933-1945.* New York: Harper Collins.

Hoffman, L. E. (1992). American psychologists and wartime research on Germany, 1941-1945. *American Psychologist, 2*, 264–273.

Hoyt, E. P. (1988). *The death of the U-boats.* New York: McGraw.

Jäckel, E., & Rohwer, J. (Eds.) (1985). *Der Mord an den Juden im Zweiten Weltkrieg* [The murder of Jews in World War II]. Stuttgart, Germany: Deutsche Verlags-Anstalt.

Kater, M. H. (1983). *The Nazi party: A social profile of members and leaders 1919-1945.* Cambridge, MA: Harvard University Press

Kater, M. H. (1989). *Doctors under Hitler.* Chapel Hill: University of North Carolina Press.

Kelley, D. M. (1946a, April). *Preliminary report of Rorschach studies of Nazi war criminals in Nuremberg.* Paper presented at the 17th annual meeting of the Eastern Psychological Association, Fordham University, New York.

Kelley, D. M. (1946b). Preliminary studies of the Rorschach records of the Nazi war criminals. *Rorschach Research Exchange, 10*, 45–48.

Kelley, D. M. (1947). *Twenty-two cells in Nuremberg: A psychiatrist examines the Nazi war criminals.* New York: Greenberg.

Kennedy, L. (1974). *Pursuit: The chase and sinking of the Bismarck.* New York: Viking.

Kennedy, R., & Rosenberg, H. (1993, March). *"Oh those crazy cards again": A test-retest analysis of the Rorschach protocols of Herman Göring.* Paper presented at the at the 53rd annual meeting of the Society for Personality Assessment, San Francisco, CA.

Klee, E., Dressen, W., & Riess, V. (Eds.). (1988). *"The good old days" The Holocaust as seen by its perpetrators and bystanders.* New York: The Free Press.

Klessmann, C. (1993). *Hans Frank: Party jurist and governor-general in Poland.* In R. Smelser & R. Zitelmann (Eds.), *The Nazi elite* (pp. 39–47). New York: New York University Press.

Klopfer, B., & Kelley, D. M. (1942). *The Rorschach technique.* New York: World Book.

Kole, D. M., & Matarazzo, J. D. (1965). Intellectual and personality characteristics of two classes of medical students. *The Journal of Medical Education, 40*, 1130–1143.

Korchin, S. J. (1976). *Modern clinical psychology: Principles of intervention in the clinic and community.* New York: Basic Books.

Kovel, J. (1976, February 6). Review of "The Nuremberg mind." *The New York Times Book Review*, p. 6.

Kren, G. M., & Rappoport, L. (1981). Resistance to the Holocaust: Reflections on the idea and the act. In Y. Bauer & N. Rotenstreich (Eds.), *The Holocaust as historical experience: Essays and a discussion* (pp. 193–222). New York: Holmes & Meier.

Langer, W. C. (1972). *The mind of Adolf Hitler.* New York: Basic Books.

Levin, H. S., Benton, A. L., & Grossman, R. G. (1982). *Neurobehavioral consequences of closed head injury.* New York: Oxford.

Lifton, R. J. (1986). *The Nazi doctors: Medical killing and the psychology of genocide.* New York: Basic Books.

Lifton, R. J., & Markuson, E. (1990). *The genocidal mentality.* New York: Basic Books.

Lubin, B., Larsen, R. M., Matarazzo, T. D., & Seever, M. (1985). Psychological test image patterns in five professional settings. *American Psychologist, 7*, 857–861.

Manson, J. M. (1990). *Diplomatic ramifications of unrestricted submarine warfare, 1939-1941.* New York: Greenwood.

McClelland, D. C. (1951). *Personality.* New York: Holt.

McCully, R. S. (1980). A commentary on Adolf Eichmann's Rorschach. *Journal of Personality Assessment, 44,* 311–318.

Meehl, P. E. (1973). *Psychodiagnosis: Selected papers.* Minneapolis: University of Minnesota Press.

Megargee, E. A. (1984). Aggression and violence. In H. E. Adams & P. B. Sutker (Eds.), *Comprehensive handbook of psychopathology* (pp. 523–548). New York: Plenum.

Merkl, P. H. (1975). *Political violence under the swastika: 581 early Nazis.* Princeton, NJ: Princeton University Press.

Merkl, P. H. (1980). *The making of a stormtrooper.* Princeton, NJ: Princeton University Press.

Miale, F. R., & Selzer, M. (1975). *The Nuremberg mind: The psychology of the Nazi leaders.* New York: The New York Times Book Company.

Milgram, S. (1963). Behavioral study of obedience. *Journal of Abnormal and Social Psychology, 67,* 371–378.

Milgram, S. (1974). *Obedience to authority.* New York: Harper & Row.

Nadler, F. (1969). *Eine Stadt im Schatten Streichers* [A city in Streicher's shadow]. Nürnberg: Fränkische Verlagsanstalt & Buchdruckerei.

Neave, A. (1978). *On trial at Nuremberg.* Boston: Little, Brown.

No geniuses. (1946, June 1). *The New Yorker, 22,* 6.

Oliner, S. P., & Oliner, P. M. (1988). *The altruistic personality.* New York: The Free Press.

Padfield, P. (1984). *Dönitz, the last Führer: Portrait of a Nazi war leader.* New York: Harper & Row.

Papen, F. (1952). *Der Wahrheit einer Gasse* [Autobiography]. München: Paul List Verlag.

Paskuly, S. (Ed.). (1992). *Death dealer: The memoirs of the SS Kommandant at Auschwitz.* Buffalo: Prometheus.

Persico, J. E. (1994). *Nuremberg: Infamy on trial.* New York: Viking.

Piotrowski, C., Sherry, D., & Keller, J. W. (1985). Psychodiagnostic test usage: A survey of the Society of Personality Assessment. *Journal of Personality Assessment, 49,* 115–119.

Pope, D. (1958). *73 North: The defeat of Hitler's navy.* Philadelphia: Lippincott.

Porpora, D. V. (1990). *How Holocausts happen.* Philadelphia: Temple University Press.

Potash, H., Crespo, A., Patel, S., & Ceravolo, A. (1990). Cross cultural attitude assessment with the Miale–Holsopple Sentence Completion Test. *Journal of Personality Assessment, 55,* 657–662.

Poythress, N., Otto, R. K., Darkes, J., & Starr, L. (1993). APA's expert panel on the Congressional review of the USS Iowa incident. *American Psychologist, 48,* 8–15.

Prisco, S. (1980). *An introduction to psychohistory: Theories and case studies.* Lanham, MD: University Press of America.

Rapaport, D., Gill, M. M., & Schafer, R. (1968). Diagnostic psychological testing (Rev. ed.). New York: International Universities Press.

Rees, J. R. (1948). *The case of Rudolf Hess; a problem in diagnosis and forensic psychiatry.* New York: Norton.

Resnick, M. N. (1984). *The Nuremberg mind redeemed: A comprehensive analysis of the Nuremberg war criminals' Rorschach records.* Unpublished doctoral dissertation, The Professional School of Psychology, San Francisco, CA.

Resnick, M. N., & Nunno, V. J. (1991). The Nuremberg mind redeemed: A comprehensive analysis of the Rorschachs of Nazi war criminals. *Journal of Personality Assessment, 57,* 19–29.

Reuth, R. G. (1990). *Goebbels.* München, Germany: Piper.

Ritzler, B. A. (1978). The Nuremberg mind revisited: A quantitative approach to Nazi Rorschachs. *Journal of Personality Assessment, 47,* 344–353.

Ritzler, B. A. (1979). *The Rorschachs of Nazi war criminals at Nuremberg.* Symposium presented at the American Psychological Association Convention, Philadelphia, PA.

Ritzler, B. A., & Nalesnik, D. (1990). The effect of inquiry on the Exner Comprehensive System. *Journal of Personality Assessment, 55,* 647–656.

Ritzler, B. A., & Saraydarian, L. (1986, August). *Sadism and the banality of evil as factors in Nazi personalities: A Rorschach analysis.* Paper presented at the American Psychological Association Convention, Washington, DC.

Ritzler, B., Zillmer, E. A., & Belevich, J. S. (1993). Comprehensive system scoring discrepancies on Nazi Rorschachs: A comment. *Journal of Personality Assessment, 61,* 576–583.

Rorschach, H. (1921). *Psychodiagnostics.* Bern: Bircher.

Rubenstein, R. L. (1976, July). Review of "The Nuremberg mind." *Psychology Today*, pp. 83–84.

Salewski, M. (1970). *Die deutsche Seekriegsleitung 1935-1945. Vol. 1: 1935-1941* [Command of German naval warfare 1935-1945 Vol. 1]. Frankfurt am Main, Germany: Bernard & Graefe.

Salewski, M. (1973). *Die deutsche Seekriegsleitung 1935-1945. Vol. 3: Denkschriften und Lagebetrachtungen 1938-1944* [Command of German naval warfare 1935-1945 Vol. 3 Memoirs and analysis of the military situation]. Frankfurt am Main, Germany: Bernard & Graefe.

Schacht, H. (1955). *76 Jahre meines Lebens* [My life of 76 years]. Bad Wörishofen: Kindler & Schiermeyer Verlag.

Schaumburg-Lippe, F. C. (1972). *Dr. Goebbels: Ein Porträt des Propagandaministers* [Dr. Goebbels: A portrait of the minister of propaganda]. Wiesbaden, Germany: Limes Verlag.

Schirach, B. (1967). *Ich glaubte an Hitler* [I believe in Hitler]. Hamburg: Mosaik Verlag.

Selzer, M. (1976). Psychohistorical approach in studying Nazis and Nazism. *Journal of Psychohistory*, 4.

Selzer, M. (1977, November 27). The murderous mind. *The New York Times Magazine*, pp. 34–37.

Shanor, C. A., & Terrell, T. P. (1980). *Military law*. St. Paul, MN: West.

Showalter, D. E. (1982). *Little man, what now? Der Stürmer in the Weimar Republic*. Hamden, CT: Archon.

Showell, J. P. M. (1989). *U-boats under the Swastika*. Annapolis: Naval Institute Press.

Simpson, C. (1972). *The Lusitania*. Boston: Little, Brown.

Smelser, R. (1988). *Robert Ley, Hitler's front leader*. New York: Berg.

Smelser, R., & Zitelmann, R. (Eds.). (1993). *The Nazi elite*. New York: New York University Press.

Smith, B. F. (1976). *Reaching judgment at Nuremberg: The untold story of how the Nazi war criminals were judged*. New York: Basic Books.

Snyder, L. L. (1947). Review of "Nuremberg diary." *American Historical Review, 53*, 167.

Snyder, G. S. (1976). *The Royal Oak disaster*. San Rafael, CA.

Speer, A. (1970). *Inside the Third Reich*. New York: Aron.

Speer, A. (1977). *Spandau: The secret diaries*. New York: Collins.

Steiner, J. M. (1976). *Power politics and social change in national socialist Germany*. Paris: Mouton.

Steinert, M. (1967). *Die 23 Tage der Regierung Dönitz* [The 23 days of the Dönitz government]. Vienna: Econ.

Swearingen, B. E. (1985). *The mystery of Hermann Goering's suicide*. New York: Dell.

Taylor, T. (1992). *The anatomy of the Nuremberg trials*. New York: Knopf.

Tec, N. (1986). *When light pierced the darkness: Christian rescue of Jews in Nazi-occupied Poland*. New York: Oxford University Press.

Thomas, C. B., Ross, D. C., & Freed, E. S. (1964). *An index of Rorschach responses*. Baltimore, MD: John Hopkins Press.

Thomas, C. S. (1990). *The German navy in the Nazi era*. Annapolis, MD: Naval Institute Press.

Thomsen, E. (1971). *Deutsche Besaztungspolitik in Dänemark 1940-1945* [German occupation policies in Denmark 1940-1945]. Hamburg: Bertelsmann Universitätsverlag.

Thompson, H. K., & Strutz, H. (1976). *Doenitz at Nuremberg: A re-appraisal*. New York: Amber.

Tusa, A., & Tusa, J. (1983). *The Nuremberg trial*. New York: Atheneum.

Waite, R. G. (1977). *The psychopathic God Adolf Hitler*. New York: Signet.

Wechsler, D. (1944). *The measurement of adult intelligence* (3rd ed.). Baltimore, MD: Williams & Wilkins.

Weinberg, G. L. (1981). *World in the balance: Behind the scenes of World War II*. Hanover, NH: University Press of New England.

Weinberg, G. L. (1994). *A world at arms*. New York: Cambridge University Press.

Weiner, I. B. (1966). *Psychodiagnosis in schizophrenia*. New York: Wiley.

Weiner, I. B. (1991). Editor's note: Interscorer agreement in Rorschach research. *Journal of Personality Assessment, 56*, 1.

Winton, J. (1983). *The death of the Scharnhorst*. New York: Anthony Bird.

Yahil, L. (1969). *The rescue of the Danish Jewry: Test of a democracy*. Philadelphia: The Jewish Publication Society of America.

Zillmer, E. A. (1991). Rorschach interpretation assistance program - version 2 (Review). *Journal of Personality Assessment, 57*(2), 381–383.

Zillmer, E. A., & Archer, R. P. (1985) *The Rorschach Data Sheet Summary and Interpretive Report for Adults* [computer program]. Indiatlantic, FL: Psychologistics Software.

Zillmer, E. A., & Archer, R. P. (1989, April). *A modern reanalysis of the Rorschach records of Nazi War criminals.* Paper presented at the 50th annual meeting of the Society for Personality Assessment, New York.

Zillmer, E. A., & Archer., R. P. (1990, July). *The Rorschach records of Nazi war criminals.* Paper presented at the 13th Congress International du Rorschach et des Methods Projectives, Paris, France.

Zillmer, E. A., Archer, R. P., & Castino, B. (1989). The Rorschach records of Nazi war criminals: A reanalysis using current scoring and interpretation practices. *Journal of Personality Assessment, 53,* 85–99.

Zillmer, E. A., & Ball, J. D. (1987). Psychological and neuropsychological assessment in the medical setting. *Staff & Resident Physician, 33,* 602–609.

Zillmer, E. A., Ball, J. D., Fowler, P. C., Newman, A. C., & Stutts, M. L. (1991). Wechsler Verbal-Performance IQ discrepancies among psychiatric inpatients: Implications for subtle neuropsychological dysfunctioning. *Archives of Clinical Neuropsychology, 6,* 61–71.

Zillmer, E. A., & Vue, J. (in press). Factor analysis with Rorschach data. *Issues and methods in Rorschach Research.* Hillsdale, NJ: Lawrence Erlbaum Associates.

Zillmer, E. A., Fowler, P. C., Newman, A. C., & Archer, R. P. (1988). Relationships between the WAIS and neuropsychological measures for neuropsychiatric inpatients. *Archives of Clinical Neuropsychology, 3,* 33–45.

Zillmer, E. A., Fowler, P. C., Waechtler, C., Harris, B., & Khan, F. (1992). The effects of unilateral and multifocal lesions on the WAIS-R: A factor analytic study of stroke patients. *Archives of Clinical Neuropsychology, 7,* 29–41.

Zillmer, E. A., Harrower, M., Ritzler, B., & Archer, R. P. (1991, March). *The Rorschach records of Nazi War criminals: Historical perspectives and current research.* Symposium presented at the 51st annual meeting of the Society for Personality Assessment, New Orleans, LA.

Zimbardo, P. G. (1972, April). Pathology of imprisonment. *Society,* 4–8.

Author Index

Subject Index